2020-2021 Edition

SAT Reading
Science and Social Studies

ISBN-13: 979-8616858337

Visit us at **PrepVantageTutoring.com**

SAT Reading: Science and Social Studies, 2020-2021 Edition
Copyright © 2020 PrepVantage Publishing

ISBN-13: 979-8616858337

Table of Contents

Part 1

Social Studies

Reading Strategy
Part 1: Social Studies

Essential Tactics

In terms of time period, the Social Studies passages that appear on the SAT represent modern trends and tendencies: so far, most of the Social Studies content has been taken from the relatively recent past. You can expect to see articles that deal with contemporary urban life, public health, popular communications platforms, and present-day trends in journalism. While consistently designed to address 21st-century problems in a rigorously evidence-based manner, Social Studies passages regularly return to a few core topics: the psychology of decision-making, population and cultural studies, economics, marketing, ethics, and the media.

What you will NEVER see in the Social Studies passages are topics that are blatantly or divisively political. As with all sections of the SAT Reading, discussions of material—religious debates, partisan arguments, sexuality, substance abuse—that could offend a large group of test-takers are strictly off-limits. Keep in mind, though, that issues such as impassioned political agendas and stances may be addressed in passing.

In general, Social Studies passages will call upon your ability to sort through different perspectives and evidence-based studies—some of which may build upon one another, some of which may be in complete disagreement. There are a few natural starting points for your analysis. Keep these in mind, but keep in mind as well that the questions may depend on fine points of passage details and passage transitions.

Topic, Sources, and Positions

There is one feature of Social Studies passages that, in the right circumstances, can make the entire reading experience move along in a wonderfully predictable manner. For SAT Fiction passages, reading the blurb that introduces a given reading can be helpful (since the Fiction blurbs can clarify character and plot points), but is not always essential (since the titles, for this passage type, can be puzzling and may not be accompanied by further information). However, for Social Studies AND for Science passages, try to make a habit of reading the short introductory content. The reason will soon become obvious.

> **ALWAYS read Social Studies and Science blurbs
> since passage titles often indicate TOPIC and MAIN IDEA.**

This approach is helpful, but is not a complete giveaway—since you will STILL need to read the passage thoroughly in order to understand how the topic, dilemma, or debate at hand is being investigated. What you should do is keep the title in mind and use it to orient your reading.

Consider the titles of some of the recent Social Studies passages that have appeared on the SAT official tests.

• "Money Can't Buy Love: Asymmetric Beliefs about Gift Price and Feelings of Appreciation" (Test 1)

• "Straphanger: Saving Our Cities and Ourselves from the Automobile" (Test 3)

• "Why You Shouldn't Trust Internet Comments" (Test 5)

• "Public Trust in the News" (Test 6)

• "How Technology Is Destroying Jobs" (Test 7)

• "Why Null Results Rarely See the Light of Day" (Test 8)

• "How the Web Affects Memory" (Test 9, New for 2020)

• "The Conundrum: How Scientific Innovation, Increased Efficiency, and Good Intentions Can Make Our Energy and Climate Problems Worse" (Test 10, New for 2020)

On their own, these titles are most helpful for helping you to understand what kinds of topics (gift giving, transportation, journalism) are being addressed. To make the best possible sense of such topics, you will need to ask the right questions as your reading moves along: how a process referenced in the title works, why a specific idea indicated in the title is important, whether a theory contained in the title is valid. The topic from Official Test 5 provides an obvious instance. Quite simply, WHY exactly are Internet comments unreliable? Your reading of the article should return an answer of some sort to this question.

Of course, passage titles do not have a perfect track record of pointing readers towards key passage information, and some of them may be too short or too cryptic to be particularly useful. You may need to work through a Social Studies passage entirely on its own terms. Knowing what to look for, in this case, is key—and, often enough, you will need to work through a few different types of information related to a key topic area.

For both Social Studies and Science passages, you must keep the following rule in mind.

> **Outside reading can help with vocabulary and comprehension
> but should NOT be relied on for answers to questions.**

Nonetheless, outside knowledge can be useful for exactly the two purposes indicated above as a form of training that supplements your work with the readings in this book. Simply visit some of the web sites for the publications favored by the official SAT—including the American Association for the Advancement of Science (www.aaas.org, used repeatedly by the College Board)—and test your comprehension on any articles at under roughly 750 words.

Part 1: Social Studies

As you read any Social Studies passage, from any source, stay alert for the following types of information.

1. Key Sources (named experts, institutions, or the author himself or herself)

2. Key Pieces of Evidence (statistics, quotations, studies, experimental outcomes)

3. Key Perspectives (common beliefs, new explanations, proposals, criticisms)

Some of these pieces of information may be quite closely related; in fact, you may naturally integrate a few of them, since you should work as much as possible to trace evidence and perspectives BACK to key sources. You should also keep in mind that how these elements are combined can vary considerably from passage to passage. Some Social Studies readings will present you with several viewpoints or studies that conflict with one another, while other readings in this category will focus on meticulously-described individual experiments— sometimes devoting almost all of the discussion to a single research project.

Notice, though, that so far you have not been called upon to weigh in on a potentially important element for any SAT Social Studies reading: the passage's thesis. The reason, here, is that the thesis will NOT occur in a single predictable place. Drawing hasty conclusions about a passage's viewpoint—even when the title seems like a giveaway—can do more harm than good. However, once you have worked through a passage's key pieces of information, you will be ready to discern what kind of thesis the passage possesses.

Working with the Thesis and Evidence

The central question with the thesis of any Social Studies passage is how strong, exactly, the author's position is. Some authors will be highly opinionated; others may simply be recording results or viewpoints. Think in terms of the following questions.

- Does the author present a single side of an issue or multiple sides?

- Does the author take a strong tone towards any side or instead avoid bias?

- Does the author endorse or set forward a theory or instead remain ambivalent or uncertain?

Note that an author may shift topic, tone, or degree of certainty considerably. These are the issues that you should keep in mind for the sake of firm reading comprehension. When in doubt, though, you can attempt to grasp the passage with the following questions.

> **What is the central topic (title, skimming, keywords) of the passage?**
> **What is the stance (positive, negative, undecided) of the author?**

Relying on these issues to determine the overall nature of the reading can be helpful. You should also notice that all of these questions are based EXCLUSIVELY on direct and indisputable evidence, not on creative interpretation or outside knowledge of any sort. Remember, while you work through the passages, to keep in mind the following guidelines.

1. DO NOT evaluate or interpret what you are reading

2. DO NOT bring in any outside knowledge

Indeed, each Reading question that you will confront is PURELY evidence-based. You should be finding important ELEMENTS of the passage as you read—elements that will give you strong comprehension for these questions—not creating independent ideas or value judgments of your own.

If you feel that you can work with the passages without ANY risk of distracting yourself from the fundamentals of evidence, details, and comprehension, you might also look for some of the following elements as you read.

1. Structure of the Passage or Patterns in the Evidence (built into or clearly articulated in the passage)

2. Significant or Recurring Phrases, Details, or Images

The danger with these issues is that, in your current coursework, you may be used to analyzing data and images for the sake of forming opinions. You CANNOT do so on the SAT (since subjective questions would be impossible to score systematically) and must instead consider literal comprehension of the passage.

Approaching the Questions

Each SAT Social Studies passage will feature roughly five different question types.

1. Major Issue (Main Idea, Overall Purpose, Overall Shift, Developmental Structure)

2. Passage Details (Inference from Evidence, Paragraph Structure, Paragraph Function, Word Function)

3. Word in Context (Identification of the meanings of individual words)

4. Command of Evidence (Either paired or individual, based on line references as answer choices)

5. Working with Visuals (Analysis of the visual either on its own or in the context of the passage)

You will find these question types dispersed in the following numbers.

•   Word in Context: 2 Normal, 1 or 3 Possible

•   Command of Evidence: 4 (Two Pairings) or 3 (One Pairing, One Individual)

•   Major Issue, Passage Details, and Visuals: Remainder, typically some in each category

There is, normally, no need to solve these questions in any special order, at least if you have your timing down to 12 or 13 minutes to complete each Social Studies passage and its question set. If you are having trouble with pacing, though, you might place special focus on questions that are less complex—typically, everything but Command of Evidence—and try for effective work in these areas.

The arrangement of questions will not change much for each 10-question passage, either in Social Studies or in Science. Aside from the fact that some individual Science passages will NOT have visuals questions (since only ONE of the two Science passages on any given full test is accompanied by a visual), the numbers above will mostly stay constant as you move through this book.

Reading 1

Questions 1-10 are based on the following passage and supplementary material.

This passage is adapted from Charlotte M. Irby, "Older workers—are they aging successfully?" an article published* in 2017 by the Bureau of Labor Statistics.

A large percentage of the U.S. labor force is 55 and over or about to turn 55. Better known as "baby boomers," these workers must now answer
Line the question: What is my optimal retirement age?
5 From the inception of Social Security in 1935 until the Social Security Amendments of 1983, the normal retirement age was 65. However, the age at which retirees could draw full benefits was increased gradually from 65 for individuals
10 born in 1937 or later to 67 for those born in 1960 or later. Thus, with the retirement age extended, many older workers are considering staying in the labor force longer.

The extended retirement age is not the only
15 motivator to persuade older people to work longer. Several other motivators exist, such as a financial need or simply that workers like their job. Another factor that they must weigh is whether they can be successful in their work as they age. In their
20 article "Who is aging successfully at work? A latent profile analysis of successful agers and their work motives," Gregory R. Thrasher, Keith L. Zabel, Reed J. Bramble, and Boris B. Baltes address this uncertainty. To help older workers
25 and their employers better understand successful aging at work, Thrasher and his colleagues look at several factors on the basis of the individual and his or her concept of aging. In addition, from their findings, they also suggest ways in
30 which employers can help their employees age successfully at work.

To determine if aging workers are working successfully, the authors began their research using a "person-centered" or individual approach,
35 which examines the characteristics of individuals together and separately. The survey involved

156 workers from ages 50 to 71. Workers were asked a series of questions concerning their concepts of age. For example, they were asked
40 about subjective (the age people feel or believe they look), functional (the age that people see themselves), and organizational (age based on job tenure) age. They were also asked questions concerning their attitude toward aging, such as
45 how they view their health and the amount of time they have left in the future or "future time perspective."

From the responses to these questions, the authors divided the participants into two groups—
50 healthy and unhealthy. Then the authors went a step further to determine who in these groups was aging most successfully. They looked at different work motivators, such as development, promotion, security, and social life. These groups
55 were then labeled as one of the following:

1. Healthy agers—those who have high levels of development and promotion motives (see themselves as very healthy) and feel more youthful
60 2. Classic agers—those who have low levels of promotion and development motives (see themselves as having poorer health) and feel less youthful

The authors went on to identify a smaller
65 subgroup of workers called organizational agers, who had longer job tenures and were older than the healthy and classic agers yet had the same developmental and promotion motives as the healthy agers.
70 Thrasher and colleagues found that the majority of older workers are aging successfully; however, much of the success is based on the older workers themselves and their concepts of aging. The authors suggest that researchers
75 performing future studies on the success of the aging worker should consider looking more into these individual subgroup differences. As for employers, the authors recommend that they look into ways to meet promotion and development
80 needs that would address the motivations of

*See Page 85 for the citation for this text.

CONTINUE

older workers. This would, in turn, help them be not only more successful but also more healthy, particularly since the number of older workers and the age of retirement will continue to increase
85   over the next several years.

1

The main purpose of the passage is to

A) offer a historical account of an overlooked social and economic trend.

B) provide practical advice to those who face a specific health risk.

C) outline the results of an inquiry that may offer guidance in the modern workplace.

D) paraphrase a variety of testimonies from two groups that contrast with one another in a clear manner.

2

On the basis of the passage, which of the following older workers would be most likely to consider "staying in the labor force longer" (lines 13-14)?

A) A worker whose job duties have gradually come to include less bureaucratic work and more travel

B) A worker who cannot leave the workforce at a common retirement age due to a lack of savings

C) A worker who fears that retirement will lead to a sense of isolation from friends and family

D) A worker who believes that there will be further changes to Social Security benefit policies

3

Which choice provides the best evidence for the answer to the previous question?

A) Lines 7-11 ("However . . . later")

B) Lines 11-13 ("Thus . . . longer")

C) Lines 16-17 ("Several . . . job")

D) Lines 17-19 ("Another . . . age")

Responses to Various Questionnaire Items, 175 Individuals Ages 65 and Over

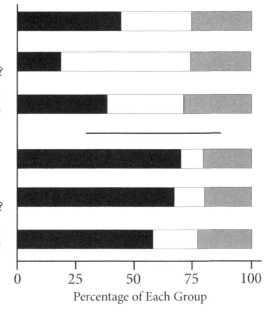

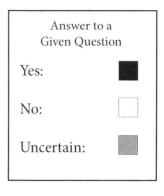

Percentage of Each Group

Part 1: Social Studies

4

The recommendations from Gregory Thrasher and his fellow researchers are based on the assumption that

A) workers of advanced age often face problems with productivity compared to younger workers.

B) previous surveys had considered an insufficient number of variables for self-reporting.

C) few aging workers make long-term career plans.

D) employers have an active interest in retaining relatively elderly workers.

5

Which choice provides the best evidence for the answer to the previous question?

A) Lines 19-24 ("In their . . . uncertainty")

B) Lines 28-31 ("In addition . . . work")

C) Lines 36-37 ("The survey . . . 50 to 71")

D) Lines 43-47 ("They . . . perspective")

6

The primary effect of the words "labeled" (line 55) and "identify" (line 64) is to create a tone that is

A) assertive, through dismissal of earlier systems.

B) concerned, through response to aging stereotypes.

C) uncommitted, through allusion to opposed ideals.

D) unbiased, through description of a method.

7

As used in line 79, "meet" most nearly means

A) hail.

B) confront.

C) satisfy.

D) join.

8

Which of the following, if true, would undermine the findings described in the passage?

A) Elderly test subjects have been shown to provide inconsistent responses to questions about aging when observed over the course of a few days.

B) Researchers have identified at least one aging subgroup that can be distinguished from both classic ager and healthy ager groups.

C) A "person-centered" approach to sociological research yields unreliable results for groups of more than 200 people.

D) An aging worker may provide quantitatively different responses when asked about subjective, functional, and organizational age.

9

According to the graph, the highest uncertainty level, in terms of percentage of individuals for the relevant group, can be traced to the question of

A) intellectually demanding activity for the control group.

B) intellectually demanding activity for the healthy agers.

C) lifespan for the control group.

D) lifespan for the healthy agers.

10

In relation to the research described in the passage (Thrasher et al.), the graph provides data that

A) resembles the information gathered at the outset of the research team's inquiry.

B) clarifies a point that the author leaves unresolved.

C) undermines one of the author's recommendations.

D) highlights a methodological shortcoming of the research team's approach.

CONTINUE

Reading 2

Questions 1-10 are based on the following passage and supplementary material.

This passage is an excerpt from Andrew J. O'Keefe II, "Welcome to the New Era of Easy Media Manipulation," an article originally published* in 2016 by SingularityHub.

Have you noticed how bizarre social media and the news cycle has been lately?

In the age of digital media, journalism
Line is changing significantly. Widely available
5 storytelling and distribution tools, misinformation spreading like wildfire, social media filter bubbles—headlines and stories are increasingly vying for attention, plastered across a smörgåsbord of platforms. Can media get any
10 stranger? Without a doubt.

The videos we watch and podcasts we listen to may themselves soon be seamlessly manipulated, distorting the truth in new ways. Photoshop was just the beginning. Advanced media creation tools
15 today are cheaper than ever, and innovative tech is accelerating the bleeding edge, further blurring the line between fantasy and reality.

One of the latest developments was introduced last week at the Adobe Max conference in San
20 Diego. Engineered to make audio editing easier, Adobe's Project VoCo allows users to edit voices by rearranging words or saying phrases never actually recorded—all via typing. The software requires a minimum of 20 minutes of recorded
25 talking to do its magic. Then you can make an edited or brand new snippet of speech. . . In short, this is the audio version of Photoshop— the ability to create something from nothing. A new generation of "sound-shopping," à la
30 photoshopping, has been born.

On the surface, many immediate practical applications like dialogue editing for video will become much easier. Gamers can also benefit from characters whose dialogue is more flexible
35 instead of defaulting to whatever the designers

initially wrote. And voice interfaces—like Siri or Alexa—are likely to sound more nuanced too.

But while the tone of the presentation was playful, the dark side of Project VoCo is hard
40 to ignore, and Adobe presenter Zeyu Jin didn't hesitate to share the negative implications. To combat misuse, he said Adobe is working on forgery prevention, using watermarks to distinguish between real or fake. It's also worth
45 noting that the tool isn't publicly available, as the project is still under development. Still, it won't be too long until such tools *are* available.

Video and sound manipulation isn't new, as anyone who's ever seen a Hollywood film can
50 attest. What's new is the affordability of such tools and the scale they can achieve nowadays versus expensive and complicated software workflows of the past. Anyone with a relatively affordable computer, hardware, and access to the internet
55 theoretically could do what once only major post-production studios could achieve.

Software alone won't devalue big budget Hollywood filmmaking—we can never seemingly have enough grandiose destruction in films these
60 days—but it will make user-generated content easier to produce at a much higher quality than previously imaginable. The future of media has already arrived, but distribution may be much more bottom-up than the top-down many have
65 come to expect, as more new tools roll out and greater numbers of people learn to use them.

Fake audio is only one facet of the larger emerging trend of audiovisual distortion. Video facial manipulation via Stanford's Face2Face
70 has shown promising results, and the software is similarly aimed at mass distribution. Beyond faces, Interactive Dynamic Video provides the ability to manipulate physical objects onscreen using software with shocking results. And there's
75 more: a newly developed machine learning algorithm can convert still images into mini videos, and it doesn't require video or audio at all, just a still image. Last but not least, we continue to see major advances in gaming graphics.

---

*See Page 85 for the citation for this text.

CONTINUE ➡

80 Each of these tools on its own isn't necessarily so harmful, but their convergence has huge implications. When computers are translating languages as well as humans and chatbots are becoming tools for communicating with dead
85 friends and relatives, piecing all these tools together is the magic glue that could one day create believable avatars of real, non-living or entirely fake personalities who can speak every language, personalize every one-on-one
90 interaction, and perform something different to a new audience every time.

Chatbot Identification
Success Rates from a 2019 Study

Response to Chatbot 1 (Monotone)

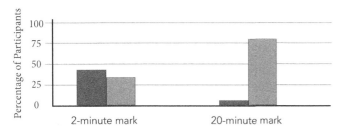

Response to Chatbot 2 (Human Inflection)

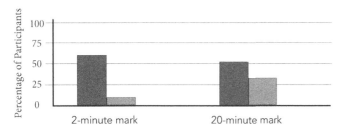

Response to Human Reading in a Monotone

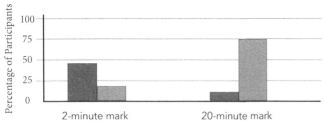

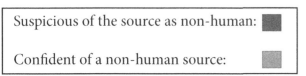

1

Which choice best describes the structure of the passage as a whole?

A) A mode of analysis is endorsed, its applicability to a recent breakthrough is explained, and adjustments to current concepts are proposed.

B) A research project is outlined, its deficiencies are explained with reference to a recent trial, and corrective measures are suggested.

C) A group of resources is described, a little-known liability is explained, and a tone of optimism in spite of reservations is established.

D) A broad tendency is delineated, its scope is explained with reference to an initiative from a single company, and consequences are assessed.

2

The author poses questions in lines 1-2 and lines 9-10 in order to

A) anticipate specific responses that help to move along a discussion.

B) pinpoint the problems that directly inspired the Adobe Max conference.

C) raise issues that are meant to provoke reflection yet do not suggest set conclusions.

D) cast doubt on the usefulness of the various technologies linked to Project VoCo.

3

As used in line 14, "Advanced" most nearly means

A) well-informed.

B) challenging.

C) sophisticated.

D) enlightened.

CONTINUE

4

As used in line 41, "share" most nearly means

A) propagate.

B) explain.

C) accommodate.

D) portion out.

5

Within the passage, the author calls attention to software-based tools that are notable for their

A) unpredictability.

B) insignificance.

C) permanence.

D) accessibility.

6

Which choice provides the best evidence for the answer to the previous question?

A) Lines 11-13 ("The videos . . . ways")

B) Lines 50-53 ("What's . . . past")

C) Lines 67-68 ("Fake . . . distortion")

D) Lines 80-82 ("Each . . . implications")

7

On the basis of the author's analysis of trends in imaging and audio software, current computer and video games are increasingly likely to feature

A) streamlined commands for how players command their in-game avatars.

B) more lifelike conversations among in-game characters

C) situations that resemble real-life predicaments.

D) extensive audio from human voice actors.

8

Which choice provides the best evidence for the answer to the previous question?

A) Lines 22-23 ("The software . . . magic")

B) Lines 33-36 ("Gamers . . . wrote")

C) Lines 62-65 ("The future . . . expect")

D) Lines 68-71 ("Video . . . distribution")

9

Which of the following statements accurately reflects the information in the three graphs?

A) A majority of listeners misidentified a human source as non-human at the 20-minute mark.

B) A majority of listeners misidentified a non-human source as human at the 20-minute mark.

C) Listeners unfailingly identified a monotone chatbot as a non-human source at the 20-minute mark.

D) Listeners remained mostly undecided for the identities of all three sources at the 20-minute mark.

10

The author of the passage would regard the information presented in the graphs as

A) representing a troubling and largely unforeseen consequence of technological progress.

B) indicating that technologies that can cause confusion among human listeners nonetheless have distinct practical purposes.

C) calling into question the idea that cutting-edge voice mimicry software is being widely used.

D) validating the idea that technological tools have been engineered to subtly and effectively mimic human speech.

Reading 3

Questions 1-10 are based on the following passage and supplementary material.

This passage is adapted from Reid Cramer, "Resilience and the contract of social insurance," an article originally published* in the digital magazine *Resilience* by NewAmerica.org.

When the Social Security Act of 1935 was signed into law, it established a far-reaching system of federal benefits that reset the terms of
Line the country's social contract. It created a federal
5 program to support retirees, the most widely-known benefit, but at the same time it created a series of grant programs so that states could provide additional assistance to the aged, the unemployed, families with dependent children,
10 and the disabled. The fundamental rationale of the entire legislative package was to erect, in President Franklin Roosevelt's words, "safeguards against misfortune." The creation of Social Security was nothing less than the advent of an
15 American system of social insurance. It rewrote the social contract.

Even before the first retirement benefits were distributed, the Act was amended in 1939 to extend benefits to the children and wives of
20 deceased or retired workers. From its earliest years, Social Security was intended as a means of providing economic security for whole families when they were most vulnerable, regardless of their stage of life. On behalf of us all, government
25 would ensure that families have access to cash to offset income involuntarily lost through a broad and diverse set of circumstances.

Fast-forward 75 years and our Social Security system has evolved in many ways. More workers
30 are covered and more benefits are provided. But the funding mechanism has stayed the same: a tax on income, collected as a deduction from every paycheck. The rate of that tax, known as "FICA" for the Federal Insurance Contributions
35 Act, had increased steadily, from two percent in the 1940s to 12.4 percent in the 1990s, where

it has plateaued. The income subject to the tax, called a wage base, has risen over time but is capped, so there is a limit on what high earners
40 pay. Qualifying for support does not depend on how much money a person made or how much has been saved. Once someone has worked enough to qualify for Social Security benefits (generally 10 years of earnings), enrollment is
45 automatic and access is universal. Benefit levels do vary so that higher earners receive marginally higher benefits, but Social Security payouts are generally progressive because they represent a higher proportion of earnings for workers at lower
50 income levels.

While some argue that this financing approach, benefit structure, and universality are important for maintaining political support for the program, my experience was revealing of the limits of the
55 public's understanding of the program's basic structure and the potential benefits at stake. In fact, contemporary discussions of the Social Security program's future usually focus on its retirement provisions, rather than its impact
60 on children. It's true that over two-thirds of beneficiaries are retired workers, so it makes sense that there's more public attention given to eligibility ages and cost-of-living adjustments for seniors than there is to the role of the program
65 in assisting families with dependent children. Yet 4.3 million children will receive Social Security benefits in 2019 because one or both of their parents are disabled, retired, or deceased. They represent about seven percent of all Social
70 Security beneficiaries. Children also benefit when others members of their household, such as grandparents, receive support as retirees. In 2017, disbursements directly to children topped $31 billion (about 3.3 percent of all Social Security
75 payments). That means the Social Security Administration pays more benefits to children than any other federal program does. . . .

"Promote the general welfare," is right there in the preamble to the Constitution: it is one of
80 the basic reasons that we have a government. Indeed, the preamble of the Social Security Act of 1935 uses the same language and states its

*See Page 85 for the citation for this text.

CONTINUE

purpose directly as to "provide for the general welfare by establishing a system of Federal old-
85 age benefits" and by enabling "more adequate provisions" for dependent children, the disabled, maternal and child welfare, public health, and the unemployed. The government programs launched in the 1930s, often considered separately, in
90 fact have a common origin. They reflect a social contract in which the government explicitly took on responsibility for the economic wellbeing of families to counterbalance arbitrary fluctuations of the economy and the uncertainties of life.

1

Based on the passage, which choice best describes how Social Security benefits relate to children?

A) Children are only eligible for benefits if they belong to families that do not have any reliable income sources.

B) Children represent a relatively small yet steadily growing proportion of all benefit recipients.

C) Children may receive benefits either due to specific adverse circumstances or through family connection to a beneficiary.

D) Children are more likely to be upwardly mobile later in life if they receive benefits in times of greatest financial need.

2

As used in the first paragraph, the words "reset" and "rewrote" help to portray Social Security as

A) preferable to comparable programs.

B) susceptible to further evolution.

C) contested at the time of its emergence.

D) transformative in its ultimate impact.

3

Which choice provides an example that most clearly fits "President Franklin Roosevelt's" (line 12) ideas about the goals of Social Security?

A) Lines 17-20 ("Even . . . workers")

B) Lines 37-40 ("The income . . . pay")

C) Lines 66-68 ("Yet . . . deceased")

D) Lines 75-77 ("That . . . program")

4

What does the chronology presented in the first two paragraphs indicate about the funds linked to Social Security?

A) Social Security was simultaneously seen as an economic necessity and a political liability.

B) No actual payments were issued in the year that the Social Security Act was signed into law.

C) The complete Social Security administrative system took four years to put in place.

D) Social Security was designed to be regularly and radically altered over time.

5

Which of the following situations would NOT fit the current structure of Social Security?

A) Social Security benefits represent a higher proportion of income for a lower-earning individual than for a higher-earning individual.

B) Social Security benefits are marginally higher for a lower-earning individual than for a higher-earning individual.

C) A lower-earning individual and a higher-earning individual pay the same Social Security tax rate.

D) A lower-earning individual and a higher-earning individual both receive annually increasing benefit payments.

CONTINUE

Part 1: Social Studies

Historical Data for the United States Social Security System

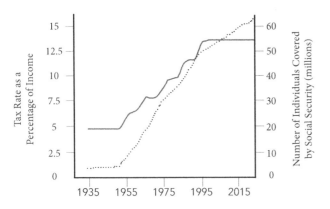

Tax Rate: ▬▬▬ Individuals Covered: •••••

8

The final paragraph of the passage primarily serves to depict Social Security as

A) mistakenly affiliated primarily with elderly Americans.

B) applicable to all Americans regardless of age and employment.

C) in accordance with longstanding American ideals.

D) immune to economic and political instability.

9

Which of the following is the most likely outcome if the trends depicted in the graph remain consistent from 1995 into the foreseeable future?

A) The Social Security tax rate increases; the number of individuals covered increases.

B) The Social Security tax rate increases; the number of individuals covered remains unchanged.

C) The Social Security tax rate remains unchanged; the number of individuals covered increases.

D) The Social Security tax rate remains unchanged; the number of individuals covered remains unchanged.

6

Which choice provides the best evidence for the answer to the previous question?

A) Lines 29-33 ("More . . . paycheck")

B) Lines 40-42 ("Qualifying . . . saved")

C) Lines 45-50 ("Benefit . . . levels")

D) Lines 60-65 ("It's true . . . children")

7

As used in line 69, "represent" most nearly means

A) advocate for.

B) portray.

C) are entitled to.

D) constitute.

10

Unlike the graph, the passage considers

A) how Social Security benefit payments vary depending on income level.

B) the increase in the total number of Americans covered by Social Security.

C) the current dollar amount of the average annual Social Security benefit payment.

D) the consistency of the Social Security tax rate in the recent past.

CONTINUE →

Reading 4

Questions 1-10 are based on the following passage and supplementary material.

This passage is an excerpt from Marta Gonzalez and Antonio Lima, "Recalculating! By not driving the optimal route, you're causing traffic jams," an article that originally appeared* in The Conversation in 2016.

If you use a car to get around, every time you get behind the wheel you're confronted with a choice: how will you navigate to your destination?
Line Whether it's a trip you take every day, such as
5 from home to work, or to someplace you haven't been before, you need to decide on a route.

Transportation research has traditionally assumed that drivers are very rational and choose the optimal route that minimizes travel
10 time. Traffic prediction models are based on this seemingly reasonable assumption. Planners use these models in their efforts to keep traffic flowing freely—when they evaluate a change to a road network, for instance, or the impact of a
15 new carpool lane. In order for traffic models to be reliable, they must do a good job reproducing user behavior. But there's little empirical support for the assumption at their core—that drivers will pick the optimal route.

20 For that reason, we decided to investigate how people make these choices in their real lives. Understanding how drivers build a route to reach their destination will help us gain insights into human movement behavior. Better knowledge
25 of individual routing can help improve urban infrastructure and GPS directions systems—not just for one driver, but for everyone. Beating congestion is a big goal: one estimate put the cost of traffic in 2014 at US$160 billion in the U.S.,
30 with 42 extra hours of travel time and $960 worth of extra fuel for every commuter.

Using GPS data collected for several months for hundreds of drivers in four European cities, we studied individuals' routing behavior, looking
35 for interesting patterns in their choices. We discovered that people use only a few routes

when moving between their relevant places, even when those trips are repeated again and again over extended periods. Most people have a single
40 favorite route for trips they perform routinely and a few alternative routes they take less frequently to the same destinations.

So did people in fact usually choose the optimal route?

45 In short, no. It turned out roughly half of the favorite routes are not the optimal routes suggested by navigation devices, such as those offered by some popular mapping apps for smartphones. If we also consider drivers'
50 alternative choices, even fewer routes are optimal—only a third overall minimize travel time. Our data provide empirical proof that drivers are not taking the optimal route, directly contradicting the shortest travel time assumption.

55 What's behind this result? A unique answer that is valid for every driver won't be easy to find. Prior small-scale studies found that many factors, some seemingly minor, might influence route preference. For example, people tend to choose
60 routes going south rather than routes of equal lengths that go north. People favor routes that are straight at the beginning, instead of shorter ones that aren't straight. Landmarks also influence route choice, by attracting more trips than travel-
65 time minimization would suggest. A novel app for iPhones builds on that very concept and allows people to find the most "interesting" route between two points.

People might not be able to determine which
70 route is optimal, among all possible choices, because of limited information and limited ability to process big amounts of information. Or, even if they can, people might deliberately make different choices, according to personal preference. Many
75 factors can influence preference, including fuel consumption, route reliability, simplicity, and pleasure.

Drivers' apparent flexibility on route choices may provide an opportunity to alleviate overall
80 congestion. For instance, smartphone apps could offer points and vouchers to drivers who are willing to take longer routes that avoid congested

*See Page 85 for the citation for this text.

CONTINUE ➤

areas. Navigation app Waze has already changed drivers' habits in some cities, so it's not so far-
85 fetched to imagine a gamification system that reduces congestion.

1

As used in line 16, "reproducing" most nearly means

A) changing.

B) emulating.

C) analyzing.

D) engaging.

2

The authors' definition of "optimal" revolves around the concept of

A) minimizing turns.

B) maximizing interesting scenery.

C) minimizing driving time.

D) minimizing fuel consumption.

3

Which choice provides the best evidence for the answer to the previous question?

A) Lines 17-19 ("But . . . route")

B) Line 51 ("only a . . . time")

C) Lines 61-63 ("People . . . straight")

D) Lines 65-68 ("A novel . . . points")

4

As used in line 55, "behind" calls attention to a factor that is notable for

A) rebutting a consensus.

B) following a prediction.

C) underlying a result.

D) emphasizing a dispute.

5

Which of the following, if true, would most serve to undermine the authors' claim that apps could help drivers to choose the fastest routes?

A) Apps do not have real-time traffic monitoring capabilities.

B) Some drivers do not like to spend money on apps.

C) Apps tend to give visual rather than auditory directions.

D) Using apps to improve navigation is a relatively new phenomenon.

6

Which of the following best supports the claim that people are generally creatures of habit when it comes to driving?

A) Lines 22-24 ("Understanding . . . behavior")

B) Lines 39-42 ("Most people . . . destinations")

C) Lines 69-72 ("People . . . information")

D) Lines 80-83 ("For instance . . . areas")

Study of U.S. Driver Preferences, 840 Individuals (2014)

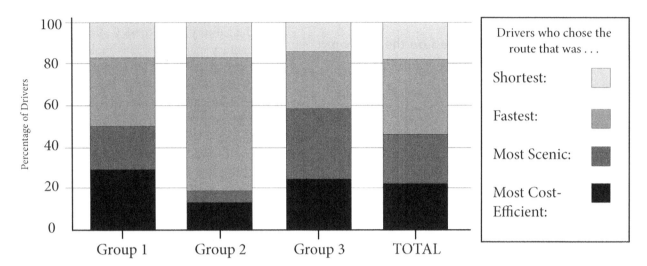

7

All of the following are mentioned by the author as being factors that affect route choice EXCEPT

A) fuel consumption.

B) simplicity.

C) avoiding tolls.

D) enjoyableness.

8

The example of Waze primarily serves to

A) offer justification for the primary point of the passage.

B) support the statement that follows the introduction of this example.

C) explain how technology leads to distracted driving.

D) posit a contrast with an earlier example of technology.

9

Which of the sub-groups represented in the graph yielded results that are most different from those across the entire 2014 study?

A) Group 1

B) Group 2

C) Group 3

D) No group, since the sub-groups all yielded similar results.

10

A driver who exhibits the behavior described in lines 63-68 ("Landmarks . . . two points") would mostly likely be placed in which category present in the graph?

A) Shortest

B) Fastest

C) Most Scenic

D) Most Cost-Efficient

CONTINUE

Reading 5

Questions 1-10 are based on the following passage and supplementary material.

This passage is adapted from Wendi Maloney and Julie Miller, "Crowdsourcing Helps to Unlock the Mystery of Cursive," an article published* in 2019 by the Library of Congress.

"That's so beautiful, but what does it say?" This is what we often hear from visitors to the Library of Congress when they see letters
Line and other documents written by hand. This
5 phenomenon—the inability of so many people to read handwriting—is the byproduct of a moment of technological change that is every bit as significant as the one that began with the introduction of the printing press by Johannes
10 Gutenberg in the middle of the 15th century. The digital age has transformed us from people who read and write by hand to people who type and read on a screen, from letter-writers to emailers, texters, and tweeters.
15   This change is so recent that our population now includes a mixture of people born before the digital age, who learned the techniques and conventions of handwriting and letter writing, and younger people, who grew up online. While older
20 people have had to learn the ways of the digital age, younger people know less and less about the ways of the analog world, even when its language and symbols persist into the digital—"cc," for example, which appears inklessly atop every
25 email message, recalls the inky blue sheets of paper typists rolled into their typewriters to make literal "carbon copies."
    Why does it matter? This isn't just a question of nostalgia, of regret for the old ways, such as the
30 lost art of cursive, which few children now learn in school. It matters because when people are unable to read old documents, they lose the ability to make personal contact with the past.
    Some very old documents necessarily require
35 interpretation by experts—for example, the Library's collection of cuneiform tablets, written

by the Sumerians on clay more than 4,000 years ago. Or the leather-bound volume of town records, in Spanish, from 16th-century Peru in
40 the Library's Harkness Collection. Or the 17th-century manuscript law books, in Shakespeare's English, collected by Thomas Jefferson.
    But documents from the 18th century, when the United States was founded, are written in English
45 that, with a couple of differences, is essentially modern. We sell ourselves short when we think we can't read them. There are a few things to learn, such as the long "s" which looks like an "f," the relatively nonstandard spelling and punctuation,
50 and some unfamiliar abbreviations. Another key to learning how to read 18th- and 19th-century writing is just to spend time looking at it, learning the writing conventions of the relatively recent past, as well as the idiosyncrasies of individual
55 writers. In time, the letters of George Washington will become as familiar to you as, say, a postcard from your Uncle Melvin.
    We saw living proof of this at a Nov. 19 event at the Library marking the 155th anniversary of
60 President Abraham Lincoln's Gettysburg Address. Members of the public and students from local Washington, D.C., schools were invited to the Library to view a copy of the Gettysburg Address and to try their hands at transcribing letters and
65 other documents in the Abraham Lincoln Papers on the Library's newly launched crowdsourcing website. Titled "By the People," the site makes images of thousands of original documents available to volunteers online, inviting them to
70 type documents, tag them with keywords to make them searchable, and review typed documents for accuracy. The transcripts are then added to the Library's website alongside the original documents.
75   At first, many of the visitors on Nov. 19, viewing 19th-century handwriting, said, "I can't read this." But when asked to pick out a letter or word anywhere on the page and then build on that kernel of understanding, they soon started to
80 identify familiar words, then phrases. By the end of a half hour, they were able to read 70 percent or more of documents. Dozens teamed up to arrange

*See Page 85 for the citation for this text.

CONTINUE

the full text of the Gettysburg Address using a large-format printed "puzzle" made of the words
85 composing Lincoln's speech. They eagerly hunted through piles, looking for letters and words that were becoming increasingly familiar.

Word Usage Over Time: Vocabulary from the Gettysburg Address

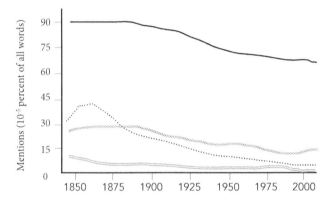

y-axis: Mentions (10^{5} percent of all words)
x-axis: 1850 1875 1900 1925 1950 1975 2000

"conceived": ▬▬▬   "consecrate": • • • • •
"hallow": ══════   "detract": ∞∞∞∞∞∞

1

One of the central ideas of the passage is that

A) interactive work with seemingly outmoded documents can make sources of this sort less daunting.

B) writing methods that are not based on technology are best suited to fostering critical thinking and attention to detail.

C) handwritten documents are valued primarily for the information that they provide about vanished cultures.

D) historical speeches should be analyzed in terms of both word choice and argumentative technique.

2

Over the course of the passage, the authors' primary focus shifts from

A) observation of a representative case to extension of the principles inherent in that case to a group of dilemmas.

B) criticism of a heavily biased outlook to advice on how to promote a more satisfying perspective.

C) narration of personal experience to depiction of varied points of view.

D) reflection on broadly-applicable conditions to description of a single endeavor.

3

The main purpose of the second paragraph (lines 15-27) is to

A) demonstrate that a technology-oriented way of writing is not automatically superior.

B) explain why specific audiences gravitate to markedly different writing practices.

C) outline the reasoning behind efforts to accustom modern readers to older documents.

D) show that terminology used by readers who are comfortable with technology often has roots in older habits.

4

As used in line 30, "lost" most nearly means

A) compromised.

B) misplaced.

C) undecided.

D) disregarded.

CONTINUE

5

Which initial response would the authors expect from a reader who has just encountered documents from an earlier century?

A) A desire to link the document to modern ideas

B) An instinctive statement of disapproval

C) A willingness to explore historical precedents

D) An expression of aesthetic appreciation

6

Which choice provides the best evidence for the answer to the previous question?

A) Lines 1-4 ("That's . . . hand")

B) Lines 4-7 ("This . . . change")

C) Lines 19-22 ("While . . . world")

D) Lines 31-33 ("It matters . . . past")

7

The authors of the passage suggest that today's readers can succeed in understanding documents from hundreds of years ago by

A) comparing them to modern documents that address similar topics.

B) identifying small yet accessible features of those documents as starting points.

C) re-writing the documents with modernized spelling and lettering.

D) quickly skimming through any given document before performing a more precise analysis of its details.

8

Which choice provides the best evidence for the answer to the previous question?

A) Lines 55-60 ("In time . . . Address")

B) Lines 67-69 ("Titled . . . online")

C) Lines 72-74 ("The transcripts . . . documents")

D) Lines 77-80 ("But . . . phrases")

9

As used in line 85, "eagerly" most nearly means

A) diligently.

B) naively.

C) impulsively.

D) creatively.

10

How does the graph that accompanies the passage build on the authors' discussion?

A) By suggesting that the Gettysburg address, while initially intimidating to some readers, had a formative influence on contemporary English

B) By indicating that technology, while often seen as diminishing historical appreciation, can enable useful analysis of the Gettysburg Address

C) By demonstrating that the Gettysburg Address, beyond presenting challenging handwriting, features increasingly uncommon words

D) By showing that subtle vocabulary choices, while often underestimated, can have an important effect on the reception of a document such as the Gettysburg Address

CONTINUE

Reading 6

Questions 1-10 are based on the following passage and supplementary material.

This passage is adapted from Chris Baraniuk, "How going hungry affects children for their whole lives," an article published* by Mosaic in 2019.

Kerry Wright didn't feel hungry. Not in the way you might expect. Her tummy grumbled, yes; she could hear it. She just couldn't feel it. She
Line called it "starvation mode." Wright, a mother of
5 three living in Aberdeen, had hit a low point. But she needed to provide for her children, who then were just entering their teens.

By the time she was faced with the prospect of watching her own children go without, she had
10 fallen out of contact with her parents and the rest of her family. She'd wanted a fresh start, except that at that moment, in 2013, a fresh start was looking pretty far off. Her partner had left and her benefits were falling short. Now and again, she
15 took paid housework jobs but never made enough money. She would scan her cupboards in despair, hoping there would be enough soup or tins of beans to at least get the next lunch together. . . .

What happened to Wright and her family
20 is common to far more households in wealthy countries than some may think. Food insecurity, also known as food poverty, is on the rise in the UK, the ninth-richest country in the world. The exact extent is unknown, but many other
25 countries are struggling with this problem. There are millions of families in Europe, the U.S., and Canada, for example, that are facing food insecurity right now.

Food banks, which hand out free supplies of
30 food to those in need, have become more and more common in places where food insecurity has become a persistent problem. But even the groups that run them, including the Trussell Trust in the UK, say that food banks cannot be a long-
35 term solution. The food they provide can vary in quantity and quality—often it is nutritionally limited. Systemic reform, charitable organisations

say, is needed to stop families from falling into the hunger trap.
40   Scientists have shown that hunger isn't just something transient. Hunger during childhood can have a ripple effect that we are only just beginning to understand. The long-term physical and psychological consequences of hunger are
45 serious and have implications for the health of society itself. Food insecurity may be a ticking time-bomb for today's hungry generations—just how dangerous is it? . . .

In a phone call to Valerie Tarasuk at the
50 University of Toronto, I mention Kerry Wright's experience and her worries about her children's mental wellbeing.

"The woman's obviously very astute," says Tarasuk. "That's exactly what we need to be
55 concerned about amongst those children."

Tarasuk is a professor of nutritional sciences and an expert on the relationship between food insecurity and health. She and colleagues have analysed national data on tens of thousands of
60 Canadians to show that the more severe a person's experience of food insecurity, the more likely that person is to seek help from healthcare services. But she also tracks research that explores the long-term effects on children who live in food-
65 insecure homes.

Studies by a team at the University of Calgary, including Sharon Kirkpatrick and Lynn McIntyre, have shown that going hungry just a handful of times is associated with poorer physical and
70 mental health. It also means that children are less likely to finish school.

In one six-year study, McIntyre and colleagues found that young people who had experienced hunger had a significantly higher risk of
75 developing depressive symptoms. And another large analysis showed that children who went hungry were similarly at risk of developing some kind of health problem within the next ten years. Hunger, the researchers wrote, had a
80 "toxic" effect: "Higher odds of chronic conditions and of asthma were observed among youth who experienced multiple episodes of hunger compared with those who were never hungry."

*See Page 85 for the citation for this text.

CONTINUE ➡

These findings held up even when other
85 things that could influence health were factored
in—hunger really does appear to play a defining
role. "The exposure that children have leaves an
indelible mark on them," says Tarasuk. "It's really
a bad idea to be leaving so many languishing in
90 this situation."

1

In the first two paragraphs of the passage, the author characterizes Kerry Wright as

A) hopeful that her children will build their lives in prosperous communities.

B) unaware of the extent of her financial struggles.

C) dedicated to some members of her family but alienated from others.

D) dependent on charity for most of her resources.

2

It can be inferred that Kerry Wright's situation is

A) the outcome of a socioeconomic transformation.

B) one of the causes of reinvigorated public attention to food insecurity.

C) a cautionary example for other low-income adults.

D) representative of a widespread form of hardship.

3

Which choice provides the best evidence for the answer to the previous question?

A) Lines 1-4 ("Kerry Wright . . . mode")

B) Lines 8-11 ("By the time . . . family")

C) Lines 11-14 ("She'd . . . short")

D) Lines 19-21 ("What . . . think")

4

Which choice supports the idea that practical measures are being taken to remedy food insecurity?

A) Lines 29-32 ("Food . . . problem")

B) Lines 46-48 ("Food . . . is it?")

C) Lines 49-52 ("In a . . . wellbeing")

D) Lines 80-83 ("Higher . . . hungry")

Food Insecurity in the United Kingdom by Year

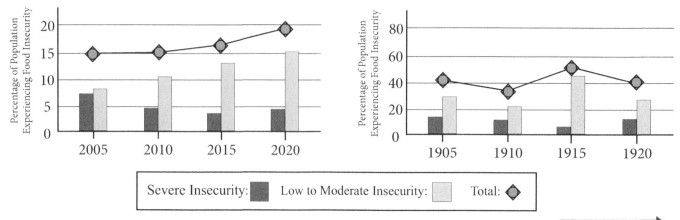

Severe Insecurity: ▮ Low to Moderate Insecurity: ▯ Total: ◈

Part 1: Social Studies

5

Which choice best captures the difference between how the word "experience" functions in line 51 and line 61, respectively?

A) To present an assumption; to raise a reservation

B) To emphasize a source of suffering; to propose a solution

C) To reference a single case; to explain a pattern of behavior

D) To address a possible bias; to establish a tone of objectivity

6

Which of the following facts, if true, would most indicate that Valerie Tarasuk's ideas are applicable beyond Canada?

A) Food insecurity and household income correlate strongly for residents of Japan.

B) Food insecurity and high school dropout rates correlate strongly for residents of Japan.

C) Residents of Japan who experience high food insecurity make a correspondingly high number of annual health clinic visits.

D) Residents of Japan who have never experienced food insecurity make fewer health clinic visits per year than residents of Canada who experience some food insecurity.

7

The author mentions Sharon Kirkpatrick and Lynn MacIntyre as two individuals who have

A) developed new terminology to describe hunger.

B) contributed to an initiative to combat food insecurity.

C) disputed some of Valerie Tarasuk's main theories.

D) linked food insecurity to educational attainment.

8

As used in line 84, "held up" most nearly means

A) became prominent.

B) began to stabilize.

C) resisted criticism.

D) remained valid.

9

Taken together, the graphs support the idea that the percentage of the U.K. population experiencing some form of food insecurity in the recent past

A) will most likely return to its historical maximum.

B) has increased but is not currently at a historic high.

C) can decrease if public policy adjustments come into play.

D) depends on the relative health of the national economy.

10

What is the relationship between the information contained in the passage and the information presented in the graphs?

A) For a population that the passage also addresses, the first graph (2005-2020) indicates the scope and proportion of food insecurity.

B) For a population that the passage also addresses, the first graph (2005-2020) explains the total number of individuals affected by food insecurity.

C) The second graph (1905-1920) indicates that a problem addressed in the passage is more severe than was once believed.

D) The second graph (1905-1920) indicates that a problem addressed in the passage is less severe that is widely assumed.

CONTINUE

Reading 7

Questions 1-10 are based on the following passage and supplementary material.

This passage is an excerpt from Vanessa Bates Ramirez, "Are Robots Coming for Our Jobs? Careful, It's a Trick Question," an article originally published* by SingularityHub in 2019.

The robots are coming, and they'll probably take your job when they get here.

Oh wait—have you heard that recently? As
Line   recently as, say, yesterday? In the news, or from
5   a coworker, or in a sinister dystopian movie,
maybe?

Sounding the alarm about job losses to automation has become commonplace—in fact, it's more of a nonstop siren these days.
10   Multiple Democratic presidential candidates are featuring their plans to combat Big Tech and solve technological unemployment as talking points of their campaigns. Dread of a robot-dominated future is mounting.
15   One of the most widely-referenced and panic-inducing figures on the topic came from a 2013 paper by two Oxford economists, Michael Osborne and Carl Benedikt Frey. Their research found that up to 47 percent of American jobs were
20   at risk of being automated by the mid-2030s. According to *The Economist*, the paper has been cited in over 4,000 articles, unnerving workers in all sectors of the economy and justifying catastrophic outlooks.
25   But last month Frey, a Swedish economic historian, published a book called *The Technology Trap: Capital, Labor, and Power in the Age of Automation* that aims to dispel some of the hysteria the paper raised. Not only must the 47
30   percent figure be deconstructed in a more nuanced manner, he says, but the public's acceptance of or resistance to technological advancement could also play a major role in job creation.

The research underlying the 2013 paper, aptly
35   titled "The Future of Employment," aimed to quantify how progress in tech could impact jobs.

The authors classified 702 occupations using a machine learning algorithm.

To train the algorithm, they chose 70 jobs
40   whose computerization label they felt confident about—such as delivery drivers, maids, civil engineering technicians, sheet metal workers, and utility meter readers—and labeled them as automatable or non-automatable. For each job,
45   they considered the question, "Can the tasks of this job be sufficiently specified, conditional on the availability of big data, to be performed by state-of-the-art computer-controlled equipment?"

The authors noted that automation will depend
50   partly on engineers overcoming computerization "bottlenecks" in increasingly complex areas, starting with perception and manipulation, then moving to creative intelligence, and finally tackling social intelligence.
55   Unsurprisingly, jobs requiring creative and social intelligence were deemed least likely to be automated: recreational therapists, mechanic and repair supervisors, and emergency management directors topped the list—no robot will be stealing
60   their jobs anytime soon. Dentists, dietitians, and elementary school teachers can settle in for the long haul, too.

On the other end of the spectrum—or in this case, the long, long list—some of the jobs
65   most susceptible to automation were insurance underwriters, telemarketers, tax preparers, and sports officials like referees. Taken as a whole, the authors found 47 percent of US employment at risk of being disrupted by automation.
70   But let's consider that wording. It doesn't say 47 percent of jobs will be automated. It says 47 out of every 100 jobs could conceivably be done by computers one day in the future if a bunch of massive engineering challenges get solved, not to
75   mention if regulations and public opposition don't get in the way.

Throughout history, technology has always created more jobs than it has destroyed. To use a generic but straightforward metaphor: if the
80   economy is a pie, tech allocates more slices to some people and fewer slices to others in the short term. But in the long term, new technologies

*See Page 85 for the citation for this text.

CONTINUE ▶

always make the whole pie bigger; thus, there's more to go around.

85   Need a concrete, recent example? Look at mobile phone usage in developing countries. A 10 percent increase in cell phone ownership among citizens of developing countries can boost per capita GDP growth by about 1 percent per 90 year. Adding mobile Internet to the equation nudges growth up even more. Farmers in Kenya and shopkeepers in India aren't as well-off as the Silicon Valley engineers who designed their phones—but they're certainly more well-off than 95 they were before. Absolute poverty rates around the world have fallen faster in the past 30 years than at any other time on record.

Composition of the United States Workforce

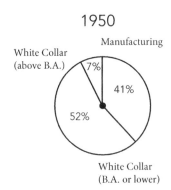

1950

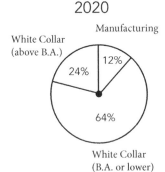

2020

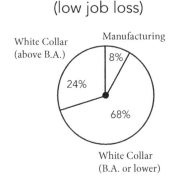

2040 estimate (high job loss)

2040 estimate (low job loss)

1

Which choice provides the most direct support for the author's assertion in lines 7-9 ("Sounding . . . days")?

A) Lines 18-20 ("Their . . . mid-2030s")

B) Lines 21-24 ("According . . . outlooks")

C) Lines 25-29 ("But . . . raised")

D) Lines 29-33 ("Not . . . creation")

2

As used in line 11, "solve" most nearly means

A) analyze.

B) remedy.

C) promote.

D) finalize.

3

As used in line 22, "unnerving" most nearly means

A) bewildering.

B) enfeebling.

C) demoralizing.

D) astounding.

4

The passage indicates that Karl Benedikt Frey regards the "47 percent" job automation estimate as

A) a loose extrapolation that has received more publicity than it deserves.

B) a misinterpreted prediction that requires subtle attention.

C) a broad yet useful starting point for further research.

D) a questionable figure that is nonetheless useful in prompting reflection.

CONTINUE

Part 1: Social Studies

5

The purpose of the discussion in the sixth and seventh paragraphs (lines 34-48) is to

A) show that automation can lead to improved efficiency and facilitate problem-solving.

B) pinpoint the procedures behind Osborne and Frey's investigation.

C) specify which jobs are most severely threatened by a shift to automation.

D) emphasize that Osborne and Frey hoped to dispel misconceptions about job loss.

6

The passage indicates that the number of jobs lost to automation may NOT reach 47 percent as a result of

A) government intervention.

B) political radicalism.

C) economic hardship

D) international collaboration.

7

Which choice provides the best evidence for the answer to the previous question?

A) Lines 55-60 ("Unsurprisingly . . . soon")

B) Lines 63-67 ("On the other . . . referees")

C) Lines 71-76 ("It says . . . way")

D) Lines 95-97 ("Absolute . . . record")

8

According to the author, social progress related to increased technology use involves

A) continuing inequality despite noted improvements in quality of life.

B) prioritization of interpersonal skills as superior to aptitudes in research and data analysis.

C) trade-offs that leave some workers suspicious of elected leaders and public institutions.

D) sequences of dislocation and adjustment that vary considerably in intensity from culture to culture.

9

Assuming that the number of workers in the United States steadily increases, which of the following categories from the graphs represents the highest quantity?

A) 1950, all white-collar workers

B) 2020, all white-collar workers

C) 2040, all white-collar workers (high job loss)

D) 2040, all white-collar workers (low job loss)

10

According to both the passage and the figures, the composition of the United States workforce

A) will in the future feature fewer manufacturing workers despite considerable increases in manufacturing productivity.

B) is susceptible to job loss even though the future extent of such a trend is unclear.

C) is unlikely to see the proportion of white-collar workers with graduate degrees rise above 40%.

D) should not exhibit a portion of manufacturing workers below 3% at any point.

CONTINUE ➡

Reading 8

Questions 1-10 are based on the following passage and supplementary material.

This passage is adapted from Alex Theng, "Watch Where I'm Going: Predicting Pedestrian Flow," an article that was originally published* in 2014 by EveryONE, the official blog of the research journal PLOS ONE.

At last check, the population of the world was around 7.1 billion and counting. As we all know, the sheer number of people on the planet presents a host of new challenges and exacerbates existing

Line 5   ones. The overarching population problem may seem daunting, but there's still plenty we can do to make a crowded, urbanized world livable. A new study in PLOS ONE focuses on the specific issue of pedestrian traffic and how to accurately model

10   the flow of people through their environment.

Researchers with Siemens and the Munich University of Applied Sciences examined video recordings of commuters walking through a major German train station on a weekday, during

15   both the morning and evening peak commute times. Scientists analyzed the videos to determine individual pedestrians' paths and walking speeds, and used the resulting data to set the parameters for a simulation of pedestrian traffic flow.

20   According to the authors, this kind of calibration of theoretical models using real-world data is largely missing from the most pedestrian flow models, which are under-validated and imprecise.

The authors utilized a cellular automaton

25   model to form the basis of this simulation. Cellular automatons are models in which cells in a grid evolve and change values through steps based on specific rules. In this instance, the authors used a hexagonal grid and a few simple rules about

30   pedestrian movement:

- Pedestrians know and will follow the shortest path to their destination unless pedestrians or other obstacles are in the way.

35   - Pedestrians will walk at their own individual preferred speeds, so long as the path is unobstructed.
- Individuals need personal space, which acts like a repelling force to other

40   pedestrians and objects.
- Walking speeds decrease as crowds get denser.
- Factors like age and fitness are all captured by setting a range of individual walking

45   speeds.

This model also borrowed from electrostatics by treating people like electrons. As the authors write, "pedestrians are attracted by positive charges, such as exits, and repelled by negative

50   charges, such as other pedestrians or obstacles."

Add to this model rules about when and where pedestrians appear, the starting points and destinations, and the relative volume of traffic from each starting point to different destinations,

55   and you've got a basic model of pedestrian traffic.

Next, the authors calibrated this model by setting parameters using real-world, observational data from the train station videos: where people at each starting point were going, distance kept from walls, the distribution of walking speeds,

60   and so on. To test their model and its parameters, the authors validated it by running predictive simulations and comparing simulated conditions to real-world scenarios. Based on the results,

65   the authors suggest that this kind of model, which includes parameters based on real-world observation, more accurately represents pedestrian flow than do other models of walkers that do not incorporate observational data.

70   The authors also changed multiple parameters to determine which ones had the largest impact on the simulation. The parameter that had the largest effect when altered was the source-target distribution (the destinations of people coming

75   from specific starting points), so the authors note that this is critical to measure accurately and precisely.

The ability to precisely predict the flow of traffic has many clear applications, from the

*See Page 85 for the citation for this text.

CONTINUE

Part 1: Social Studies

80 design of buildings and public spaces to the prediction and prevention of unsafe crowd densities during large events or emergencies.
Next research question: when it's crowded, does pushing really not make it go faster?

1

The main purpose of the passage is to

A) overturn faulty yet common assumptions about how pedestrians navigate their surroundings.

B) call attention to the value of using scientific methods to clarify ethical practices by focusing on a single project at length.

C) provide a series of user-friendly guidelines for effectively navigating public spaces.

D) describe an interdisciplinary endeavor that illuminates everyday behaviors and decisions.

2

As described in the passage, what deficiency in earlier studies did researchers from Siemens and the Munich University of Applied Sciences want to correct?

A) Modeling of unrealistic simulated obstacles

B) Overly simplistic positive and negative inputs

C) Use of generally low-quality video footage

D) Insufficient attention to the experiences of actual pedestrians

3

Which choice provides the best evidence for the answer to the previous question?

A) Lines 11-16 ("Researchers . . . times")

B) Lines 16-19 ("Scientists . . . flow")

C) Lines 20-23 ("According . . . imprecise")

D) Lines 46-50 ("This model . . . obstacles")

4

Which of the following situations would represent a departure from the "few simple rules" (line 29) for the simulation mentioned in the passage?

A) Two pedestrians walking together achieve faster and more efficient movement than either pedestrian does individually.

B) Two pedestrians moving in the same direction vary their walking paces and their distance from one another considerably.

C) One pedestrian naturally slows down if he is approaching a large and stationary crowd.

D) One pedestrian walks through an area with no obstacles at twice the speed of another pedestrian.

5

Which choice provides the best evidence for the answer to the previous question?

A) Lines 31-34 ("Pedestrians . . . way")

B) Lines 35-37 ("Pedestrians . . . unobstructed")

C) Lines 38-42 ("Individuals . . . denser")

D) Lines 43-45 ("Factors . . . speeds")

6

The statement in lines 46-47 ("This model . . . electrons") suggests that the authors of the study

A) would have achieved unreliable results had they relied solely on a cellular automaton model.

B) were unaware of the usefulness of an electrostatic model when they were first designing the study.

C) used a further set of conventions to complement elements of a cellular automaton model.

D) believe that their work with pedestrian movement will be of use to particle physicists.

CONTINUE

Movement Efficiency of a "Model" Pedestrian, Multiple Sequences

	Sequence of Inputs (P = positive; N = negative) for pedestrian model								Efficiency (1-10 scale)
1	N	P	N	P	N	P	N	P	2.00
2	P	N	P	N	P	N	P	N	2.50
3	N	N	P	P	N	N	P	P	2.00
4	P	P	N	N	P	P	N	N	3.50
5	P	P	N	P	N	N	P	N	3.50
6	N	N	P	N	P	P	N	P	2.50
7	P	P	P	N	N	N	P	N	2.50

7

As used in line 60, "distribution" most nearly means

A) circulation.

B) administration.

C) occurrence.

D) handling.

8

As used in line 76, the word "critical" could mean all of the following EXCEPT

A) imperative.

B) pivotal.

C) essential.

D) unforgiving.

9

According to the table, the movement efficiency of a "model" pedestrian is most clearly dependent on

A) the configuration of positive and negative inputs.

B) the duration of each positive or negative input.

C) the initial speed enabled by the early positive inputs.

D) the initial delay occasioned by the early negative inputs.

10

The authors of the study mentioned in the passage and the researchers who produced the table understand positive and negative inputs in the same way. Which could thus be the input sequence for Pedestrian 7?

A) Pedestrian (3); Exit sign (3); Pedestrian (2)

B) Pedestrian (2); Obstacle (1); Exit Sign (3); Pedestrian (2)

C) Exit Sign (3); Pedestrian (3); Exit Sign (2)

D) Exit Sign (3); Obstacle (1); Pedestrian (2); Exit Sign (1); Pedestrian (1)

29

Part 1: Social Studies

Reading 9

Questions 1-10 are based on the following passage and supplementary material.

This passage is adapted from Fleur Macdonald, "Urban living makes us miserable. This city is trying to change that," an article that originally appeared* in 2019 in Mosaic Science.

If you live in Glasgow, you are more likely to die young. Men there die a full seven years earlier than their counterparts in other UK cities.
Line Until recently, the causes of this excess mortality
5 remained a mystery. "Deep-fried Mars bars," some have speculated. "The weather," others suggested. For years, those reasons were as good as any. In 2012, *The Economist* described the situation thus: "It is as if a malign vapour rises
10 from the Clyde at night and settles in the lungs of sleeping Glaswegians." The phenomenon has become known as the Glasgow Effect. But David Walsh, a public health programme manager at the Glasgow Centre for Population Health who
15 led a study on the excess deaths in 2010, wasn't satisfied with how the term was being used. "It turned into a Scooby-Doo mystery but it's not an exciting thing. It's about people dying young; it's about grief."
20   Walsh wanted to work out why Glaswegians have a 30 per cent higher risk of dying prematurely—that is, before the age of 65—than those living in similar post-industrial British cities. In 2016 his team published a report looking
25 at 40 hypotheses—from vitamin D deficiency to obesity and sectarianism. "The most important reason is high levels of poverty, full stop," says Walsh. "There's one in three children who is classed as living in poverty at the moment."
30   But even with deprivation accounted for, mortality rates in Glasgow remained inexplicable. Deaths in each income group are about 15 per cent higher than in Manchester or Liverpool. In particular, deaths from "diseases of despair"—
35 drug overdoses, suicides, and alcohol-related deaths—are high. In the mid-2000s, after adjusting for sex, age and deprivation, there was almost a 70 per cent higher mortality rate for suicide in Glasgow than in the two English
40 cities. Walsh's report revealed that radical urban planning decisions from midcentury onwards had made the physical and mental health of Glasgow's population more vulnerable to the consequences of deindustrialisation and poverty.
45   Shifting theories of city planning have profoundly altered people's lives everywhere, and particularly over the past half-century in Glasgow. The city's population stands at about 600,000 now. In 1951, it was nearly double this.
50 Glasgow's excess mortality, the report suggests, is the unintended legacy of urban planning that exacerbated the already considerable challenges of living in a city.
     Studies have consistently linked city living
55 with poorer mental health. For example, growing up in an urban environment is correlated with twice the risk of developing schizophrenia for growing up in the countryside. By 2050, 68 per cent of the world's population will live in cities,
60 according to UN figures. The consequences for global health are likely to be significant.
     Can we learn from what happened in Glasgow? As an increasing number of people move to or are born in cities, questions of fragmented
65 communities, transient populations, overcrowding, inequality, and segregation—and how these affect the wellbeing of residents—will become more acute.
     Are urban dwellers doomed to poor mental
70 health or can planners learn from the mistakes of the past and design cities that will keep us healthy and happy? In postwar Glasgow, local authorities decided to tackle the city's severe overcrowding. The 1945 Bruce report proposed housing people
75 in high-rises on the periphery of the city centre. The Clyde Valley report published a year later suggested encouraging workers and their families to move to new towns. In the end, the council adopted a combination of both. . . .
80   The rapid change in the city's make-up was soon recognised as disastrous. Relocating workers and their families to new towns was described

---

*See Page 85 for the citation for this text.

CONTINUE

in mid-1960s parliamentary discussions as "skimming the cream." In an internal review in
85 1971, the Scottish Office noted that the manner of population reduction was "destined within a decade or so to produce a seriously unbalanced population with a very high proportion [in central Glasgow] of the old, the very poor, and the almost
90 unemployable . . . "

Although the government was soon aware of the consequences, these were not necessarily intentional, says Walsh. "You have to understand what sort of shape Glasgow was in, in terms of
95 the really lousy living conditions, the levels of overcrowded housing and all the rest of it," he says. "They thought the best approach was to just start afresh."

1

A central idea of the passage is that

A) attempts to decrease urban population density have an unfortunate tendency to result in overcrowding.

B) urban planning that combines economic and mental health considerations is a regarded as both unprecedented and useful.

C) well-intentioned urban planning projects can backfire in a manner that harms economic conditions and quality of life.

D) urban planners are unlikely to understand the forms of suffering faced by the poorest city residents.

2

The first paragraph of the passage serves to characterize the "Glasgow Effect" as

A) a bizarre fact of life that has become a source of dismissive commentary.

B) a concerning reality that has eluded explanation.

C) a problem traceable to a single city landmark.

D) an illusory condition that has been widely publicized.

3

As used in line 20, "work out" most nearly means

A) pursue new measures for.

B) optimize results as to.

C) resolve the question of.

D) display discipline on.

4

Which choice offers the best support for the thesis set forward in "Walsh's report" (line 40)?

A) Lines 24-26 ("In 2016 . . . sectarianism")

B) Lines 58-61 ("By 2050 . . . significant")

C) Lines 63-68 ("As an increasing . . . acute")

D) Lines 80-81 ("The rapid . . . disastrous")

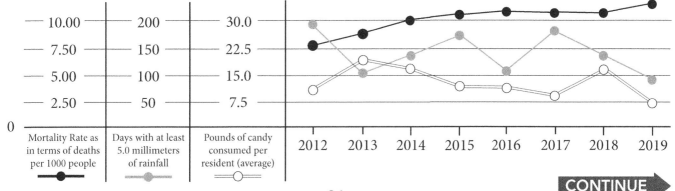

Mortality Rate, Weather, and Food Consumption Data for Glasgow

CONTINUE

Part 1: Social Studies

5

The author suggests that the correlation between city life and poor mental health, as seen in Glasgow, is

A) aggravated principally by climate and weather conditions in Glasgow.

B) linked to the life expectancy of elderly residents in a fairly predictable fashion.

C) distinct and observable in other urban contexts.

D) evident in the same proportions in nearby cities.

6

Which choice provides the best evidence for the answer to the previous question?

A) Lines 30-33 ("But even . . . Liverpool")

B) Lines 54-55 ("Studies . . . health")

C) Lines 69-72 ("Are urban . . . happy?")

D) Lines 84-90 ("In an internal . . . unemployable")

7

As used in line 68, "acute" most nearly means

A) incisive.

B) direct.

C) pronounced.

D) sensitive.

8

According to the passage, David Walsh regards the recommendations of the Bruce report and the Clyde Valley report as

A) informed by a planning approach that has succeeded in locations other than Glasgow.

B) only loosely related to the "mystery" of excess mortality in Glasgow.

C) efficient in method but uncharitable in intent.

D) understandable in aim yet ultimately misguided.

9

The graph for conditions in Glasgow indicates a strong positive correlation for

A) mortality rate and annual number of rainy days.

B) mortality rate and candy consumption per person per year.

C) all three of the factors measured.

D) none of the three factors measured.

10

Which topic from the passage is the graph most useful in helping to analyze?

A) Specific proposed causes of "excess mortality" (line 4) in Glasgow

B) The role of "high levels of poverty" (line 27) as a cause of Glasgow's problems

C) The link between city living and "poorer mental health" (line 55)

D) Outcomes of a past "approach" (line 97) to revitalizing Glasgow

CONTINUE

Reading 10

Questions 1-10 are based on the following passage and supplementary material.

This passage is adapted from Maureen Soyars, "Big-box stores pay workers good wages," an article published* in 2014 by the Bureau of Labor Statistics.

As the labor market has struggled to recover from the recent recession, there's been a lot of talk about the creation of "good jobs"—jobs that
Line pay high wages and offer good benefits. There is
5 concern that many middle-class "good jobs," such as those in manufacturing, have been replaced with minimum wage jobs, such as those in retail. A new study looks at the recent expansion of the retail industry, especially the growth of big-box
10 chain stores, and examines the wages that go along with jobs at these stores. Jobs in retail are plentiful, but are these jobs good for workers?

In their article "Do large modern retailers pay premium wages?" Brianna Cardiff-Hicks,
15 Francine Lafontaine, and Kathryn Shaw show that workers can make more money working for large chain stores than for mom-and-pop shops, that wages grow as the firm and establishment size grow, and that promotion potential increases at
20 larger stores, which can potentially lead to higher wages. An establishment usually has one location where business is conducted. Most firms have a single establishment, but the majority of workers are employed by firms that comprise several
25 establishments under the same ownership.

The retail industry has flourished in recent years. The segment with the most growth is the modern retail industry, which is made up of firms, such as Starbucks or Wal-Mart, that have
30 developed regional or national chains in the past few decades. Retail has grown more concentrated, with fewer firms making up a larger percentage of the pie. The authors indicate that the four-firm concentration ratio—that is, the market share of
35 the four largest firms—grew from 5.2 percent in 1987 to 12.3 by 2007. And larger firms have become more common, as big-box retailers continue to pop up across the country. According to the article, 41 percent of full-time workers in
40 retail work in firms of 1,000 or more workers.

According to the authors' calculations, large firms pay higher wages than smaller, mom-and-pop retailers. For example, large firms (with 100 to 499 workers) pay workers with a high school
45 education 20.9 percent more than small firms (with fewer than 10 workers) do. Workers with some college or a college degree or earn 30.1 percent more at a large firm than at a small firm.

Larger establishments pay higher wages, too.
50 According to the study, a store with at least 500 employees pays 26 percent more to high-school educated workers and 36 percent more to workers with some college education (including college degree or more) than stores with fewer than 10
55 workers. The authors attribute the wage gains to the ability of large firms and establishments to "hire and promote the more able."

Larger retailers offer employees more opportunities for promotion within the company,
60 and managers at big-box stores earn more than managers at mom-and-pop stores. There is a wide pay gap between managers and non-managers: a high-school educated manager in a small store earns 12.6 percent more than a nonmanager; a
65 high-school educated manager at a large store earns 28.2 percent more than a nonmanager.

The authors suggest that these statistics on retail wages can help to inform policy decisions intended to increase middle-class jobs.
70 Employment opportunities in modern retail chains are growing, while employment in manufacturing has shrunk. And although the retail sector pays considerably less than the manufacturing sector, there are ample opportunities in retail for well-
75 paid management positions. Instead of focusing resources on bringing outsourced manufacturing jobs back to the United States, the authors note that a more successful strategy may be to improve training for workers in modern retail firms, with
80 an eye toward preparing workers to be managers.

---

*See Page 85 for the citation for this text.

CONTINUE ➡

Part 1: Social Studies

Data for Big Box Store Employees

Figure 1: Survey results for 1073 employees

Are you at present . . .	Yes	No	Unsure
satisfied with your wages?	732	145	196
enjoying your job duties?	669	102	302
trying to get promoted?	565	377	131
hoping to find a new job?	266	576	231

Figure 2: Entry-level hourly wages (nationwide average for each company, February 2020)

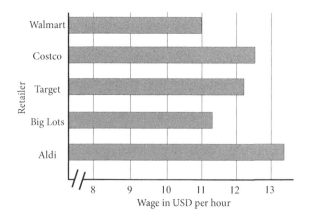

1

Based on the passage, what relationship between company size and employee wages does the study by Brianna Cardiff-Hicks, Francine Lafontaine, and Kathryn Shaw suggest?

A) Larger companies pay higher wages almost entirely to college-educated employees.

B) Larger companies pay higher wages to employees at all education levels.

C) Smaller companies pay higher wages only in order to retain college-educated employees.

D) Smaller companies pay lower wages in order to fuel their expansion into large companies.

2

Which of the following would NOT fit the concept of a "good job" as explained in the first paragraph?

A) A manufacturing job that demands long hours but offers an industry-leading wage and extensive benefits

B) A sales job that is structured to offer commission, benefits, and a reasonable base wage

C) An administrative job that provides a traditional wage and benefits structure even though the job itself is premised on telecommuting

D) A managerial position that features substantial take-home pay in place of a formal employee benefits program

3

The author indicates that big box stores are capable of providing some preferable employment conditions because

A) they use technology to facilitate better hiring and workflow decisions.

B) they attract top talent to an extent that smaller stores do not.

C) they have experienced rapid growth in the past few decades.

D) they can draw on larger worker bases to identify the best candidates for promotion.

4

Which choice provides the best evidence for the answer to the previous question?

A) Lines 8-11 ("A new . . . stores")

B) Lines 27-31 ("The segment . . . decades")

C) Lines 38-40 ("According . . . workers")

D) Lines 55-57 ("The authors . . . able")

CONTINUE

5

As used in line 38, "pop up" most nearly means

A) surprise observers.

B) promote innovation.

C) expand operations.

D) react instantaneously.

6

By referring to some retailers as "mom-and-pop" (lines 17, 42-43, and 61) businesses, the author characterizes these retailers as

A) limited in extent.

B) unusual in nature.

C) inefficient in structure.

D) subtle in approach.

7

The author suggests that manufacturing jobs

A) have not been fully eliminated but have been shifted out of the United States.

B) require many of the same skills that are valued by managers of big box stores.

C) will be prioritized once again as the result of a new policy initiative.

D) are becoming less popular because employers have gradually lowered manufacturing wages.

8

Which choice provides the best evidence for the answer to the previous question?

A) Lines 67-69 ("The authors . . . jobs")

B) Lines 70-72 ("Employment . . . shrunk")

C) Lines 72-75 ("And . . . positions")

D) Lines 75-80 ("Instead . . . managers")

9

According to the information contained in figure 1, which response would NOT apply to a majority of participants in the survey?

A) "I would prefer to remain at my current job even if given a chance to work at a smaller company."

B) "I genuinely look forward to coming to work as expected by my employer."

C) "I have not performed an extensive job search since being hired for my current position."

D) "I hope to stay in my current position without any change of wage or responsibilities."

10

Does the information in figure 2 help to clarify the claims in lines 49-57 ("Larger . . . able")?

A) Yes, because figure 2 calls attention to the fact that there are meaningful differences in terms of entry-level wages at larger companies.

B) Yes, because figure 2 demonstrates that a worker without a college degree can earn industry-leading wages at a big box store.

C) No, because figure 2 does not consider different levels of experience or contrasting levels of company size in any capacity.

D) No, because figure 2 does not assess the overall job satisfaction expressed by big box store employees.

CONTINUE

Part 1: Social Studies

Reading 11

Questions 1-10 are based on the following passage and supplementary material.

This passage is adapted from "Researchers identify brain circuits that help people cope with stress," a 2016 news release* from the National institutes of Health.

Research supported by the National Institutes of Health has identified brain patterns in humans that appear to underlie "resilient coping," the
Line
5　healthy emotional and behavioral responses to stress that help some people handle stressful situations better than others. People encounter stressful situations and stimuli everywhere, every day, and studies have shown that long-term stress can contribute to a broad array of health problems.
10　However, some people cope with stress better than others, and scientists have long wondered why. The new study, by a team of researchers at Yale University, New Haven, Connecticut, is now online in the Proceedings of the National
15　Academy of Sciences.

"This important finding points to specific brain adaptations that predict resilient responses to stress," said George F. Koob, Ph.D., director of the National Institute on Alcohol Abuse
20　and Alcoholism (NIAAA), part of NIH and a supporter of the study. "The findings also indicate that we might be able to predict maladaptive stress responses that contribute to excessive drinking, anger, and other unhealthy reactions to stress."

25　In a study of human volunteers, scientists led by Rajita Sinha, Ph.D., and Dongju Seo, Ph.D., used a brain scanning technique called functional magnetic resonance imaging (fMRI) to measure localized changes in brain activation during
30　stress. Study participants were given fMRI scans while exposed to highly threatening, violent and stressful images followed by neutral, non-stressful images for six minutes each. While conducting the scans, researchers also measured non-brain
35　indicators of stress among study participants, such as heart rate and levels of cortisol, a stress hormone, in blood.

The brain scans revealed a sequence of three distinct patterns of response to stress, compared
40　to non-stress exposure. The first pattern was characterized by sustained activation of brain regions known to signal, monitor, and process potential threats. The second response pattern involved increased activation, and then decreased
45　activation, of a circuit connecting brain areas involved in stress reaction and adaptation, perhaps as a means of reducing the initial distress related to a perceived threat.

"The third pattern helped predict those who
50　would regain emotional and behavioral control to stress," said Dr. Sinha, professor of psychiatry and director of the Yale Stress Center.

This pattern involved what Dr. Sinha and colleagues described as "neuroflexibility," in
55　a circuit between the brain's medial prefrontal cortex and forebrain regions including the ventral striatum, extended amygdala, and hippocampus during sustained stress exposure. Dr. Sinha and her colleagues explain that this neuroflexibility
60　was characterized by initially decreased activation of this circuit in response to stress, followed by its increased activation with sustained stress exposure. "This seems to be the area of the brain which mobilizes to regain control over our
65　response to stress," said Dr. Sinha.

The authors note that previous research has consistently shown that repeated and chronic stress damages the structure, connections, and functions of the brain's prefrontal cortex. The
70　prefrontal cortex is the seat of higher order functions such as language, social behavior, mood, and attention, and also helps to regulate emotions and more primitive areas of the brain.

In the current study, the researchers
75　reported that participants who did not show the neuroflexibility response in the prefrontal cortex during stress had higher levels of self-reported binge drinking, anger outbursts, and other maladaptive coping behaviors. They hypothesize
80　that such individuals might be at increased risk for alcohol use disorder or emotional dysfunction problems, which are hallmarks of chronic exposure to high levels of stress.

*See Page 85 for the citation for this text.

CONTINUE ➡

Part 1: Social Studies

1

According to the author, the research findings regarding brain adaptations are useful because such discoveries

A) shed light on the evolutionary origins of the human race.

B) will help to mitigate and possibly prevent brain damage.

C) explain a variety of non-brain stress indicators.

D) enable researchers to predict unhealthy stress responses.

2

Which choice provides the best evidence for the answer to the previous question?

A) Lines 10-12 ("However . . . why")

B) Lines 21-24 ("The findings . . . to stress")

C) Lines 25-31 ("In a study . . . stress")

D) Lines 38-40 ("The brain . . . exposure")

3

Which of the following is NOT a pattern of response to stress seen in the fMRI experiment?

A) Neuroflexibility

B) Activation of brain regions that process threats

C) Frontal cortex repair

D) Varying levels of activation of brain regions that respond to stress

4

As used in line 47, "a means" most nearly means

A) a connivance.

B) a method.

C) a definition.

D) an instinct.

5

The author of the passage implies that people who have low neuroflexibility have a relatively hard time

A) learning new tasks.

B) recovering from brain injuries.

C) assessing potential threats.

D) regaining control over their responses to stress.

6

Which of the following best supports the notion that stress can physically alter the sufferer's body?

A) Lines 33-37 ("While conducting . . . blood")

B) Lines 66-69 ("The authors . . . cortex")

C) Lines 74-79 ("In the current . . . behaviors")

D) Lines 80-83 ("such individuals . . . stress")

7

As used in line 64, "mobilizes" most nearly means

A) activates.

B) overrides.

C) aims.

D) inspires.

CONTINUE ▶

Part 1: Social Studies

Brain Activity in Response to Stressful Situations

Trial 1: Lower-Stress Stimulus

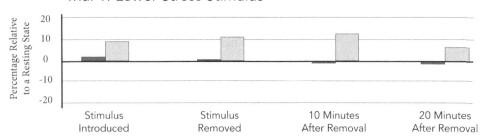

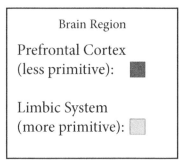

Brain Region

Prefrontal Cortex
(less primitive):

Limbic System
(more primitive):

Trial 2: Higher-Stress Stimulus

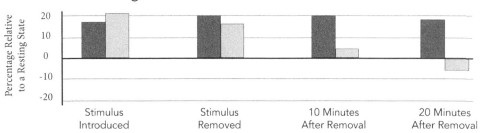

8

The list that appears in lines 71-72 ("language . . . attention") primarily serves to

A) present the components encompassed by a term.

B) enumerate a few promising areas of study.

C) illustrate what occurs during a stress response.

D) show how humans are more advanced than ancestor species were.

9

It can be reasonably inferred from the graph that

A) a long-term high-stress situation will eventually lead to a loss of emotional control.

B) a low-stress situation can have negligible short-term effects on the prefrontal cortex.

C) high-stress situations can damage the prefrontal cortex.

D) the limbic system is the crucial component in regulating basic emotional responses to stress.

10

Which choice best describes the relationship between the figure and the passage?

A) The figure draws a distinction between more and less primitive brain regions, while the passage does not consider such categories.

B) The figure indicates that stress responses are relatively similar regardless of stress intensity, while the passage outlines three different approaches to stress management.

C) The figure indicates the neurological effects of repeated exposure to stress, while the passage considers the same possibility from the perspective of social behavior.

D) The figure categorizes stressful experiences in terms of relative intensity, while the passage mostly contrasts stressful and non-stressful experiences.

CONTINUE

Reading 12

Questions 1-10 are based on the following passage and supplementary material.

This passage is an excerpt from Bruce Mutsvairo, "What is news in the 21st century?" an article published* in 2016 by The Conversation in partnership with Northumbria University.

When celebrated media and communication theorist Dennis McQuail proposed in 1992 that news was a selective, socially manufactured
Line product with the power to determine and define
5 events, he hadn't heard of social media. Not every occurrence is necessarily news, he wrote. His argument was based on the notion that the "gatekeepers" (who are mostly journalists and editors) decide what is news and how it should be
10 reported and disseminated.

McQuail would be the first to admit that that's no longer the case. From Malawi to Myanmar, Chad to China, social media's growing influence has become a potent symbol of citizen
15 empowerment across the globe. That's because in several parts of the world, social networks such as Twitter and Facebook have become the norm for day-to-day communication, inadvertently replacing mainstream media as a source of news.
20 In so doing, such networks are not only redefining the ways news and content can be shared but also forcing us to rethink the meaning and significance of "news" itself. When citizen journalists, digital activists or any other non-professionals produce
25 and share news on Twitter, who is going to stop them, and who is going to deny them the opportunity to produce news?

With the news industry changing at such a dizzying speed, it would seem as if the time has
30 come for us to accept citizen journalists as active players in the news business. Indeed, teaching a student how to gather, write, and edit stories isn't enough anymore. Students need to know that their main competitor isn't just a journalist from the
35 crosstown rival newspaper; it's anyone owning a smartphone.

The audiences, who for several generations have largely been sleeping partners in the news production business, have suddenly become more
40 active. In the past, they only purchased news content. And if they were angry after reading biased or inaccurate stories, drafting a "letter to the editor" was their only possible way of showing concern.

45 Today they have direct access to the editor via Twitter, they directly comment on stories anonymously and instantly, and as alternative players they produce content and share it online. They have also become a legitimate source of
50 information for conventional journalists. But can the blogosphere be considered a reliable and vital part of ethical news production? Most professional journalists I talk to would say no. But while not everything bloggers are producing
55 is reliable, you just cannot exclude social media content from a 21st-century journalism degree course. It's impossible to remove the unrelenting digital enthusiasts from the news matrix.

Some scholars have defined news as the
60 information that people need to make rational decisions about their lives. Meanwhile, Pamela J Shoemaker and Akiba Cohen, preferring a market-based definition, have called news "a commodity. It can be bought, sold, and traded." Then of course
65 there are the "big" world stories: wars, outbreaks of disease or famine, elections. Some of these will make a difference in our lives—for example, the Syrian crisis and the flow of migrants into Europe, or the U.S. election which has repercussions far
70 beyond North America.

But to most people who now spend time on social media, if you've got something "new" to share, rational or irrational, then you've got news—or at least you believe so. When
75 newlyweds share stories and pictures of their marriage, they are distributing news. And the fact that this news doesn't fit some market-oriented criteria doesn't mean that they're wrong.

*See Page 85 for the citation for this text.

CONTINUE

News isn't only what a major outlet like the
80 British Broadcasting Corporation (BBC) tells
you is news. The BBC will come up with a news
bulletin reporting on major international, national
and local events. It's a package of news put
together by the BBC. Citizens, however, can and
85 should decide what's news to them.

1

A central idea of the passage is that

A) free expression on social media has radically changed social and political norms.

B) the rise of social media was the direct result of distrust of traditional sources of authority in the news.

C) trained journalists and editors are not the only sources of important modern media content.

D) older standards of writing quality have vanished due to technological advances.

2

In the first paragraph, the author cites the ideas of Dennis McQuail for the purpose of

A) pointing out that McQuail's beliefs were deeply flawed even when these arguments were first developed.

B) depicting McQuail's lack of foresight as the result of journalistic integrity.

C) setting the context for analysis that reveals a historical departure from McQuail's conceptions.

D) anticipating the thesis that contemporary media commentators should return to values promoted by McQuail.

3

As used in lines 29, "a dizzying" most nearly means

A) an entertaining.

B) a destructive.

C) an unclear.

D) an intense.

Activities of Five Social Media Users, with Use by Percentage of Total Time Investment

User	Occupation	Why is social media most useful for you?	News and Entertainment	Friends and family contact	Networking	Other
1	foreign affairs journalist	posting articles and performing research	60%	15%	15%	10%
2	fashion blogger	networking and blog publicity	50%	10%	25%	15%
3	school principal	staying in touch with family	15%	75%	5%	5%
4	media consultant	networking and obtaining clients	20%	5%	65%	10%
5	financial planner	contacting friends and family	10%	75%	10%	5%

Part 1: Social Studies

4

The author of the passage would agree that specialists in contemporary journalism are obliged to

A) disregard past editorial standards in order to remain employed.

B) account for reporting that is factually incorrect.

C) consent to the idea that "news" is an undefinable concept.

D) interact with readers on a daily basis.

5

Which choice provides the best evidence for the answer to the previous question?

A) Lines 20-23 ("In so . . . itself")

B) Lines 31-33 ("Indeed . . . anymore")

C) Lines 37-40 ("The audiences . . . active")

D) Lines 54-56 ("But . . . course")

6

The passage indicates that it is possible to define "news" based on the concept of

A) sensationalism.

B) utility.

C) complexity.

D) truth.

7

Which choice provides the best evidence for the answer to the previous question?

A) Lines 59-61 ("Some . . . lives")

B) Lines 64-66 ("Then . . . elections")

C) Lines 71-74 ("But . . . so")

D) Lines 76-78 ("And . . . wrong")

8

As used in the final paragraph, the phrases "come up with" (line 81) and "put together" (lines 83-84) characterize the actions of the BBC as

A) reliant on clever manipulation.

B) questionable in ultimate impact.

C) improvised for broad appeal.

D) premised on a specific end goal.

9

Based on the table, which person spends the greatest amount of time on social media?

A) The foreign affairs journalist

B) The fashion blogger

C) The media consultant

D) There is not enough information to provide a definitive answer.

10

What objection to the organization of the table would be expected from the author of the passage?

A) Contact that primarily deals with family events can also be classified as "news."

B) Activity classified as "other" could involve consumption of unreliable news.

C) News generation and professional networking are not comparable activities.

D) Equating "news" and "entertainment" causes distrust of modern news organizations.

CONTINUE ▶

Copyright 2020 PrepVantage, online at prepvantagetutoring.com

41

Reading 13

Questions 1-10 are based on the following passage and supplementary material.

This passage is adapted from Glenn Jackson, "Ripe for the Picking: Wild weeds may provide a new food source," an article that originally appeared* in 2019 on EveryONE, the community blog of the research journal PLOS ONE.

Line
The overgrown lots and sidewalks of California cities might not seem like a great place to seek out nutritious greens, but in a recent study published in PLOS ONE, Professor Philip Stark
5 and his team have found evidence of a potentially untapped bounty of drought-resistant, edible weeds growing in the dense urban environments of three cities in the San Francisco East Bay region of California. Furthermore, the University
10 of California, Berkeley research team's findings suggest that even while soil in these environments may have higher levels of lead, cadmium, and other heavy metals, certain varieties of wild-growing greens are still safe to eat (after a
15 thorough rinsing, that is!).

Over several months between 2014 and 2015, Stark (who is the Principal Investigator of the Berkeley Open Source Food project) and his team set out to conduct field observations, soil
20 tests, and nutritional and toxicology tests on plant tissues pulled from three separate sites in the East Bay cities of Berkeley, Richmond, and Oakland. During this time, Stark and his team set out to visit various sites throughout the East Bay;
25 each site was approximately nine square blocks and focused on areas where residential buildings bordered busy roadways and active industrial zones. At each location, the team conducted field observations and collected plant specimens and
30 soil samples for additional tests back in the lab. In essence, the researchers were interested in testing the soil and plants from what could be considered "food deserts," usually impoverished urban areas where it is difficult to buy affordable

35 or good-quality fresh food due to a lack of grocery stores or markets where healthy food is offered. "According to the USDA, the areas in Richmond and Oakland are more than a mile from any shop that sells fresh produce, and the area in Berkeley
40 is more than half a mile from such a shop," say Stark and his team. "All have below-average income, according to the U.S. Census."

Yet all around them, Stark and his colleagues saw an overlooked food source: wild, edible
45 weeds. Using iNaturalist (an open-source citizen science database of observations of plants and animals), Stark utilized teams of observers to help record estimates of the number of servings of edible weeds that were either "accessible"
50 (defined as within an arm's reach of a public space, such as a sidewalk or road) or "visible" (defined as visible and available to those with access to the property where the weeds have grown) within the chosen sites. What they found
55 was that wild edible plants such as mallow, bristly ox tongue, cat's ear, English plantain, wild lettuce, nasturtium, dandelion, sweet fennel, sourgrass, and chickweed were available and visible in abundance, growing without human
60 aid and persisting even during record droughts in California.

But how is one to know whether or not it is safe to eat the edible plants growing in these environments? To answer this question, Stark
65 and his team collected soil samples from various sites in the cities of Richmond and Oakland (specifically, the West Oakland neighborhood), and sent the samples to a lab in order to test for the concentration of metals such as zinc, copper,
70 arsenic, lead, cadmium, and other toxic metals present in the soil. Then, plant tissue samples were collected from locations where the soil testing had shown the highest concentration of metals, including a few samples from plants
75 growing between patches of asphalt. The plant tissue samples were rinsed in tap water and then dried before being sent to a lab to be tested for metal contaminants. In addition, the team also had fresh samples tested for nutritional value as well

*See Page 85 for the citation for this text.

CONTINUE ➡

80 as for potential chemical contaminants (such as man-made chemicals, glyphosate, multi-residue pesticides, and oxalic acid).

When the results were in, the study found that while a few soil samples showed levels of

85 lead and cadmium near or exceeding EPA limits, toxic metals detected in most soil samples were far below the US EPA maximum acceptable daily dose for children and adults. In addition, approximately 330 pesticides, herbicides, and

90 other toxins did not turn up in soil sample tests.

The takeaway? While these plants weren't cultivated on an organic farm tucked away in the bucolic pastures of California's central valley, they appear not only safe to eat but also

95 surprisingly nutritious compared to some of their store-bought counterparts. While this research is promising, you shouldn't just start eating every leafy green you see growing between your front door and your office.

1

The main point of the passage is that various wild plants

A) are generally both safe and nutritious.

B) may have dangerous levels of toxins.

C) do not grow in abundance in food deserts.

D) are healthier than grocery store produce.

2

As used in line 6, "untapped" most nearly means

A) underutilized.

B) elegant.

C) misunderstood.

D) uncompromised.

3

The main purpose of the quotation in lines 37-40 ("According . . . Census") is to

A) explain a plan to revitalize specific areas.

B) rebut a claim that appeared earlier in the passage.

C) show that the sites being discussed are food deserts.

D) argue for a different approach to land usage.

4

As used in line 75, "patches" most nearly means

A) connections.

B) recuperations.

C) potholes.

D) areas.

5

Which of the following best supports the notion that the researchers described in the passage wanted a worst-case scenario estimate of metal contamination?

A) Lines 9-14 ("Furthermore . . . to eat")

B) Lines 64-71 ("To answer . . . the soil")

C) Lines 71-75 ("Then, plant . . . of asphalt")

D) Lines 75-78 ("The plant . . . contaminants")

6

According to the passage, most of the weeds in urban areas are

A) concentrated in industrial settings.

B) not laden with chemical contaminants.

C) located in food deserts.

D) both visible and accessible.

43

CONTINUE →

Opinions of 1073 East Bay City Residents

Question: Would you willingly eat the following?

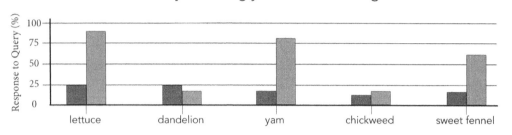

Response

Yes (when source is an urban area): ■

Yes (when source is a supermarket): ▪

7

Which choice provides the best evidence for the answer to the previous question?

A) Lines 25-28 ("each site . . . zones")

B) Lines 31-36 ("In essence . . . offered")

C) Lines 47-54 ("Stark . . . sites")

D) Lines 86-90 ("toxic . . . tests")

8

The tone of the last sentence of the passage can best be described as

A) moderately fearful.

B) cautiously optimistic.

C) unabashedly sarcastic.

D) thoroughly ambivalent.

9

Which information would be necessary in order to determine whether the chart is relevant to the issue of "food deserts" that interested Stark and the other researchers?

A) The the total income of the 10 lowest-earning respondents over a five-year period

B) The amount of money that a respondent spends, on average, on meals that are not home-cooked on an annual basis

C) The individual amounts of money that the 10 highest-earning respondents typically spend on food on an annual basis

D) The median annual income of the respondents as compared to the median annual income in the United States

10

On the basis of the passage, one of the ironies present in the chart is that some East Bay residents

A) do not recognize that various locally-occurring plants are in fact edible.

B) consciously shun food sources that have well-demonstrated nutritional value.

C) believe that more expensive types of produce are intrinsically healthier.

D) have aversely over-reacted to research concerning pesticides and other contaminants.

Reading 14

Questions 1-10 are based on the following passage and supplementary material.

This passage is adapted from Spandana Singh, "Special Delivery: How Internet Platforms Use Artificial Intelligence to Target and Deliver Ads," a study originally published* by NewAmerica.org.

In the early 2000s, a Minnesota father found Target ads for maternity clothing and nursery furniture addressed to his teenage daughter in
Line
5 the mail. According to Target statistician Andrew Pole, the company was able to use historical buying data on all of the women who had signed up for Target baby registries to identify purchasing patterns. This information was used to create an algorithm that could identify women who
10 were likely pregnant. Target then delivered ads to women who had been identified as pregnant. For example, the company's statisticians found that women on the baby registry were buying more quantities of unscented lotion around the
15 beginning of the second trimester. Additionally, many pregnant women purchased supplements such as calcium, magnesium, and zinc during the first 20 weeks. By bundling pattern-based data points such as these together, Target was able to
20 calculate and assign each shopper a "pregnancy prediction score" and estimate each pregnant woman's due date within a narrow window. In the case of the Minnesota teen, this meant that the company knew that she was pregnant and acted on
25 this knowledge before she decided to tell her own family.

This was over 10 years ago. Since then, the digital advertising ecosystem has significantly changed, and such practices have become even
30 more refined, more pervasive, more automated, and less visible. Today, the industry relies on and monetizes user data at an unprecedented scale. In this way, data have become the lifeblood of the digital advertising industry. Simultaneously,

35 these rampant data collection and monetization practices have raised a number of concerns.

As Harvard Business School scholar Shoshana Zuboff outlined, the digital advertising industry can be situated within the framework of
40 "surveillance capitalism." In her book *The Age of Surveillance Capitalism: The Fight for a Human Future at the New Frontier of Power*, Zuboff describes how, in the twentieth century, companies such as General Motors and Ford sparked the rise
45 of mass production and managerial capitalism. In the twenty-first century, companies such as Google and Facebook have initiated the rise of surveillance capitalism. These platforms commodify "reality" by tracking the behaviors of
50 individuals online and offline, making predictions about how they may act in the future, and constructing mechanisms to influence these future behaviors, whether such behaviors are voting or making purchases.

55 In this new digital advertising model, internet platforms might not sell access to user data. But they do sell the attention of these consumers to brands and companies that are willing to pay for it. Additionally, these platforms monetize data by
60 using it to facilitate ad targeting. These practices are extensive and invasive. Such pervasive online and offline surveillance, along with the subsequent monetization of users' behaviors and ideas, treats the "private human experience as raw material for
65 product development and market exchange." This model incentivizes internet platforms to collect as much data on users as possible, as this process will make precise targeting and delivery tools available to advertisers. In addition, the digital
70 advertising ecosystem incentivizes rampant data collection, as these systems require vast datasets in order to operate and improve. . .

In addition, political advertisements on internet platforms have come under increased scrutiny.
75 This concern was in part triggered by revelations that Russian operatives had used political advertising services on a number of internet platforms to influence and suppress voting in the 2016 U.S. presidential election. Since then, these

*See Page 85 for the citation for this text.

45

CONTINUE

80 platforms have come under increased scrutiny and pressure to provide greater transparency and accountability around their advertising operations, and to develop clearer policies and processes governing who can purchase and run

85 political advertising campaigns. Some companies, such as Pinterest and most recently Twitter, have opted to ban political advertising on their platforms altogether. However, because political advertisements cannot be easily categorized or

90 defined, and given that some of these decisions were made fairly recently, the impact of these new bans is yet to be seen.

1

The main purpose of the passage is to

A) call attention to the unfortunate implications of a fairly common advertising practice.

B) promote procedural adjustments that would address ethical problems in digital advertising.

C) explain why a few economic and political systems appear to contradict their own core principles.

D) show how both professionals and the public reacted to a troubling episode.

2

The discussion of the Minnesota teen calls attention to advertising practices that can result in

A) suspicion of companies that claim to be assisting families and communities.

B) the creation of harmful stereotypes about large social groups.

C) the disclosure of information without an individual's consent.

D) the marketing of products that do not function as hoped.

3

Which choice provides the best evidence for the answer to the previous question?

A) Lines 4-8 ("According . . . patterns")

B) Lines 8-10 ("This . . . pregnant")

C) Lines 18-22 ("By . . . window")

D) Lines 22-26 ("In the . . . family")

Advertising During the 2016 U.S. Presidential Election

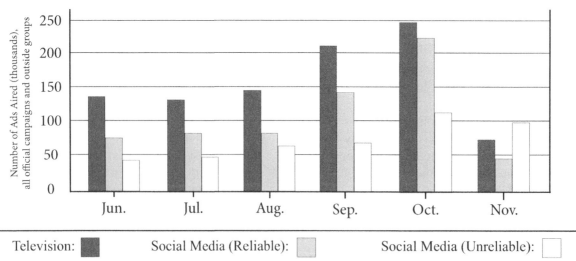

Television: ▮   Social Media (Reliable): ▢   Social Media (Unreliable): ☐

CONTINUE

4

As used in line 22, "narrow" most nearly means

A) precise.

B) simplistic.

C) challenging.

D) unyielding.

5

As used in line 44, "sparked" most nearly means

A) inflamed.

B) initiated.

C) incentivized.

D) illuminated.

6

According to the passage, "surveillance capitalism" can best be characterized as

A) dependent on interactions that do not take place exclusively online.

B) reliant on uninterrupted improvement in computing speed and efficiency.

C) antagonistic to government oversight and regulation.

D) impervious to the problems that befell managerial capitalism

7

Which choice provides the best evidence for the answer to the previous question?

A) Lines 37-40 ("As Harvard . . . capitalism")

B) Lines 43-45 ("in the twentieth . . . capitalism")

C) Lines 48-54 ("These . . . purchases")

D) Lines 69-72 ("In addition . . . improve")

8

Which irony of political advertising does the author highlight in the passage?

A) Political ads can be used to depress rather than stimulate voter participation.

B) The creators of political ads seldom have strong political biases of their own.

C) Non-political users of social media are likely to encounter an abundance of political ads.

D) The United States does not run political ads in countries known to target American citizens with political messaging.

9

During which month in 2016 did the largest number of unreliable political ads appear on social media?

A) August

B) September

C) October

D) November

10

The author of the passage would most likely argue that the presence of unreliable political ads on social media, as represented in the graph, is the result of

A) the disproportionate profitability of running political ads on a social media platform.

B) the prioritization of free and uncensored expression by some social media companies.

C) the difficulty of distinguishing political from non-political content.

D) the use of political ads in surveillance of unlawful activity.

CONTINUE

Reading 15

Questions 1-10 are based on the following passage and supplementary material.

This passage is adapted from "Unique Mapping Tool Brings Unprecedented Look at Land Cover Change in West Africa," a 2018 news release* from the United States Geological Survey.

They say that there are forests in West Africa where spirits abide—where people walk among woodland burial grounds and speak to the dead,
Line where life plays out from beginning to end. Places
5 of myths and taboos, of proverbs and songs, forests have played key roles within the cultural rhythms of West Africans for centuries. According to the native traditions in Ghana, a family would plant a tree in the woods for each child born. Each
10 year then, the development of that son or daughter was measured by the growth of the tree. As the seasons passed and the branches began to bear fruit, it became time for the child to marry. And when the circle of life was complete, it's said that
15 one's spirit became eternally linked to one's own personal birthright tree.

"That's why when the forests began to disappear, there were significant impacts, socioeconomically, environmentally, even
20 culturally," says Francis Dwomoh, a native Ghanaian who recently completed his doctoral degree in Geospatial Science and Engineering at South Dakota State University in Brookings, SD. "For us, if you are losing your forests, you're also
25 losing part of your culture."

Ghana is in fact losing its forests. By some estimates, the country's primary rainforest declined by 90 percent in the past half century. Logging, wildfires, agricultural expansion,
30 climate variability, population growth—all have exacted heavy tolls on forest resources, not simply in Ghana but throughout the 17 countries that comprise a West African sub-region roughly the size of the United States.
35 It's a loss felt at all levels of West African life, from governments facing declining timber exports

to local villagers who no longer have ready sources of wood for cooking and housing. But now there are indications that the trend could be
40 reversing, at least in some places. Now it appears that many West African policy and decision makers are looking at new, innovative ways to better nurture and preserve their forests and other natural resources.
45 A prime example of that innovation is a unique mapping tool created by West Africans and the U.S. Geological Survey's (USGS) Earth Resources Observation and Science (EROS) Center, with financial support from the U.S.
50 Agency for International Development (USAID). Led by USGS Geographer Gray Tappan at EROS, the West Africa Land Use and Land Cover Trends Project produced maps and datasets that represent an unprecedented look at how land cover has
55 changed in that part of the world over 40 years, both at regional and national scales. This new tool captures where forests have faded away beneath the advance of creeping desertification. Where booming population growth has spurred
60 urban sprawl. Where croplands have replaced woodlands. And, in what many view as a positive trend, where the greening of the landscape by new tree growth is now occurring.

Remotely sensed time-series data from
65 Landsat's rich archive have been crucial in capturing these changes, Tappan said. But the maps and datasets also are products of decades of boots-on-the-ground visual mapping and analysis—much of it done by native West Africans
70 themselves—as well as thousands of aerial photographs.

Tappan and his team understood that they could have simply relied on automation to take multispectral information from satellite sensors
75 and use the reflectances they captured to map land cover classes. But the accuracy of such an approach wouldn't have met their needs, he said. So, they decided early on to take Landsat images and manually do the mapping "with just good old-
80 fashioned visual analysis," noted Tappan. It not only dramatically improved the maps' accuracy, but also brought other important dimensions to

*See Page 85 for the citation for this text.

CONTINUE ➤

them, such as texture, pattern, shape, size, even shadows. For example, roads can be seen coming
85 together at villages in the middle of agricultural areas. "All these other dimensions allowed us to really bring the accuracy way up," Tappan said.

1

Over the course of the passage, the focus shifts from

A) a theoretical proposition to a hypothesis to a tentative conclusion.

B) background information to an evident problem to a new program.

C) a synopsis of a cultural practice to an endorsement of the modernization of that practice.

D) an analysis of a widely-acknowledged problem to the revelation of an unanticipated solution.

2

The tone of the first two sentences of the passage can best be described as

A) skeptical.

B) flattering.

C) captivated.

D) disconcerted.

3

The function of the description in lines 7-16 ("According . . . tree") is to

A) explain a term.

B) defend a culture.

C) rebut a claim.

D) provide an example.

4

As used in line 57, "captures" most nearly means

A) overtakes.

B) catches.

C) remembers.

D) records.

CONTINUE

Part 1: Social Studies

5

As used in line 58, "creeping" most nearly means

A) expanding.

B) prying.

C) spying.

D) dragging.

6

According to the passage, the benefits of manual mapping include

A) facilitated collaboration between nations.

B) a large array of information types.

C) the ability to promote ecological restoration.

D) increased income for local residents.

7

Which choice provides the best evidence for the answer to the previous question?

A) Lines 45-56 ("A prime . . . scales")

B) Lines 61-63 ("And in . . . occurring")

C) Lines 80-86 ("It not . . . areas")

D) Lines 86-87 ("All these . . . said")

8

Which of the following choices best supports the notion that, compared to manual mapping, land cover mapping by machines relies on indirect methods?

A) Lines 56-58 ("This new . . . desertification")

B) Lines 64-66 ("Remotely . . . Tappan")

C) Lines 66-71 ("But the . . . photographs")

D) Lines 72-76 ("Tappan . . . classes")

Rainforest Area Loss in Three West African Countries

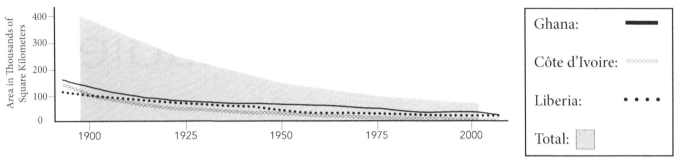

Total Rainforest Area Rehabilitated in Three West African Countries

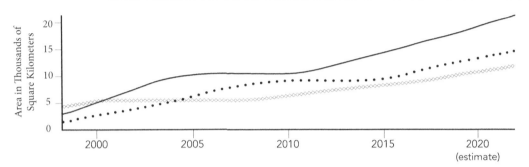

9

The graphs indicate that rainforest rehabilitation in the three African countries represented

A) has not facilitated a return to pre-1900 levels of rainforest area coverage.

B) is the outcome of a policy shift unique to Ghana.

C) has fluctuated wildly over a short timespan.

D) was a response to crisis conditions that arose a few years into the 21st century.

10

In the context of the accompanying graphs, the passage primarily

A) connects trends documented in the two graphs to specific causes.

B) suggests that a problem documented in the first graph is not as severe as some of the existing data may suggest.

C) explains why pre-1900 measurements of rainforest area loss are unreliable.

D) posits that visual resources such as the second graph will be rendered unnecessary by improvements in mapping technology.

STOP
**If you have finished this section, consult the relevant answers and explanations.
Do not turn to any other section.**

Answer Key
Part 1: Social Studies

Reading 1	Reading 2	Reading 3	Reading 4	Reading 5
1. C	1. D	1. C	1. B	1. A
2. B	2. A	2. D	2. C	2. D
3. C	3. C	3. C	3. B	3. B
4. D	4. B	4. B	4. C	4. D
5. B	5. D	5. B	5. A	5. D
6. D	6. B	6. C	6. B	6. A
7. C	7. B	7. D	7. C	7. B
8. A	8. B	8. C	8. B	8. D
9. C	9. A	9. C	9. B	9. A
10. A	10. D	10. A	10. C	10. C

Reading 6	Reading 7	Reading 8	Reading 9	Reading 10
1. C	1. B	1. D	1. C	1. B
2. D	2. B	2. D	2. B	2. D
3. D	3. C	3. C	3. C	3. B
4. A	4. B	4. A	4. D	4. D
5. C	5. B	5. C	5. C	5. C
6. C	6. A	6. C	6. B	6. A
7. D	7. C	7. C	7. C	7. A
8. D	8. A	8. D	8. D	8. D
9. B	9. C	9. A	9. D	9. D
10. A	10. B	10. D	10. A	10. C

Reading 11		Reading 12		Reading 13		Reading 14		Reading 15	
1.	D	1.	C	1.	A	1.	A	1.	B
2.	B	2.	C	2.	A	2.	C	2.	C
3.	C	3.	D	3.	C	3.	D	3.	D
4.	B	4.	B	4.	D	4.	A	4.	D
5.	D	5.	D	5.	C	5.	B	5.	A
6.	B	6.	B	6.	B	6.	A	6.	B
7.	A	7.	A	7.	D	7.	C	7.	C
8.	A	8.	D	8.	B	8.	A	8.	D
9.	B	9.	D	9.	D	9.	C	9.	A
10.	D	10.	A	10.	B	10.	C	10.	A

Answer Explanations

Passage 1, Pages 6-8

1. <u>C</u> is the correct answer.

The passage focuses on describing a recent article which explores factors that contribute to successfully aging at work. Since the article also offers recommendations about "ways employers can help their employees age successfully at work" (lines 30-31), C is the most appropriate answer. A and B can be eliminated since the passage focuses on what aging at work looks like in contemporary society (NOT on a historical survey of this topic), and explores aging overall, NOT any single specific health risk. D can also be eliminated since, while the study did identify two distinct groups (healthy agers and classic agers), the focus was NOT on reproducing testimony from either group.

2. <u>B</u> is the correct answer.

In lines 16-17, the author states, in reference to older people who work longer, that "Several other motivators exist, such as a financial need or simply that workers like their job." This content implies that an older worker may remain in the workforce due to financial need created by a lack of adequate retirement savings; choose B as appropriate. A and C can be eliminated since the passage does NOT identify any specific duties or connect these to remaining in the work force, and also does NOT discuss any connection between retirement and fears of isolation (even though POSITIVE enjoyment of a job is discussed). D can also be eliminated since, while one specific change to Social Security policy is mentioned, there is no discussion of FUTURE changes.

3. C is the correct answer.

See the previous answer explanation for analysis of the correct line reference. A describes a change in Social Security policy, while B describes changes in the workforce which may have resulted from this policy change. D describes a factor in workplace success which reflects the central research questions explored by the study. None of these other answers establish a connection between financial security and older workers remaining in the workforce, and therefore they should all be eliminated.

4. D is the correct answer.

In describing the authors of an article, lines 29-31 state that "In addition, from their findings, they also suggest ways employers can help their employees age successfully at work." Since the researchers offered recommendations about employers supporting older employees, it follows that researchers assume that employers are invested in the performance and success of older workers. Choose D as appropriate. B and C can be eliminated since previous (as opposed to present) research into this topic is NOT discussed in this passage, and since the career planning of older workers is not analyzed within the study. Be careful not to choose A, since while the study does offer an examination of what factors might lead someone to age successfully and remain productive as an older worker, it does NOT negatively follow that many or most older workers experience lower rates of productivity.

5. B is the correct answer.

See the previous answer explanation for analysis of the correct line reference. A identifies a question and a research study which explored that question, while C outlines the methodology of the study. D identifies some of the questions posed to participants in the study. Since none of these other answers establish the assumption that employees generally want to retain older workers, they should all be eliminated.

6. D is the correct answer.

Specific words in lines 55 and 64 describe the actions of researchers in a way that indicates that the researchers were systematic, methodical, and unbiased in their actions over the course of the study. Choose D to reflect the tone created by this language. A and B can be eliminated since these lines simply describe the actions that researchers carried out in conducting their study and do NOT constitute a discussion of stereotypes or prior studies. C can be eliminated, since these lines focus on methods and do NOT articulate any particular ideals.

7. C is the correct answer.

In line 79, "meet" refers how strategies could satisfy the requirements of older workers. Choose C to reflect this meaning. A (inappropriately implying summoning or verbally alerting someone), B (inappropriately implying engaging with someone in a hostile or aggressive manner), and D (inappropriately implying becoming part of a group or unit) all introduce improper contexts and should therefore be eliminated.

8. A is the correct answer.

The study relied on elderly individuals being classified as either healthy or classic agers based on their responses to questions about aging. However, if there were evidence that elderly individuals were typically inconsistent in their responses about aging, this information would undermine the ability to conclusively classify someone as either a healthy or classic ager. Choose A to reflect this content. B can be eliminated since the presence of a third group would NOT necessarily undermine the patterns displayed by the two initial groups of agers, while C can be eliminated since the study only looked at a group of 156 workers. D can be eliminated since it is in fact quite likely that someone's subjective, functional, and organizational ages would all be different (on the basis of lines 37-43), and this pattern would not undermine the findings of the study.

9. <u>C</u> is the correct answer.

The graph shows that when members of a control group were asked about whether or not they believed they would be alive in 10 years, more than a quarter of them were uncertain. In contrast, when the control group members were asked about enjoying intellectually demanding activities, a smaller percentage rated themselves as uncertain, and when the healthy agers were asked the same question, the percentage was smaller still. When the healthy agers were asked if they believed that they would be alive in 10 years, there was significant uncertainty, but still less than existed in the control group. Based on this data, the highest rate of uncertainty emerged when the control group was asked about life expectancy; choose C, and dismiss the other answers.

10. <u>A</u> is the correct answer.

At the start of the study, researchers found that elderly adults could display tendencies towards being "healthy agers" and that these individuals typically reported feeling younger and healthier than their peers did. The data in the graph display a similar trend, with the healthy agers group reporting higher levels of confidence than a control group. Choose A to reflect this content. B and C can both be eliminated since the graph does not display any data which extend beyond the questions of the research study, nor does it present any information which would generate or contradict a recommendation. D can also be eliminated, since the graph only presents findings without offering any insight into the methodology of how this data was gathered.

Passage 2, Pages 9-11

1. <u>D</u> is the correct answer.

The passage begins with a description of a general trend towards media representations becoming manipulated and even distorted, and then focuses on Adobe's Project VoCo. The passage describes this project; then, the author hones in on the potential risks associated with it. Choose D to reflect this content. Be careful not to choose A, since manipulation of media does not qualify as a form of analysis, and the author's tone towards this trend is clearly critical and NOT supportive. B and C can readily be eliminated since the passage describes the development of a new product, NOT a research product, and since the author's tone throughout the passage is skeptically foreboding, NOT optimistic, about these technological advancements.

2. <u>A</u> is the correct answer.

In lines 1-2, and 9-10, the author uses questions for which the potential response of a reader can most likely be predicted and is suggested in the lines that follow soon after. Since the outcomes of these questions is known, they function rhetorically to advance the author's argument. Choose A as appropriate. Be careful not to choose B, since the author sees Adobe Max as a symptom of a problem, NOT an attempt to resolve it. C and D can also be eliminated since the questions are fairly direct and immediate (NOT intended to provoke deep reflection) and since the questions are introduced BEFORE the discussion of Project VoCo.

3. C is the correct answer.

In line 14, "advanced" refers to media creation tools that are highly refined and capable of achieving a wide array of effects. Choose C to reflect this meaning. A (inappropriately implying someone who has researched or studied a given topic), B (inappropriately implying someone or something which is not easy to engage with) ,and D (inappropriately implying someone who has seen beyond conventional beliefs or values) all introduce improper contexts and therefore should be eliminated.

4. B is the correct answer.

In line 41, "share" refers to an Adobe presented openly and directly communicating some of the risks associated with Project VoCo. Choose B to reflect this meaning. A (inappropriately implying something reproducing or duplicating itself), C (inappropriately implying making changes in order to make a structure or process easier for someone to access), and D (inappropriately implying distributing set amounts of a substance) all introduce improper contexts and therefore should be eliminated.

5. D is the correct answer.

In lines 50-53, the author describes how "What's new is the affordability of such tools and the scale they can achieve nowadays versus expensive and complicated software workflows of the past." This content indicates that software-based editing tools are becoming more accessible due to being less expensive and less complicated to use; choose D as appropriate. A and B can be eliminated since, if tools were either unpredictable or insignificant, their usage would not be an increasingly significant phenomenon. C can also be eliminated since the passage suggests that such tools are rapidly being developed and are currently evolving, rather than remaining permanent.

6. B is the correct answer.

See the previous answer explanation for analysis of the correct line reference. A describes a potential negative outcome which could occur due to technological advancements, while C situates a specific example within a broader trend. D qualifies and adds nuance to the argument that the author is making about the harmful consequences of technology. None of these other answers imply that editing software is becoming more widely accessible, and therefore they should all be eliminated.

7. B is the correct answer.

Lines 33-36 describe how "Gamers can also benefit from characters whose dialogue is more flexible instead of defaulting to whatever the designers wrote." This content indicates that technological shifts will make it increasingly possible for video and computer games to feature more lifelike conversations; choose B as the best answer. A and C can be eliminated since the passage does not primarily focus on gaming and does NOT clearly address either commands or the situations that characters encounter. Be careful not to choose D, since the changes that the author describes would involve the players being able to edit existing audio within the game, NOT to change the type of audio included in the first place.

8. <u>B</u> is the correct answer.

See the previous answer explanation for analysis of the correct line reference. A describes a technical requirement of the software, while C identifies a prediction related to how the market for software editing tools will shift in the future. D identifies another emerging product while indicating the risks that it could create. None of these other answers suggest that technological advancements could change the way in which gamers interact with audio within their games, and therefore they should all be eliminated.

9. <u>A</u> is the correct answer.

The third chart shows that when participants were listening to a human voice, at the twenty minute mark almost 75% of the participants were confident that they were hearing a non-human voice, and a small percentage were suspicious that they might be hearing a non-human voice. This data implies that many listeners misidentified a human source as non-human; choose A as appropriate. B and C can be eliminated since, when listening to a chatbot, most were either confident or suspicious that they were hearing a non-human voice. D can also be eliminated since, at the twenty minute mark, a strong majority of listeners responded to a monotone voice (either human or artificial) by reporting confidence that the voice in question was artificial.

10. <u>D</u> is the correct answer.

The data from the charts show that many individuals cannot correctly identify whether a voice is human or artificial. This information indicates that voice mimicking tools are sophisticated and effective; choose D as appropriate. A and B can be eliminated since the data reveal evidence of a trend, but NOT direct consequences of it, while the charts themselves do not communicate anything about the benefits of voice mimicking software. C can also be eliminated since the charts represent data from a controlled study and do NOT reflect how widely used the relevant tools are.

Passage 3, Pages 12-14

1. <u>C</u> is the correct answer.

The passage indicates that "4.3 million children will receive Social Security benefits in 2019 because one or both of their parents are disabled, retired, or deceased . . . Children also benefit when others members of their household, such as grandparents, receive support as retirees" (lines 66-72). This content implies that children may receive benefits directly due to family circumstances, or access benefits indirectly if a relative is receiving such assistance; choose C to reflect this content. Be careful not to choose B, since the passage does indicate that children make up a significant population of benefit recipients but does NOT specify whether they are a growing percentage of Social Security recipients. A and D can also be eliminated since children's access to Social Security is not directly tied to family income, and the passage does NOT describe the impact of children receiving or not receiving benefits.

2. <u>D</u> is the correct answer.

In the first paragraph, words like "reset" and "rewrote" indicate that, when Social Security was introduced, it created significant change and had a substantial impact on the American social landscape. Choose D as the best answer. A and C can be eliminated since the first paragraph does not compare Social Security to any other programs, or indicate whether or not it was controversial when introduced. B can also be eliminated since the first paragraph focuses on the PAST impact of Social Security, NOT further directions for the program.

3. <u>C</u> is the correct answer.

In line 12, the author states that Roosevelt's vision for Social Security focused on creating safeguards against misfortune. Lines 66-68 indicate that children are eligible to receive Social Security benefits if "one or both of their parents are disabled, retired, or deceased." Having a parent who meets one or more of these criteria indicates a case in which someone is experiencing misfortune, and therefore this example best reflects Roosevelt's vision of the goals of Social Security. Choose C as appropriate. A describes an early amendment which expanded the scope of Social Security, while B describes some details of how the program works. D states a fact which might be surprising to readers about Social Security and children. None of these other answers provide evidence of how Social Security supports individuals experiencing misfortune as directly linked to Roosevelt's conception, and therefore they should all be eliminated.

4. <u>B</u> is the correct answer.

In the first section of the passage, the author explains that "the Social Security Act of 1935 was signed into law" (lines 1-2) and then continues on to explain that "Even before the first retirement benefits were distributed, the Act was amended in 1939" (lines 17-18). Logically, this content indicates that there was lag between when Social Security was established (1935) and when benefits began to be paid out (some time after 1939). Choose B as appropriate. Be careful not to choose C, because the passage does NOT specify whether benefits were first paid out in 1939 or whether administrative logistics were the reason for the delay in benefit payment. A and D can also be eliminated because, based on the chronology established between 1935 and 1939, it cannot be inferred that Social Security was politically controversial, or designed to be significantly altered, since the author is mostly providing a somewhat approving account of historical events.

5. <u>B</u> is the correct answer.

Lines 45-50 explain that, while higher earners may earn slightly higher benefits, lower earners will receive a higher percentage of their earnings, so that there is minimal variation in the amounts received. This content is contradicted by the statement made in B, so that B should be identified as the correct answer. A (instead of CONTRADICTING) reflects the same content found in lines 45-50, while C reflects the description of how Social Security tax rates are applied. D fits within the current Social Security structure because both high and low earners can receive benefit payments. Since all of these other answers make statements which are aligned with the current structure of Social Security, they should all be eliminated.

6. <u>C</u> is the correct answer.

See the previous answer explanation for analysis of the correct line reference. A identifies something which has remained consistent about Social Security as well as something which has changed, while B provides part of the explanation of how Social Security benefits are distributed. D offers a justification as to why aspects of the program related to elderly recipients tend to be the most widely discussed aspects. None of these other answers would indicate that a lower-earning individual does NOT receive higher benefits than a higher-earning individual; at most, they present points about seemingly relevant topics (Social Security and related benefits) that are not DIRECTLY contradicted by any of the answers to the previous question.

7. <u>D</u> is the correct answer.

In line 69, "represent" refers to how children make up a small but significant portion of Social Security recipients. Choose D to reflect this meaning that relates to being part of a group. A (inappropriately implying someone arguing in favor of something), B (inappropriately implying or describing someone or something), and C (inappropriately implying being designated as the appropriate recipient of something, a meaning appropriate in OTHER contexts) all introduce improper contexts and should therefore be eliminated.

8. <u>C</u> is the correct answer.

The final paragraph moves from objective description of how Social Security functions and who benefits from it to a more philosophical reflection on how Social Security reflects values which have long been embedded in American society. Choose C to reflect this content. B and D can both be eliminated since the author's impassioned defense of Social Security suggests that it is NOT in fact immune to the "fluctuations" and "uncertainties" mentioned in the paragraph, and since the description of how the program works has made it clear that Social Security is not universally accessible. Be careful not to choose A, since a part of the passage does focus on explaining that children also benefit from Social Security (not just the elderly), but this discussion is NOT the primary focus of the last paragraph.

9. <u>C</u> is the correct answer.

The graph indicates that between 1995 and 2015, the tax rate associated with Social Security remained stable at 12.5%, but in the same time period, the number of individuals covered by Social Security increased from approximately 50 million individuals to 60 million. This trend is described in C, which is thus the best answer. B can readily be eliminated since it reverses the relationship of the data shown in the graph. A can be eliminated because since at least 1995, the social security tax rate has remained stable, and D can be eliminated since the graph shows that the number of individuals covered by Social Security has steadily increased since at least 1955.

10. <u>A</u> is the correct answer.

The graph only shows data about how, over time, taxes have been collected to fund Social Security, and how more and more individuals have become eligible for coverage. It does NOT provide any data about actual payments and whether they vary by income level, whereas the passage does provide information about this aspect of the program (lines 42-50). Choose A as appropriate. B and D can be eliminated since the content of these answers is represented in BOTH the graph and the passage. C can be eliminated since the content of this answer is discussed in NEITHER the graph nor the passage.

Passage 4, Pages 15-17

1. <u>B</u> is the correct answer.

In line 16, "reproducing" refers to the way in which traffic models must mirror or replicate the behavior of actual drivers. Choose B to reflect this meaning. A (inappropriately implying the alteration of behavior, not simply a modeling of GIVEN behavior), C (inappropriately implying using intellectual effort to arrive at greater understanding), and D (inappropriately implying the establishment of a relationship) all introduce incorrect contexts and therefore should be eliminated.

2. <u>C</u> is the correct answer.

In lines 50-51, the authors explain that "even fewer routes are optimal—only a third overall minimize travel time." This content reveals that the authors' definition of an optimal route relies on the route using the lowest total amount of driving time; choose C as appropriate. A and B refer to other factors (the fewest turns, or the most interesting scenery) which the passage describes as factors in a driver's decision making, but NOT as indications that the route is optimal. These answers should be eliminated. D can also be eliminated, since the relationship between driving behavior and fuel consumption (a factor which is NOT brought up in the passage's actual discussion of short, efficient routes) is not discussed in the passage.

3. <u>B</u> is the correct answer.

See the previous answer explanation for the analysis of the correct line reference. A challenges a seemingly logical assumption, while C describes a factor that influences actual driving behavior. D describes a technological tool designed to reflect the preference of some drivers for interesting and picturesque routes. None of these other answers define an optimal route as one that minimizes driving time (though some answers do broadly relate to the topic of a driver's behavior), and therefore they should all be eliminated.

4. <u>C</u> is the correct answer.

In line 55, the authors transition to an explanation of a conclusion documented in the study: drivers often do not choose the shortest route. By opening up a discussion about what might be behind this result, the authors emphasize that this conclusion has ALREADY been documented. Choose C to reflect this content. Be careful not to choose A, since the notion that drivers often do not choose the optimal route DOES challenge a commonly held belief, but this perception is an assumption, NOT a validated consensus. B and D can both be eliminated since the idea of drivers not following the shortest route challenges rather than follows a prediction, and does not evoke a dispute; the idea of different driver preferences that is present in the passage does NOT justify such a strong negative tone.

5. <u>A</u> is the correct answer.

If apps were not able to monitor traffic conditions, then apps themselves would be seriously limited in their ability to accurately recommend the fastest route to drivers; such a situation would therefore undermine the authors' claim that apps can help drivers to choose the fastest route. Choose A as the best answer. B can be eliminated since, if some drivers were unwilling to spend money on apps, that tendency might limit the number of individuals who utilize an app but NOT the efficacy of the app itself. C and D can also be eliminated since there is no reason to assume that visual directions would be unsuccessful at helping drivers to choose efficient routes, and since a new phenomenon would still help drivers to subsequently make decisions about route optimization.

6. <u>B</u> is the correct answer.

In lines 39-42, the authors state that most people typically take the same route to destinations which they visit regularly; this content indicates that many drivers are creatures of habit. Choose B to reflect this content. A provides a justification for why research into driving behavior is important, while C provides an acknowledgment that drivers may genuinely be unable to determine the most efficient route. D offers a suggestion about how technology could be used to improve drivers' experiences. None of the other answers substantiate the claim that drivers favor taking the same route over and over, and therefore they should all be eliminated.

7. <u>C</u> is the correct answer.

In lines 74-77, the authors explain that "Many factors can influence [route] preference, including fuel consumption, route reliability, simplicity, and pleasure." The only factor NOT mentioned here is the avoidance of toll fees; choose C. Since all of the other answers reflect factors which DO appear to influence the choice of a route, they should all be eliminated.

8. <u>B</u> is the correct answer.

In lines 83-86, the authors introduce the app Waze as evidence of technological innovation which appears to have already influenced driver behavior. This example is used to support a subsequent broader claim that technological tools, such as apps or gamification, may be the solution to traffic congestion. Choose B to reflect this content. Be careful not to choose A, since the possibility of technology increasing traffic efficiency is one idea raised in the passage, but NOT the central idea. C and D can also be eliminated, since technology is presented as positive force and is not (despite its apparently transformative potential) explicitly contrasted with a previous example.

9. <u>B</u> is the correct answer.

According to lines 45-54, optimal or fastest routes were NOT preferred by the participants in the 2014 study; in contrast, the participants in Group 2 had an overwhelming preference for fast routes (second lightest bar) that would signal a departure from this finding. Choose B and eliminate all other answers, since the other groups exhibited considerable variety in route preference by person (a finding of the study) and featured significant percentages of participants who chose routes based on factors NOT clearly related to speed (such as whether a route is scenic or cost-efficient).

10. <u>C</u> is the correct answer.

Lines 63-68 describe a driver who would choose a longer route in order to pass by a notable landmark; this driver could best be placed in the category of those who choose the most scenic route. Choose C as appropriate. A, B, and D can all be eliminated since a driver who extends a route in order to observe a landmark is taking a route which is not NECESSARILY fast, short, and cost-efficient, since the route is longer and since passing a landmark is the key objective.

Passage 5, Pages 18-20

1. <u>A</u> is the correct answer.

The passage describes how many people today initially feel disengaged from, and confused by, written documents, especially those from past centuries. However, the authors go on to make an argument that, if people have the chance to actively engage with handwritten historical documents, these individuals can often come to a better understanding; in order to make this argument, the passage provides a specific example from an event held in 2019 (lines 58-87). Choose A as appropriate. B and D can be dismissed since the authors argue for the value of both handwritten and printed documents, NOT that handwritten documents are superior in promoting critical thinking; the authors also do NOT discuss only speeches, since "letters" (line 3) are mentioned early on. C can be eliminated since the authors do highlight the value of handwritten historical documents for the information that they can provide about earlier cultures, but this is NOT the main point of the article, which focuses on accessibility to non-specialists in terms of format and medium.

2. <u>D</u> is the correct answer.

The authors begin by discussing why modern audiences feel alienated by handwritten documents in general, and then focuses more specifically on documents from the 18th and 19th centuries. The authors then move to explain a specific event held at the Library of Congress in 2019. This is a pattern of moving from describing a broad trend to describing a specific initiative, as D reflects. A and C can be eliminated since the passage does not begin with any particular representative example (as opposed to several examples), and the authors do not open by discussing personal experiences (not to be confused with accounts of the event LATER in the passage). Be careful not to choose B, since the authors do move from a less-than ideal-reality to a more optimistic example, but does NOT link the historical problems inherent in reading handwriting to personal bias.

3. <u>B</u> is the correct answer.

The second paragraph identifies generational changes in how individuals learn to read, write, and engage with texts. By identifying these differences between older and younger generations, the authors demonstrate one reason that different individuals will feel more or less at ease with different writing practices; choose B as appropriate. A and C can be eliminated because the paragraph offers a fairly neutral description without portraying one form of writing as superior, and because at this point the authors have not yet started to make a case for introducing readers to older documents (a priority of lines 28-33). D can also be eliminated since, while the paragraph does identify some features of technology which have roots in older practices, this is NOT the primary point of the paragraph, which mostly uses the "carbon copy" description to indicate a trend.

4. <u>D</u> is the correct answer.

In line 30, "lost" refers to how cursive writing is no longer popular or regarded as necessary. Choose D to reflect this meaning. A (inappropriately implying something which has been reduced in integrity or quality), B (inappropriately implying something which has been moved to a different or unknown location), and C (inappropriately implying a lack of clear consensus or action) all introduce improper contexts and should therefore be eliminated.

5. <u>D</u> is the correct answer.

Lines 1-4 quote visitors who encounter handwritten historical documents as often remarking "That's so beautiful, but what does it say?" This quote indicates that individuals who first encounter documents from another century often initially respond to the aesthetic qualities ("beautiful") of the documents; choose D as appropriate. A and C can both be eliminated since nothing indicates that most viewers would immediately engage in a complex analysis of how documents connect to modern ideas or historical precedents (even though the AUTHORS undertake such analysis). B can readily be eliminated since most individuals seem to initially respond to historical documents in a positive manner.

6. <u>A</u> is the correct answer.

See the previous answer explanation for analysis of the correct line reference. B identifies a specific phenomenon and argues for the significance of that phenomenon, while C differentiates between how older and younger people engage with handwritten texts. D makes an argument about the potential negative impact of individuals losing the ability to read handwriting. None of these other answers indicate that many individuals admire the beauty of handwritten documents, and therefore they should all be eliminated.

7. <u>B</u> is the correct answer.

Lines 77-80 describe a technique which was used successfully to prompt modern readers to gain confidence in reading handwritten historical documents: "when asked to pick out a letter or word anywhere on the page and then build on that kernel of understanding, they soon started to identify familiar words, then phrases." Choose B to reflect this content. A and C can be eliminated since there is no explicit mention in the passage of comparing or rewriting documents, even though these are interactive activities. Be careful not to choose D, since it articulates a reading strategy similar but NOT identical to one used at the Library of Congress event.

8. <u>D</u> is the correct answer.

See the previous answer explanation for analysis of the correct line reference. A makes an optimistic claim and then provides an example as evidence. B describes a resource which was used to increase confidence in reading historical documents, and C describes an additional positive outcome associated with having readers engage with historical documents. None of these other answers identify a strategy that readers can use to engage with handwritten historical documents, and therefore they should all be eliminated.

9. <u>A</u> is the correct answer.

In line 85, "eagerly" refers to how Library of Congress visitors engaged in an activity in a thoughtful and focused way. Choose A to reflect this meaning. B (inappropriately implying a lack of knowledge or sophistication), C (inappropriately implying a lack of foresight or planning), and D (inappropriately implying an ability to behave in unconventional or unexpected ways) all introduce improper contexts or wrongly negative tones.

10. <u>C</u> is the correct answer.

The graph does not provide any information about the handwriting of the Gettysburg Address, but it does show that all of the identified words chosen from the Address have declined in usage since the date of the

Address itself. This information indicates that readers of historical documents may encounter a dual challenge of both unfamiliar cursive handwriting and unfamiliar vocabulary; choose C as the best answer. A and D can both be eliminated since there is insufficient information presented in the graph (which only indicates a decline in word usage frequency) to indicate that the Address had a significant influence on the evolution of language or on a document's reception. B can be eliminated since nothing in the graph (which considers word usage WITHOUT designating a specific technology for gathering data) indicates that technology has proven useful for arriving at a better understanding of the Gettysburg Address.

Passage 6, Pages 21-23

1. C is the correct answer.

The beginning of the passage (lines 1-18) describes Kerry Wright as very devoted to the welfare of her children; this segment also describes how she has separated from her partner and no longer had a relationship with her parents and other family members. It is accurate to characterize this situation as a state of being devoted to some family members while being alienated from others; choose C as an effective answer. A and B can both be readily eliminated since the passage clearly indicates that Kerry felt a pronounced sense of stress due to her financial situation and was worried about the future of her children. D can also be eliminated since there is NOT a mention of Kerry receiving charity support for MOST of her needs; though charity might have been helpful, she did perform work in an attempt to earn money.

2. D is the correct answer.

While the passage begins with a description of the specific experiences of one individual (Kerry Wright), this example is meant to be representative of a wider trend among individuals who experience food insecurity. As the author notes in lines 19-21, "What happened to Wright and her family is common to far more households in wealthy countries than some may think." Choose D as appropriate. B and C can be eliminated because nothing about Kerry's situation indicates that her story, though dramatic and regrettable, was widespread enough to attract public attention or that it could be used as a preventative case. A can also be eliminated since this choice implies that Kerry's situation was tied to a drastic change, not to ongoing challenges that concerned poverty and food insecurity.

3. D is the correct answer.

See the previous answer explanation for analysis of the correct line reference. A describes a physical sensation experienced due to food deprivation, while B identifies a factor which exacerbated economic instability and food scarcity. C provides additional context about Kerry Wright's situation. None of these other answers connect Kerry's situation to a wider pattern of food scarcity (since these choices, instead, primarily describe the situation ITSELF), and therefore they should all be eliminated.

4. A is the correct answer.

Lines 29-32 identify one effort to combat hunger by describing how "Food banks, which hand out free supplies of food to those in need, have become more and more common in places where food insecurity has become a persistent problem." Choose A as the best answer. B uses a rhetorical question to transition to a different subtopic, while C identifies an instance in which the author of the passage sought the perspective of an expert. D describes some diseases which may be more prevalent in cases in which individuals experienced food scarcity during childhood. None of these other answers (which focus on problems and perspectives) identify measures being taken to combat food insecurity, and therefore they should all be eliminated.

5. C is the correct answer.

In line 51, "experience" refers to the specifics of Kerry's life, while in line 61 "experience" refers to a general pattern shared by the majority of individuals who have to endure food scarcity. Choose C to reflect this difference. A can be eliminated because there are no reservations expressed about the commonalities of food scarcity, while B can be eliminated because in neither of these line references does the author of the passage propose a solution. D can also be eliminated since the straightforward and factual description of Kerry's situation focuses on a specific example but does NOT necessarily indicate a source of bias.

6. C is the correct answer.

Tarasuk's research, conducted in a Canadian context, indicates that "the more severe a person's experience of food insecurity, the more likely they are to seek help from healthcare services." If it were found that Japanese individuals visited clinics more frequently when they experienced food insecurity, that fact might indicate that Tarasuk's findings were applicable in Japan as well as in Canada. Choose C as appropriate. A and B can be eliminated since Tarasuk's research (despite its focus on specific social patterns) did NOT investigate household income or high school dropout rates. D can also be eliminated since the pattern relevant to this answer would indicate that trends in Japan are different from trends in Canada, NOT similar.

7. D is the correct answer.

The research conducted by Kirkpatrick and McIntyre indicates that experiencing food scarcity means "that children are less likely to finish school." Choose D as appropriate. A and B can be eliminated since the passage identifies additional research contributions made by these researchers but does NOT suggest that they developed new terminology or contributed to a direct response to food insecurity. C can also be eliminated since there is no description of a relationship between these researchers and Tarasuk, despite some apparently similar concerns.

8. D is the correct answer.

In line 84, "held up" is used to explain that research findings remained consistent even when variables were changed. Choose D to reflect this meaning. A (inappropriately implying something becoming more notable or more visible), B (inappropriately implying something which had previously been inconsistent or erratic coming to show a reliable pattern), and C (inappropriately implying something which could withstand questioning and challenges) all introduce improper contexts and should be eliminated.

9. B is the correct answer.

The graphs show that food insecurity in the UK has been increasing steadily between 2005 and 2020. However, in 2020, only slightly more than 15% of the total population experienced low to moderate food insecurity, whereas in 1915 more than 40% of the total population experienced low to moderate food insecurity. The graphs indicate that while hunger is increasing, it is still nowhere the peak historical rates; choose B as the best answer. A and C can be eliminated since both of these answers reflect hypothetical predictions of how rates of hunger could change, whereas the graphs only retrospectively report actual hunger rates at specific moments in time. D can also be eliminated since this answer reflects a relationship which cannot be substantiated based on the data shown in the graph, since the health of the ENTIRE economy is never explicitly measured.

10. A is the correct answer.

The passage explains that individuals who experience food insecurity suffer potential long-term impacts, whereas the graph shows how widespread the phenomenon of food insecurity is in the United Kingdom (an area also significant to the passage). Choose A to reflect this relationship. B can be eliminated since the graph only shows the individuals affected as a percentage of the total UK population, NOT the complete numbers of individuals experiencing hunger. C and D can both be eliminated since the passage focuses on experiences of hunger in relatively recent times whereas the second graph shows historical data about rates of hunger in much earlier times and is thus only vaguely related to the passage.

Passage 7, Pages 24-26

1. B is the correct answer.

In lines 7-9, the author asserts that it has become commonplace to express alarm and worry about job losses due to automation. Lines 21-24 explain that a statistic indicating a huge potential decline in jobs has "been cited in over 4,000 articles, unnerving workers in all sectors of the economy and justifying catastrophic outlooks." Choose B to reflect that lines 21-24 substantiate the claim initially made in lines 7-9. A describes a grim statistic about potential job loss, while C describes emerging research which challenges existing claims. D elaborates on some of the findings of this new research. None of these other answers provide supporting evidence for the idea that there is widespread alarm about jobs declining due to automation, and therefore they should all be eliminated.

2. B is the correct answer.

In line 11, "solve" refers to how presidential candidates propose to address and resolve the negative effects of job loss due to technological advancement. A (inappropriately implying thinking deeply about or examining, NOT taking action), C (inappropriately implying encouraging efforts or heightening public attention, NOT signaling a problem), and D (inappropriately implying completing the last remaining steps to arrive at an intended outcome, NOT an initiative) all introduce improper contexts and therefore should be eliminated.

3. C is the correct answer.

In line 22, "unnerving" refers to how readers became alarmed and despairing based on statistics about impending job loss. Choose C to reflect this clearly negative meaning. A (inappropriately implying confusion and lack of comprehension), B (inappropriately implying weakening someone's physical abilities) and D (inappropriately implying shock and astonishment) all introduce improper contexts despite some negative tones and should therefore be eliminated.

4. <u>B</u> is the correct answer.

The author of the passage quotes Frey as arguing that "the 47 percent figure be deconstructed in a more nuanced manner." Choose B to reflect this context of subtlety and moderation. A and C should both be dismissed since Frey does NOT argue that the 47% figure was a generalization and broad assumption; he believes that while this number may have been obtained in a methodical way, it could still require additional scrutiny. Be careful not to choose D, since this answer wrongly indicates that Frey would dismiss the number; like A, this choice balances positive and negative tones, yet here the grounds of Frey's criticism are misrepresented.

5. <u>B</u> is the correct answer.

The sixth and seventh paragraphs provide a more detailed explanation of the research methodology which led to the conclusions in a widely-cited 2013 study of automation and work. Choose B as the best answer. A and C can be rejected since the paragraphs only present a method by which research was conducted, NOT any conclusions which were generated. D can also be rejected since these paragraphs describe the method through which Osborne and Frey arrived at their initial conclusion predicting widespread job loss; a focus on motives would wrongly reference an EARLIER stage of the work of these researchers.

6. <u>A</u> is the correct answer.

In lines 71-76, passage indicates that "47 out of every 100 jobs could conceivably be done by computers one day in the future if a bunch of massive engineering challenges get solved, not to mention if regulations and public opposition don't get in the way." This content suggests that government intervention ("regulations") could reduce the number of jobs lost to automation; choose A as appropriate. B and D distort the focus on government to bring in loosely-related political themes that the author does NOT discuss, while C cites a possible EFFECT of job loss, NOT a cause.

7. <u>C</u> is the correct answer.

See the previous answer explanation for analysis of the correct line reference. A identifies jobs which are unlikely to be at risk due to automation, while B identifies jobs which have a high likelihood of being impacted by automation. D states a statistic about the overall decline in global poverty. None of these other answers connect government intervention to the protection of employment (even though some answers do address broad economic themes), and therefore they should all be eliminated.

8. <u>A</u> is the correct answer.

The author states that "Farmers in Kenya and shopkeepers in India aren't as well-off as the Silicon Valley engineers who designed their phones—but they're certainly more well-off than they were before." This content indicates that technological progress involves ongoing inequity along with overall improvements in prosperity. Choose A to reflect this content. B and C can be eliminated since the author does NOT mention specific skills which increase or decline in importance, nor does the author describe a connection between technology and a worker's relationship to authority (since economic prosperity is the true focus of the discussion). D should also be eliminated because the author does NOT discuss cultural (as opposed to economic) variations, even though the passage does designate different geographic regions.

9. C is the correct answer.

The graphs predict that, in a high-job-loss scenario, by 2040, 97% of all jobs will be white collar jobs (whether requiring a B.A. or not). This projection represents the category with the highest quantity of jobs from any graph; choose C as appropriate. A can be eliminated since in 1950, only 59% of all jobs were white collar, while B can be eliminated since in 2020, 88% of all jobs were white collar. D can also be eliminated, since in a low-job-loss projection, by 2040, 92% of jobs will be white collar.

10. B is the correct answer.

By way of the parenthetical labels "low job loss" and "high job loss," the graphs indicate that some job loss is likely to occur between 2020 and 2040, even if the rate of that loss is not clear. Choose B to reflect this content, which recalls the passage's major premise that some jobs will disappear due to automation. A can be eliminated since, while the graphs do demonstrate a steady decline in manufacturing jobs, they do NOT demonstrate any data about manufacturing productivity. C can be eliminated since the graphs suggest that in a high-job loss scenario, 36% of jobs could require a B.A. or higher by 2040, and nothing indicates that this number would not continue to grow from there since later years are not considered. D can be eliminated since the graphs suggest that in a high-job loss scenario, by 2040, only 3% of jobs would be manufacturing jobs and nothing indicates that this number would not continue to decline; for its part, the passage does not define a numerical limit to the manufacturing job losses in any way.

Passage 8, Pages 27-29

1. D is the correct answer.

The passage focuses on describing a study which modeled the flow of pedestrian traffic by borrowing from principles usually associated with cells and electrons (as noted in lines 46-50). Choose D to reflect this content. A and B can both be eliminated since the study focused primarily on modeling actual behavior, NOT testing and disproving assumptions, and since there were no significant ethical implications to the behavior examined by the study (which was mainly modeled and explained). C can be eliminated since the purpose of the study was to validate how pedestrians typically move through space, NOT to recommend how they should move.

2. D is the correct answer.

Lines 20-23 state that "calibration of theoretical models using real-world data is largely missing from the most pedestrian flow models, which are under-validated and imprecise." This content indicates that previous research had not adequately included data based on tracking actual pedestrian movements; choose D as appropriate. A and B can be eliminated since there is no mention of whether previous studies incorporated simulated obstacles or what type of inputs they relied on; real-world considerations are the main deficiency. C can also be eliminated since the researchers (as opposed to the author) do NOT critique video footage usage.

3. C is the correct answer.

See the previous answer explanation for analysis of the correct line reference. A describes how the study gathered information about pedestrian movements, while B describes the calculations and analysis which researchers conducted based on the movements they observed. D identifies another type of model from a different discipline which proved useful to the researchers. None of these other answers critique previous studies for failing to account for the movement of actual pedestrians, and therefore they should all be eliminated.

4. <u>A</u> is the correct answer.

The passage summarizes a series of rules governing pedestrian movements, including the idea that "Individuals need personal space, which acts like a repelling force to other pedestrians and objects" (lines 38-42). This rule would be contradicted by a situation in which two pedestrians walking together, rather than maintaining personal space, achieved greater speed and efficiency. Choose A as the best answer. B can be eliminated since it in fact aligns with rules about pedestrians keeping distance from one another and walking at different speeds. C and D can be eliminated since these scenarios align with rules about speed decreasing due to crowd density and natural variation in speed among pedestrians.

5. <u>C</u> is the correct answer.

See the previous answer explanation for analysis of the correct line reference. A explains how pedestrians will seek out the shortest route, while B explains that pedestrians tend to maintain their preferred speeds. D identifies some factors which may contribute to someone having a slower or faster walking speed. None of these answers would explain why a situation in which two pedestrians walk quickly together is unusual (thus introducing the needed counter-example), and therefore they should all be eliminated.

6. <u>C</u> is the correct answer.

In lines 46-47, the authors state that they used principles developed for modeling the behavior of electrons to model pedestrian behavior. It is indicated that these principles helped to complement the understanding that the authors developed using a cellular automaton model; choose C as appropriate. A can be eliminated since there is no specific explanation of what would have happened if the researchers relied solely on an automaton model. B can be eliminated since the authors integrated an electrostatic model, implying they WERE aware of its utility, and D can be eliminated since there is no mention of pedestrian movement studies being applicable to other disciplines; at most, another discipline was used to FORMULATE the pedestrian model.

7. <u>C</u> is the correct answer.

In line 60, "distribution" refers to the different walking speeds which took place during the research. Choose C to reflect this content. A (inappropriately implying fluid movement through designated channels), B (inappropriately implying rules and policies governing processes), and D (inappropriately implying physical manipulation and touch) all introduce improper contexts and therefore should be eliminated.

8. <u>D</u> is the correct answer.

In line 76, "critical" refers to the significance of measuring source-target distribution accurately. Since this is a very significant factor, the connotations of "critical" include A (appropriately implying essential to the success of an outcome), B (appropriately implying an action on which success or failure depends), and C (appropriately implying something vital and non-optional). D (inappropriately implying an emotional context, and someone withholding forgiveness after a slight) is the only answer which introduces an improper context and therefore represents the correct answer.

9. A is the correct answer.

The table documents how different sequences of positive and negative inputs contribute to greater or lower movement efficiency. Therefore, the table can be used to infer that the configuration of different inputs will impact movement efficiency; choose A as appropriate. B can be eliminated since the table does not present any data about the duration of the inputs (which are simply either positive or negative) and simply shows the sequence in which they were introduced. C and D can also both be eliminated since the table does NOT provide any information about how speed or delay were impacted by inputs; it only shows the sequence of inputs and the overall movement efficiency.

10. D is the correct answer.

According to the study (lines 46-50) and the table, exit signs would be interpreted as positive inputs (and represented as a P in the table), whereas obstacles and other pedestrians would be interpreted as negative inputs (and therefore represented as N in the table). If Pedestrian 7 encountered 3 exit signs, followed by 1 obstacle, followed by 2 Pedestrians, followed by 1 exit sign and then followed by 1 pedestrian, this pattern of inputs would be scored as PPPNNNPN. This sequence is described by D and accurately reflects what is documented in the table. Choose D. All other answers (A and B starting with negative inputs, C ending with a positive input) reflect sequences of inputs which do not align with the data described in the table.

Passage 9, Pages 30-32

1. C is the correct answer.

The passage moves from discussing a problem (poor rates of health and other urban consequences in Glasgow) to identifying one possible cause of that problem: recommendations from the 1940s which led to changes to housing and population distribution. This content indicates that an urban planning project which was intended to improve quality of life actually ended up decreasing quality of life: choose C as the best answer. A and D can be eliminated since the passage focuses on problems which are NOT limited only to overcrowding and does NOT explicitly connect problems with urban planning projects to a lack of understanding on the part of the planners. B can also be eliminated since the passage focuses primarily on problems which have been created due to urban planning, NOT positive new developments.

2. B is the correct answer.

The Glasgow Effect is a documented problem in which residents of this city tend to die relatively young and experience poor health overall (lines 1-19). No one understands exactly why this problem occurs (lines 30-31). Choose B to reflect this content. A and D can both be eliminated since the passage indicates that this problem is taken seriously (NOT dismissed) and that the problem is real and documented (NOT an illusion, even though the problem may appear to be unusual). C can also be dismissed as illogical, since nothing in the passage indicates that a widespread social phenomenon has any causal relationship to a particular landmark (even though the problem is localized to one city and related to some unusual explanations).

3. C is the correct answer.

In line 20, "work out" refers to Walsh's desire to resolve and explain the mystery of low life expectancy in Glasgow. Choose C to reflect this meaning. A (inappropriately implying trying to extend rather than resolve a phenomenon), B (inappropriately implying increasing performance rather than simply arriving at an understanding) and D (inappropriately implying exerting corrective force) all introduce improper contexts and should therefore be eliminated.

4. D is the correct answer.

In line 40, the key finding of Walsh's report is summarized; apparently, Glasgow's poverty and social problems can be mainly attributed to urban planning decisions. Lines 80-81 support this thesis by explaining how, after specific urban planning measures were put in place, "The rapid change in the city's make-up was soon recognized as disastrous." Choose D as appropriate. A describes some possible causes (NOT a more definitive cause) which were examined to see if they contributed to social problems in Glasgow. B cites a statistic about populations shifting to urban centers all over the world. C explains why increasing urbanization raises complex social questions and potential challenges. None of these other answers provide support for Walsh's claim that urban planning decisions had significant negative consequences in Glasgow, and therefore they should all be eliminated.

5. C is the correct answer.

Lines 54-55 state that "Studies have consistently linked city living with poorer mental health," an assertion which indicates that a problem documented in Glasgow also exists in other contexts. Choose C as appropriate. A and B can be dismissed since weather is not presented as a significant contributing factor in Walsh's research, and since poor mental health seems to affect younger residents of Glasgow more strongly by decreasing their life expectancy. D can also be dismissed since the passage looks at Glasgow specifically, and then at overall global trends, but does not provide any extended comparative context for Glasgow and other nearby regions.

6. B is the correct answer.

See the previous answer explanation for analysis of the correct line reference. A argues that cities with comparable levels of poverty experience much lower death rates, while C uses a rhetorical question to transition to a detailed analysis of a specific example. D provides further evidence that the negative repercussions of urban planning decisions quickly became apparent. None of these other answers connect problems in Glasgow to a broader global pattern, and therefore they should all be eliminated.

7. C is the correct answer.

In line 68, "acute" refers to how problems associated with urban life will likely become heightened as more and more people move into urban centers. Choose C to reflect this meaning. A (inappropriately implying someone being astute and sharply observant), B (inappropriately implying someone or something being assertive and clear), and D (inappropriately implying something or someone being highly responsive to stimuli) all introduce improper contexts and should therefore be eliminated.

8. <u>D</u> is the correct answer.

Walsh does not condemn the intentions of urban planning measures taken in Glasgow in the 1940s, but he does connect these measures to subsequent poverty and suffering. Choose D to reflect this content. A and B can be eliminated since there is no discussion of whether similar measures were implemented in other cities, and Welsh argues for a very strong relationship between these measures and current mortality rates. C can also be eliminated since it reverses the actual relationship: Walsh finds fault with the outcome, and NOT the intent, of these measures.

9. <u>D</u> is the correct answer.

The graph shows that, between 2012 and 2019, the mortality rate in Glasgow climbed steadily. During that same time period, patterns of rainy days and candy consumption were much more erratic, and no correlation is observed between any of these three factors. Choose D to reflect this data accurately. A, B, and C can be eliminated since they all assume clear correlations and thus articulate patterns which are NOT accurate representations of the data shown in the graph.

10. <u>A</u> is the correct answer.

Line 4 of the passage indicates that, in an effort to explain Glasgow's mysteriously high mortality rate, various factors have been considered, including food consumption and weather patterns. The graph provides data relevant to such factors, substantiating that they do not seem to contribute to mortality rates since there is no correlation with the upward-trending mortality rate data. Choose A as appropriate. B and C can be eliminated since the graph does NOT show any data about income levels in Glasgow or data about mental health among urban dwellers (factors that are nonetheless somewhat relevant to the PASSAGE on its own). D can also be eliminated since the graph does NOT show any data which would make it possible to analyze or assess revitalization efforts (so that this answer raises another topic unique to the passage).

Passage 10, Pages 33-35

1. <u>B</u> is the correct answer.

The study discussed in the passage finds that large companies consistently pay employees higher wages, regardless of the education level of those employees (lines 13-21 and 41-48). Choose B to reflect this content. A can be eliminated since the passage clearly states that employees with a high school education are paid more by larger companies than by small ones. C can be eliminated since the study finds that larger companies pay higher wages than smaller ones, and D can be eliminated since the passage does NOT explain how a smaller company can expand, despite noting the prevalence of the trend involving lower wages.

2. <u>D</u> is the correct answer.

The first paragraph defines a "good job" according to two criteria: "jobs that pay high wages and offer good benefits" (lines 4-5). A job which does NOT provide any employee benefits therefore would not meet these criteria, and D should be chosen as the one answer which does NOT describe a good job. All of the other answers describe jobs which provide both good wages and access to strong benefits, regardless of their other features. Therefore, these other answers can be eliminated based on the definition presented in the passage.

3. B is the correct answer.

In reference to large companies, lines 55-57 state that "The authors attribute the wage gains to the ability of large firms and establishments to hire and promote the more able." Choose B to reflect the idea that larger employers are able to hire top talent. A and C can be eliminated since there is no mention of how technology is used differently by larger and smaller employers, and since while the growth of large retailers is described in the passage, this growth is NOT connected to the ability to pay higher wages. Be careful not to choose D, since the passage indicates large firms can be more discriminating BOTH in whom they hire and promote, NOT just in whom they promote.

4. D is the correct answer.

See the previous answer explanation for analysis of the correct line reference. A identifies the focus of the research study described in the passage, while B identifies some recent trends in the retail industry. C provides a statistic about the distribution of retail workers across employers. None of these other answers highlights how a large employer's ability to hire and retain top talent allows it to pay higher wages, and therefore all of these other answers should be eliminated.

5. C is the correct answer.

In line 38, "pop up" refers to how big box operators continue to expand and open franchise locations. Choose C to reflect this meaning. A (inappropriately implying that someone is watching something physically appear at once), B (inappropriately implying pursuing new or novel ideas), and D (inappropriately implying an immediate response) all introduce improper contexts, and therefore they should all be eliminated.

6. A is the correct answer.

By characterizing some retail operations as "mom-and-pop shops," the author indicates that these retailers operate on a small scale, with few locations, and with only a limited number of employees. Throughout, larger firms CONTRAST with these smaller operations. Choose A to reflect this content. B and C can be eliminated since "mom and pop shops" are NOT an unusual or surprising concept (since many exist, and since the principle is well-known) and being small in scope does NOT necessarily imply that they are inefficient (despite the somewhat lower wages that they pay). D can be eliminated as outside of the scope of the passage since there is no way of knowing what philosophy and approach small retailers take to their business; after all, the choices of LARGER firms are of primary interest to the author.

7. A is the correct answer.

In reference to management and labor decisions, lines 75-80 state that "Instead of focusing resources on bringing outsourced manufacturing jobs back to the United States, the authors note that a more successful strategy may be to improve training for workers in modern retail firms . . . " This content indicates that manufacturing jobs continue to exist, but are now located mainly outside of the United States. Choose A to reflect this content. B and C can be eliminated since there is NO description of the skills required for either manufacturing or retail jobs, and since the study clearly indicates that manufacturing jobs are unlikely to increase in number. D can also be eliminated since the passage indicates that manufacturing jobs have become more scarce, but NOT that the wages for these jobs (not to be confused with wages for jobs in smaller firms) have decreased.

8. D is the correct answer.

See the previous answer explanation for analysis of the correct line reference. A describes a real-world implication which can be extrapolated from the research, while B contrasts job outlooks in two different sectors. C provides an important qualification to a hypothetical objection to the argument of the researchers. None of these others answers identify a shift in manufacturing jobs to regions outside of America, and therefore they should all be eliminated.

9. D is the correct answer.

According to figure 1, a total of 565 respondents were trying to get promoted, while 131 were unsure. This situation indicates that the majority of respondents either wanted, or were considering, moving to a different position with higher wages and responsibilities. Choose D, since this statement contradicts the data represented in the figure. A and B can be eliminated since a majority of respondents report high satisfaction with their duties and wages. C can also be eliminated since only a small percentage of respondents indicated that they were looking for a new job.

10. C is the correct answer.

Lines 49-57 explain that larger employers are able to pay higher wages, and that this trend is consistent across employee categories. Figure 2 provides data about entry-level wages at different retail employers but does NOT indicate how these wages might differ for employees with different education or experience levels. The figure also does NOT show any measurable differences in size between employers. Choose C to reflect this content. A can be eliminated since figure 2 DOES indicate wage differences, but this data does not further the argument of the study since size considerations are mostly avoided in the figure. B can be eliminated since figure 2 does NOT show wages broken down according to the education level of the worker. D can also be eliminated because figure 2 does NOT reveal any data which can accurately be correlated with employee satisfaction (while figure 1 in fact does).

Passage 11, Pages 36-38

1. D is the correct answer.

In lines 21-24, the passage quotes an expert describing how "findings also indicate that we might be able to predict maladaptive stress responses that contribute to excessive drinking, anger, and other unhealthy reactions to stress." This content supports the idea that research into brain adaptation may predict cases in which stress triggers an unhealthy response; choose D as appropriate. A and B can both be eliminated since evolutionary responses are not discussed in the context of this research study, and since the study focuses on brain adaptation which occurs without exposure to accident or injury. C can be eliminated because the research study did track non-brain stress indicators but did NOT focus on this data in its findings and conclusions.

2. <u>B</u> is the correct answer.

See the previous answer explanation for an analysis of the correct line reference. A describes the research question which led to the genesis of the study, while C provides an overview of how the study was conducted. D identifies the core finding of the study. None of these answers indicate that studying brain adaptations can help researchers to predict unhealthy stress responses, and therefore they should all be eliminated.

3. <u>C</u> is the correct answer.

During the fMRI experiment, researchers observed that some participants displayed activation of brain regions known to process threats, and some participants displayed a pattern which the researchers dubbed "neuroflexibility." Another group showed varying patterns of activation in stress response areas. None of the participants displayed indications of frontal cortex repair during the experiment. Based on this content, choose C as appropriate. A, B, and D all indicate patterns of response which at least some of the participants displayed during the experiment.

4. <u>B</u> is the correct answer.

In line 47, "means" refers to how cycling patterns of activation and deactivation provide a way for the brain to mitigate a stress response. Choose B to reflect this meaning. A (inappropriately implying deliberately constructed schemes), C (inappropriately implying the meaning associated with a particular term), and D (inappropriately implying a response to a particular stimulus) all introduce incorrect contexts and therefore should be eliminated.

5. <u>D</u> is the correct answer.

The passage states that "participants who did not show the neuroflexibility response in the prefrontal cortex during stress had higher levels of self-reported binge drinking, anger outbursts, and other maladaptive coping behaviors" (lines 75-79). Based on this content, choose D as the best answer. A and B can readily be eliminated since the study did NOT explore the ability to learn new tasks or assess individuals with brain injuries; responses and coping mechanisms were the major concerns. Be careful not to choose C, since the study did expose participants to threatening imagery but focused only on how they responded to those threats, NOT on participants' ability to assess threats for potential danger.

6. <u>B</u> is the correct answer.

In lines 66-69, the author explains that "The authors note that previous research has consistently shown that repeated and chronic stress damages the structure, connections, and functions of the brain's prefrontal cortex." This content indicates the possibility that stress instigates physiological changes (in this case, to the brain); choose B to support this content. A describes other variables monitored during the experiment, while C describes a significant finding from the study. D connects a research finding to potential broader implications. None of these other answers establish a connection between stress and physical changes in the body, and therefore they should all be eliminated.

7. <u>A</u> is the correct answer.

In line 64, "mobilizes" refers to how the brain initiates a cycling pattern of activation and deactivation in order to constrain the effects of a stressor. Choose A to reflect this meaning. B (inappropriately implying using one process to dominate or halt another), C (inappropriately implying goals or priorities), and D (inappropriately implying an emotional response to a valued outcome) all introduce incorrect contexts and therefore should be eliminated.

8. <u>A</u> is the correct answer.

In lines 71-72, the author introduces the concept of "higher-order functions" and then lists examples of these functions. This list of examples makes it easier for a reader to understand what types of brain activity belong to this classification. Choose A as appropriate. B and C can readily be eliminated since these categories refer to brain function (not study areas) or signs of a stress response. D can also be eliminated since these brain functions (which are mostly related to present-day research in the passage) are NOT represented as features separating humans from their ancient ancestors.

9. <u>B</u> is the correct answer.

In trial 1, when a lower stress stimulus was introduced, the prefrontal cortex barely showed a response and returned to a percentage comparable to a resting state as soon as the stimulus was removed. This data indicates that a low-stress situation has a negligible effect on the prefrontal cortex; choose B as the best answer. A can be eliminated since the graph does not document the loss of emotional control, only highly specific brain activity, while C can be eliminated since the graph portrays the prefrontal cortex returning to a normal state even after exposure to high stress stimuli. D can also be eliminated since the graph shows BOTH the prefrontal cortex and the limbic system responding to stress stimuli and therefore playing a role in emotional regulation.

10. <u>D</u> is the correct answer.

The figure documents the differing responses for high stress and low stress stimuli, whereas in the experiment discussed in the passage, participants were only exposed to one category of stress stimuli. As a result, the experiment contrasts a stressful situation with a non-stressful context, whereas the data in the figure represents a contrast between low stress and high stress situations. Choose D as appropriate. A can be eliminated since the passage ALSO explores different brain regions and their different responses, while B can be eliminated because the figures clearly show a much stronger stress response when individuals were exposed to high stress stimuli. C can be ruled out since the graph documents changes in stress response over a brief time lapse, but only in response to one exposure and NOT in response to repeated exposure to stressors.

Passage 12, Pages 39-41

1. <u>C</u> is the correct answer.

The author of the passage argues that the rise of social media has made it possible for many different individuals to participate in reporting and sharing news, and that therefore journalists and editors are no longer the sole producers of news content (lines 20-31). Choose C to reflect this content. Be careful not to choose B, because while the rise of social media has changed systems of power and authority, the passage does NOT connect the rise of social media to a mistrust of authority. A and D can also be eliminated since the passage focuses specifically on changes to news media, NOT social and political norms more broadly, and the passage also does NOT comment specifically on writing quality despite noting other changes in communication.

2. C is the correct answer.

The first paragraph summarizes McQuail's theories in a neutral way, setting the stage for a subsequent argument that these theories are no longer accurate (lines 11-12). Choose C to reflect this content. A and B can be eliminated since the paragraph initially presents McQuail's theories in a neutral and objective way, without critiquing them ITSELF. D can also be eliminated since the passage uses the reference to McQuail to indicate how values have changed, NOT to advocate for a return to those values.

3. D is the correct answer.

In line 29, "dizzying" refers to the extremely rapid pace of evolution in the news industry. Choose D to reflect this meaning. A (inappropriately implying deriving pleasure from watching or experiencing something), B (inappropriately implying something which leads to negative consequences), and C (inappropriately implying a lack of instruction or process) all introduce improper contexts, and therefore they should be eliminated.

4. B is the correct answer.

Lines 54-56 state that "But while not everything bloggers are producing is reliable, you just cannot exclude social media content from a 21st-century journalism degree course." This content indicates that trained journalists have to contend with the expansion of social media while also remaining ethical and attentive to potentially inaccurate information. Choose B to reflect this content. A can be eliminated since the passage does NOT identify a conflict between previous editorial standards and current requirements (despite noting changes in news production), while C can be eliminated since the passage suggests that news has grown increasingly complex but NOT necessarily undefinable. D can be eliminated since there is no DIRECT discussion of a requirement to interact with readers on a daily basis (even though social media seems to promise new modes of frequent interaction).

5. D is the correct answer.

See the previous answer explanation for analysis of the correct line reference. A identifies the broad philosophical implications of the rise of social media, while B identifies how a traditional approach to journalistic training is no longer adequate. C describes one of the key changes resulting from the rise of social media. None of these other answers identify a journalist's responsibility to investigate the accuracy of information, and therefore they should all be eliminated.

6. B is the correct answer.

Lines 59-61 state that "Some scholars have defined news as the information that people need to make rational decisions about their lives." This content indicates that utility can be a key feature of what defines information as newsworthy or not; choose B as the best answer. A and D can both be eliminated since sensationalism and truth are NOT identified as key features which can be used to distinguish if news is informative or not (even though real-world debates OUTSIDE the passage focus on these features). C can also be eliminated since the passage discusses how the concept of news is now associated with complexity in terms of available options, but NOT necessarily defined by complexity.

7. A is the correct answer.

See the previous answer explanation for analysis of the correct line reference. B provides some examples of events which are obviously news, while C describes a popular mindset which has significantly broadened concepts of what qualifies as news. D provides a qualification to add complexity and ambiguity to an argument. None of these other answers articulate a connection between utility and the definition of news (and some seem to avoid an explicit definition entirely), and therefore they should all be eliminated.

8. D is the correct answer.

The final paragraph describes the BBC as taking particular actions driven by the corporation's goals and priorities. Choose D as appropriate. A and B can be eliminated since the passage (in mostly providing historical information here) does NOT negatively indicate that the corporation is manipulating information or that the news it delivers is inconsequential. C can be eliminated for raising a faulty concept, since the passage does NOT suggest that news delivered by the BBC is presented in an "improvised" or loosely directed way.

9. D is the correct answer.

The table provides percentages for HOW different individuals allot the time they spend on social media, but does NOT provide any information about the total amount of time they spend on social media. Choose D as the best answer. All of the other answers can be eliminated since they specify specific individuals who spend more time on social media, whereas the table does NOT provide any data to substantiate such claims.

10. A is the correct answer.

The passage argues that under current and complex definitions of what "news" means, family events can qualify as news to the people impacted by or interested in these events (lines 71-78). However, the table separates "news and entertainment" and "staying in touch with family and friends" into two different and distinct categories. Choose A to reflect this disagreement between the table and the passage. B and C can be eliminated since the passage does NOT focus specifically on unreliable news sources or on whether networking and news are comparable. D can also be eliminated because the passage is NOT primarily concerned with individuals losing trust in modern news organizations. All of these debates are commonly linked to social media in OTHER modern sources but not in the passage itself.

Passage 13, Pages 42-44

1. A is the correct answer.

The passage focuses on presenting research which ultimately indicates that wild plants growing in California "appear not only safe to eat but also surprisingly nutritious compared to some of their store-bought counterparts" (lines 94-96). Choose A to support this content. Be careful not to choose D, since while the passage suggests that wild plants are nutritious and possibly comparable to store-bought plants, it does NOT focus on an argument that wild plants are nutritionally superior. B and C can readily be eliminated since the passage establishes that wild plants grow abundantly and tend to be quite safe to eat, thus avoiding a clear negative tone.

2. <u>A</u> is the correct answer.

In line 6, "untapped" refers to a source of food which has not yet been appreciated or used. Choose A to reflect this meaning. B (inappropriately implying aesthetic beauty and simplicity), C (inappropriately implying that incorrect beliefs attached to someone or something), and D (inappropriately implying that something has not been altered or damaged) all introduce improper contexts and should be eliminated.

3. <u>C</u> is the correct answer.

Lines 37-40 feature a quote from an expert who explains that some regions in California qualify as "food deserts" because there is no place to access fresh produce located in close proximity. Choose C to reflect this content. A and D can be eliminated since, in this portion of the passage, the expert simply identifies an existing reality and does NOT propose an alternative or a solution. B can also be eliminated since this statement is NOT preceded by any claims suggesting that produce is readily accessible in these regions; such claims would logically FOLLOW such a discussion.

4. <u>D</u> is the correct answer.

In line 75, "patches" refers to portions of asphalt with space left in between. Choose D to reflect this meaning. A (inappropriately implying objects with a link holding them together), B (inappropriately implying objects which have sustained damage and then been repaired), and C (inappropriately implying damage to asphalt, concrete, and other surfaces) all introduce improper contexts and therefore should be eliminated.

5. <u>C</u> is the correct answer.

Lines 71-75 describe how researchers chose to test plants growing in areas where the concentration of toxic metals was highest. This choice shows that researchers wanted to know the toxicity of plants growing in the worst possible conditions; choose C as appropriate. A highlights the research finding that plants can grow in toxic soil and still be safe to eat, while B describes the research methodology used in the study. D gives more details about how the study was carried out. None of these other answers reveal an intentional decision to examine the plants growing in the most toxic conditions, and therefore they should all be eliminated.

6. <u>B</u> is the correct answer.

Lines 86-90 explain that "toxic metals detected in most soil samples were far below the US EPA maximum acceptable daily dose for children and adults. In addition, approximately 330 pesticides, herbicides, and other toxins did not turn up in soil sample tests." This content indicates that most of the wild plants in urban areas are not toxic; choose B as the best answer. Be careful not to choose A or C, since some of the weeds growing in urban areas may appear in industrial areas and food deserts, yet the passage does NOT state that the majority of these plants grow in such areas. D can also be eliminated since the research prioritized sites where wild plants were visible and accessible, but this fact does NOT necessarily indicate that the majority of wild plants grow under these conditions.

7. <u>D</u> is the correct answer.

See the previous answer explanation for analysis of the correct line reference. A provides detailed information about how locations were selected for the research study, and B summarizes a key goal of the research project. C describes additional criteria utilized in the research study. None of these answers support the claim that wild plants growing in urban areas display low levels of toxicity, and therefore they should all be eliminated.

8. <u>B</u> is the correct answer.

The last sentence of the passage instructs readers to continue to be careful about selecting which wild plants to eat, introducing a note of caution into an otherwise optimistic perspective on the relative safety of wild plants. Choose B to reflect this content. A and D can both be eliminated since the author of the passage is cautious but generally focused on emphasizing the safety of wild plants and is willing to make a conclusive statement about their safety. C can be eliminated since the overall tone of the passage has been straightforward and sincere, and nothing indicates the use of sarcasm in the final lines, despite a somewhat informal tone here.

9. <u>D</u> is the correct answer.

The chart provides data drawn from 1073 individuals living in the East Bay City about which plants they would willingly eat, but it does not provide any information about the income levels of these individuals. In order for the chart to be relevant to Stark's research, the individuals surveyed would need to live in a "food desert" region. One way to determine whether they likely do so would be to verify whether their income is lower than the typical median income; choose D as appropriate. A would provide some information on the income of some of the respondents, but only a limited subset, which would make it hard to generalize about the entire group. B and C would only provide information about the ways in which individuals spend money for food-related expenses, and this information would not necessarily help to explain whether or not the individuals live in food desert regions. Since none of these other answers would directly address the concept of a food desert as related to ALL test subjects, these false answers can all be eliminated.

10. <u>B</u> is the correct answer.

The data displayed in the chart indicate that in the case of some food items (lettuce, yams, and sweet fennel) a significant portion of the respondents would eat the item when it comes from a supermarket source. This willingness to eat indicates an awareness of the nutritional value (on the basis of the passage) or the overall desirability of these items. However, the respondents reported much lower willingness to eat these items when they were grown in an urban environment. This distinction indicates that individuals may reject food items known to have nutritional value based on where those items were grown; choose B as appropriate. A and C can be rejected since some respondents indicate a willingness to eat wild-grown plants (suggesting that respondents understand that these plants are safe to eat) and no data is explicitly present about whether supermarket or wild-sourced plants are more or less expensive. D can also be eliminated since it is outside of the scope of the graph even when the passage is taken into account and speculates about the motivations of respondents, which cannot be ascertained based on the data available.

Passage 14, Pages 45-47

1. <u>A</u> is the correct answer.

The passage focuses on describing the common advertising practice of gathering and monetizing user data (lines 27-31), yet highlights some of the negative consequences associated with these practices. Choose A as appropriate. B and C can be eliminated since the passage does NOT identify specific changes which could improve digital advertising and does NOT focus on contrasting economic and political systems; the author notes a linkage between data collection and political messaging (lines 73-79) but does not argue for any corrective measures. D can be eliminated, since the passage does begin with a description of a troubling episode, but does NOT indicate that this household event was widely known or triggered a public reaction.

2. <u>C</u> is the correct answer.

Lines 22-26 state that, in terms of data collection related to pregnancy, "In the case of the Minnesota teen, this meant that the company knew that she was pregnant and acted on this knowledge before she decided to tell her own family." This content indicates that digital advertising can lead to information (such as a pregnancy) being disclosed without consent; choose C as the best answer. A and B can be eliminated since there was NOT an implication that Target was trying to assist individuals in need, nor did the company's action lead to harmful stereotypes (since the goal throughout was to target customers efficiently). D can also be eliminated since the passage does NOT discuss whether the products performed as advertised (only that a problem in terms of information privacy was created).

3. <u>D</u> is the correct answer.

See the previous answer explanation for analysis of the correct line reference. A describes how Target was able to devise an algorithm, while B describes what that algorithm was used to predict (whether a woman is pregnant). C extends the explanation of what type of information this algorithm was used to predict. Since none of these other answers explain how targeted digital advertising can violate privacy and consent (despite mentioning OTHER elements of a relevant example), they can all be eliminated.

4. <u>A</u> is the correct answer.

In line 22, "narrow" refers to the specificity and precision with which Target was able to predict a woman's due date. Choose A to reflect this meaning. B (inappropriately implying a lack of sophistication or complexity), C (inappropriately implying something being difficult or rigorous), and D (inappropriately implying something which refuses to change or submit) all introduce improper contexts and should therefore be eliminated.

5. <u>B</u> is the correct answer.

In line 44, "sparked" refers to how certain companies triggered or catalyzed the rise of mass production. Choose B to reflect this meaning. A (inappropriately implying an increase or heightening of tensions and anger), C (inappropriately implying offering a reward in order to promote specific behavior), and D (inappropriately implying something being revealed or clarified) all introduce improper contexts and should therefore be eliminated.

6. <u>A</u> is the correct answer.

Lines 48-54 describe how surveillance capitalism functions: "platforms commodify "reality" by tracking the behaviors of individuals online and offline, making predictions about how they may act in the future, and constructing mechanisms to influence these future behaviors, whether such behaviors are voting or making purchases." This content supports the idea that surveillance capitalism functions in both online and offline spaces; choose A as appropriate. B and C can be eliminated since a link is NOT established between surveillance capitalism and computer speed (despite the reference to online activity), nor does the passage describe the role that government oversight plays in this system (despite references to political dilemmas in the final paragraphs). D can also be eliminated since different epochs of capitalism are NOT explicitly contrasted in the passage; though seemingly advanced, surveillance capitalism ALONE is the focus.

7. <u>C</u> is the correct answer.

See the previous answer explanation for analysis of the correct line reference. A identifies a useful theoretical model, while B provides a specific example of how a system came to be dominant. D identifies one requirement in order for digital advertising to function successfully. Since none of these other answers stipulate that surveillance capitalism has implications for both online and offline life, they should all be eliminated.

8. <u>A</u> is the correct answer.

The passage describes how "Russian operatives had used political advertising services on a number of internet platforms to influence and suppress voting in the 2016 U.S. presidential election." This content indicates that political advertising does not function solely to influence voters to vote in a particular way, and that it can also serve to discourage eligible individuals from voting at all. Choose A as appropriate. B and C can be eliminated since no information is present in the passage about the beliefs held by individuals who create political ads (despite the author's focus on negative political outcomes) or how non-political social media users experience different types of political advertisements (though non-political users are considered on their own in the first paragraph). D can be dismissed as outside the scope of the passage since countries that target the U.S. (NOT countries that the U.S. itself TARGETS) interest the author.

9. <u>C</u> is the correct answer.

In October 2016, more than 100,000 unreliable political ads aired. In every other month documented in the table, the number of unreliable ads was 100,000 or fewer. Since October was the month with the highest number of these ads, choose C as the best answer. Other answers may wrongly reference high quantities for television (NOT social media) and reliable ads.

10. <u>C</u> is the correct answer.

The graph shows that political ads are displayed on social media and can be either reliable or unreliable. The author of the passage argues that, while some social media platforms have attempted to ban political content, "because political advertisements cannot be easily categorized or defined" (lines 88-90), problematic political content continues to appear. Choose C to reflect this explanation. A and B can be eliminated since the author (in mostly avoiding analysis of company motives) does NOT argue that profitability or free expression is likely to explain why social media platforms continue to run political ads. D can also be eliminated since the author does NOT connect the use of political ads to law enforcement (as opposed to swaying public opinion).

Passage 15, Pages 48-51

1. <u>B</u> is the correct answer.

The passage begins with a section contextualizing the rich cultural significance of forests in Ghanaian culture (lines 1-16), and then highlights the challenge of significant deforestation happening in the region. The passage then moves to a discussion of a new tool designed to make it easier to visualize changes to land cover (lines 45-50). The structure of the passage is best described by B, which is thus correct. A can be eliminated since the author does not propose a hypothesis, but rather highlights research which has already been concluded. C and D can also be ruled out since the description of the land mapping tool does NOT reflect a modernization of existing cultural practices (drawing a false linkage between actual topics), and since the tool is best described as a possible contribution to understanding the problem of deforestation, NOT a solution.

2. <u>C</u> is the correct answer.

In the first two sentences of the passage, the author describes some West African beliefs about forests and analyzes why forests play a pivotal cultural role. The author refers to these beliefs in a genuine, sincere, and respectful way; choose C as the best answer. A and D can be dismissed since both of these answers refer to a negative perspective, whereas the author's tone in these lines is positive. Be careful not to choose B, since the author's tone is intended to introduce these fundamental beliefs to an audience unfamiliar with them, NOT to flatter someone who already holds these beliefs.

3. <u>D</u> is the correct answer.

Lines 7-16 focus on a specific Ghanaian custom in which trees are used to commemorate movement through life stages. This custom is an example of cultural practices in which trees and forests play a central role, and serves to illustrate a broader example of why trees are important in Ghanaian culture. Choose D as appropriate. A can be eliminated since no single specific term is used to identify this practice (despite its distinctive and specialized nature), while B can be eliminated since the author describes the practice from a neutral perspective. C can also be eliminated since no conflicting argument has been introduced prior to this mostly informative example.

4. <u>D</u> is the correct answer.

In line 57, "captures" refers to how the visualization tool creates images of landmass. Choose D to reflect this meaning. A (inappropriately implying surpassing someone or something else), B (inappropriately implying seizing hold of someone or something), and C (inappropriately implying recalling a previous experience) all introduce improper contexts and therefore should be eliminated.

5. <u>A</u> is the correct answer.

In line 58, "creeping" refers to how a landscape is slowly becoming less forested and more desert-like. Choose A to reflect this meaning. B (inappropriately implying expressing an interest in something outside of one's appropriate scope), C (inappropriately surveilling someone for information or gain), and D (implying slowly moving someone by force) all introduce improper contexts and therefore should be eliminated.

6. B is the correct answer.

Lines 80-86 explain that manual mapping allows for the inclusion of different types of information; choose B as appropriate. A and D can be eliminated since the research project may have spanned multiple countries but did NOT exist specifically to foster international collaboration, and the project did not aim to increase the income of local residents. Be careful not to choose C, since mapping was an initial step towards a larger goal of ecological restoration, but offered the PRIMARY advantage of including additional types of detail.

7. C is the correct answer.

See the previous answer explanation for analysis of the correct line reference. A introduces a specific tool and research project designed to provide information about West African deforestation, while B identifies one trend observed using the new mapping tool. D describes the positive impact of the additional features provided by manual mapping. None of these other answers identify the additional features made possible by the use of manual mapping (despite references to mapping generally), and therefore they should all be eliminated.

8. D is the correct answer.

Lines 72-76 describe how machine-based land mapping relies on data acquired passively through satellite sensors. This content indicates that machine-based land mapping is indirect; choose D as the best answer. A describes one trend which has been confirmed using images from the land mapping tool, while B describes why it has been possible to use this tool to track changes in land mass over time. C describes how a blended approach and partnerships with local communities have made it possible to achieve the research goals of the project. None of these other answers describe how machine-based land mapping functions, and therefore they should all be eliminated.

9. A is the correct answer.

Between 1900 and 2000, up to 150,000 thousand hectares of West African rainforest have been lost per year. Between 2000 and 2020, up to a maximum of 20,000 hectares per year have been restored. Due to the much faster rate of deforestation, and the longer time period in which deforestation has been occurring, it can be inferred that rainforest rehabilitation has not yet been successful at restoring rainforest coverage to pre-1900 levels. Choose A as appropriate. B and D can be eliminated since increasing levels of rainforest rehabilitation have been observed in multiple countries (not only Ghana), and since nothing about the data (which simply measures area coverage) indicates why rainforest rehabilitation efforts began or how they compared to efforts before the 21st century. C can be eliminated since the graph shows a steady and consistent increase in hectares rehabilitated, NOT dramatic fluctuations.

10. A is the correct answer.

Together, the graphs indicate that West African rainforests have gradually been reduced in land mass, but that efforts are also occurring to rehabilitate them. The passage reinforces this data with more specific information about forest loss in Ghana and about a research study designed to provide specialized data about deforestation. Choose A as appropriate. B and C can be eliminated since the passage corroborates the data by indicating that forest loss in Ghana is a significant problem and does not discuss differences in data relevant to forest loss over time. D can be eliminated since mapping technology serves to gather data, while graphs such as those presented along with the passage are used to visualize that same data and make it easy to understand.

NOTES

- Passage 1, "Older workers—are they aging successfully?" is adapted from the article of the same name by Charlotte M. Irby and published by the United States Bureau of Labor Statistics. May 2018, BLS. https://www.bls.gov/opub/mlr/2018/beyond-bls/older-workers-are-they-aging-successfully.htm. Accessed 25 February 2020.

- Passage 2, "Welcome to the New Era of Easy Media Manipulation," is an excerpt from the article of the same name by Andrew J. O'Keefe II and published by SingularityHub. 13 November 2016, SingularityHub. https://singularityhub.com/2016/11/13/welcome-to-the-new-era-of-easy-media-manipulation/. Accessed 25 February 2020.

- Passage 3, "Resilience and the contract of social insurance," is adapted from the article of the same name by Reid Cramer and published by the NewAmerica.org. *Resilience: a digital magazine exploring the boundaries of resilience*. https://resilience.newamerica.org/resilience-and-the-contract-of-social-insurance/. Accessed 25 February 2020.

- Passage 4, "Recalculating! By not driving the optimal route, you're causing traffic jams," is an excerpt from the article of the same name by Marta Gonzalez and Antonio Lima and published by The Conversation. 15 March 2016, The Conversation. https://theconversation.com/recalculating-by-not-driving-the-optimal-route-youre-causing-traffic-jams-56135. Accessed 25 February 2020.

- Passage 5, "Crowdsourcing Helps to Unlock the Mystery of Cursive," is adapted from the article of the same name by Wendi Maloney and Julie Miller and published by the Library of Congress. 23 January 2019, Official Blog of the Library of Congress. https://blogs.loc.gov/loc/2019/01/crowdsourcing-helps-to-unlock-the-mystery-of-cursive/. Accessed 25 February 2020.

- Passage 6, "How going hungry affects children for their whole lives," is adapted from the article of the same name by Chris Baraniuk and published by Mosaic. 9 April 2019, Mosaic Science. https://mosaicscience.com/story/food-poverty-nutrition-health-austerity-child-development-diet-benefits/. Accessed 25 February 2020.

- Passage 7, "Are Robots Coming for Our Jobs? Careful, It's a Trick Question," is an excerpt from the article of the same name by Vanessa Bates Ramirez and published by SingularityHub. 22 July 2018, SingularityHub. https://singularityhub.com/2019/07/22/will-robots-take-our-jobs-careful-its-a-trick-question/. Accessed 25 February 2020.

- Passage 8, "Watch Where I'm Going: Predicting Pedestrian Flow," is adapted from the article of the same name by Alex Theng and published by EveryONE, the PLOS ONE community blog. 22 January 2014, PLOS ONE. https://blogs.plos.org/everyone/2014/01/22/watch-im-going-predicting-pedestrian-flow/. Accessed 25 February 2020.

- Passage 9, "Urban living makes us miserable. This city is trying to change that," is adapted from the article of the same name by Fleur Macdonald and published by Mosaic. 15 October 2019, Mosaic Science. https://mosaicscience.com/story/urban-living-city-mental-health-glasgow-cities-happiness-regeneration/. Accessed 25 February 2020.

- Passage 10, "Big-box stores pay workers good wages," is adapted from the article of the same name by Maureen Soyars and published by the Bureau of Labor Statistics. November 2014, BLS. https://www.bls.gov/opub/mlr/2014/beyond-bls/big-box-stores-pay-workers-good-wages.htm. Accessed 25 February 2020.

- Passage 11, "Researchers identify brain circuits that help people cope with stress," is adapted from the article of the same name published by the National Institues of Health. 29 July 2016, NIH. https://www.nih.gov/news-events/researchers-identify-brain-circuits-help-people-cope-stress. Accessed 25 February 2020.

- Passage 12, "What is news in the 21st century?" is an excerpt from the article of the same name by Bruce Mutsvairo and published by The Conversation. 7 March 2016, The Conversation in partnership with Northumbria University. https://theconversation.com/what-is-news-in-the-21st-century-55073. Accessed 25 February 2020.

- Passage 13, "Ripe for the Picking: Wild weeds may provide a new food source," is adapted from the article of the same name by Glenn Jackson and published by EveryONE, the PLOS ONE community blog. 12 April 2019, PLOS ONE. https://blogs.plos.org/everyone/2019/04/12/wild-weeds-may-provide-new-food-source/. Accessed 25 February 2020.

- Passage 14, "Special Delivery: How Internet Platforms Use Artificial Intelligence to Target and Deliver Ads," is adapted from the article of the same name by Spandana Singh and published by NewAmerica.org. 18 February 2020, New America. https://www.newamerica.org/oti/reports/special-delivery/. Accessed 25 February 2020.

- Passage 15, "Unique Mapping Tool Brings Unprecedented Look at Land Cover Change in West Africa," is adapted from the article of the same name published by the United States Geological Survey. 14 August 2018, USGS. https://www.usgs.gov/center-news/unique-mapping-tool-brings-unprecedented-look-land-cover-change-west-africa?qt-news_science_products=1#qt-news_science_products. Accessed 25 February 2020.

About the Figures: The various visual resources that accompany the passages in this section are primarily meant to facilitate critical thinking skills and may not reflect historical data.

Part 2

Science, Single

Reading Strategy
Part 2: Science, Single

Essential Tactics

The two Science passages that appear on each SAT Reading section can be drawn from a variety of topics: biology, chemistry, physics, ecology, earth science, and astronomy among them. In fact, passages that address issues in psychology and technology—fields that may seem oriented towards Social Studies—are eligible to appear under Natural Science. Keep in mind, also, that one graph WILL always appear and that one paired passage MAY appear in this passage category.

Fortunately, the designated Science passages can be quite approachable at times. Although you may be challenged to adapt to a new scientific concept, you will ALWAYS be given enough background information to approach such content; as ever on the SAT, outside knowledge may help but is not in any way a necessity. Moreover, there will be relatively few stylistic difficulties. Because Science passages are almost always taken from the past 75 years—and often from the extremely recent past—the possibility of encountering older-fashioned expressions and syntax decreases considerably.

Perhaps the most fortunate feature of Science passages, though, is their relative predictability in structure and intent. Though there are certainly some exceptions, a typical Science passage will be devoted to a single well-defined area of inquiry that is addressed in the following format.

1. Inquiry or Issue Established

2. Experiment or Research Explained

3. Broader Outcomes Addressed (Applications, Problems, Debates, Future Inquiries)

In some cases, Science passages will break down into EXACTLY these stages, with one following the next in an orderly fashion. In other cases, the different stages may be harder to discern—that is, until you learn to identify and comprehend each stage with speed and efficiency. For the sake of at least a preliminary sense of how the characteristic topics and format of Science passages have played out recently, here are the Science passages that have appeared on the most recent official SAT tests.

- "Why Birds Fly in a V Formation" by Patricia Waldron (how and whether birds utilize wind currents when flying together, Test 7)

- "How the Higgs Boson Was Found" by Brian Greene (how an important concept in physics was regarded and understood over time, Test 7)

- "Salt Stretches in the Nanoworld" by Rachel Ehrenberg (how salt exhibits varying properties, Test 8)

- Excerpt from *What a Plant Knows: A Field Guide to the Senses* by Daniel Chamovitz (how a Venus flytrap responds to prey stimuli, Test 8)

- Excerpt from *Paleofantasy: What Evolution Really Tells Us about Sex, Diet, and How We Live* by Marlene Zuk (how guppies can be used to model evolutionary change, Test 9)

- "Pleasant to the Touch" by Sabrina Richards (how human nerves detect specific sensations, Test 10)

- Excerpt from *Life Under the Sun* by Peter A. Ensminger (how plowing times affect weed control, Test 10)

Inquiry or Issue

Your first priority should be to determine what theory, fact, or problem in scientific inquiry the author has chosen to address. This is in some ways a fairly straightforward task since 1) the TITLE can be extremely informative in some cases and 2) the FIRST FEW PARAGRAPHS can lay out a considerable amount of information. Of course, there may be SAT passages that deal with main issues that are extremely complex, that are elaborated over the course of rather long paragraphs, or that are accompanied by several counter-examples and counter-arguments. If you find yourself faced with such a passage, maintain high precision with the following questions—which are relevant to ANY Science passage.

- What information does the title provide? What ADDITIONAL questions does it raise?

- What is the theory, idea, or assumed fact that is being evaluated in the passage? Is there an EXPLICIT statement that defines the topic under investigation?

- What factors COMPLICATE the main inquiry or issue? Are competing theories, explanations, or examples mentioned anywhere?

Once you have clarified these issues by finding the needed information—whether provided by the author or by researchers quoted in the article—you can easily move on to consider how, exactly, the investigations described in the passage proceeded.

Experiment or Research

In some passages, "experiments" and "research" may seem loosely defined at best. Official SAT passages have included informative and theoretical discussions of topics such as DNA and the Higgs boson particle; in these cases, the authors provided overviews of major scientific issues. Still, passages that are walk-throughs of specific experiments and research projects continue to dominate the test, and passages that deviate from this classic format can still be approached using a similar method.

As you read any given Science passage, divide up information in terms of methods of inquiry. These are often experiments, but can sometimes be ideas or proposals (such as the nature of a molecule or a particle) that are given some logical explanation. Be aware, also, that experiment-oriented passages may proceed in stages, with two or even three related inquiries outlined one after another. Overall, try to think in terms of the following questions for every method or mode of investigation present.

- What idea or premise is this experiment, project, or line of reasoning meant to evaluate?

- What are the fine points of design and execution for the research? Did the researchers meet any obstacles?

- What are the immediate outcomes? Do they confirm or contradict any ideas—or lead to a new inquiry?

If you can think about immediate outcomes, you will also have a firm basis for considering the broad research outcomes that, frequently, are addressed in the final stages of Science passages.

Broader Outcomes

The last few paragraphs of a Science passage will, with some regularity, broaden the topic outward. A variety of new issues raised by the topic or research at hand may be considered, and some of the most common are listed below.

- Validation of an earlier theory
- Proposal for a new or modified experiment

- Contradiction of an assumed explanation
- Intensification of a debate or dispute

- Formulation of a new or improved theory
- Approval or agreement from the scientific community

- Sources of continuing uncertainty
- Dissent from a specific expert or a group of specialists

These issues may be raised by the author, by researchers quoted or described throughout the passage, or by researchers who are quoted for the first time near the passage's closing. Note also that some passages may terminate WITHOUT raising broad issues such as these, or may raise them towards a midpoint. Your task is to use your comprehension skills to approach each passage on its unique terms, as helpful as knowing the standard Inquiry/Research/Outcome format can be.

Passages Begin on the Next Page

Reading 16

Questions 1-10 are based on the following passage.

This passage is adapted from Bryn Nelson, "Umbilical cord blood: a new lifeline after a nuclear disaster?" an article published* by Mosaic in 2017.

Two days after the inauguration of US President Donald Trump, the Bulletin of the Atomic Scientists warned of the "terrifying
Line geography of nuclear and radiological insecurity
5 in South Asia." The journal's analysis of vulnerabilities within India and Pakistan raised the spectre of an attack on a nuclear power plant, construction of a "dirty bomb" containing radioactive material, theft of a nuclear weapon,
10 or other terrorist act. Less than two weeks later, Japanese utility officials reported sky-high radiation levels within the country's crippled Fukushima nuclear plant.
    Away from the heated debates around national
15 and global security, a handful of research groups are exploring whether treatments based on umbilical cord blood could provide a temporary lifeline in the immediate aftermath of an accidental or deliberate release of radiation.
20   Following a nuclear disaster, survivors exposed to high-dose ionising radiation can fall victim to acute radiation syndrome. Around 30 people died from this illness in the first few months after the Chernobyl meltdown in 1986.
25   Radiation can brutalize the body's bone marrow, which makes platelets and white and red blood cells. While radiation strong enough to wipe out someone's marrow would likely prove fatal due to damage elsewhere, a potentially survivable
30 dose could still wreak havoc on the spongy tissue.
    Seattle start-up Nohla Therapeutics is one research group exploring the use of umbilical cord blood cells as a countermeasure. Their strategy is to isolate blood-forming stem cells
35 from donated cord blood, multiply them in the lab until they number in the hundreds of millions

or even billions, and then infuse them into a patient. Until that patient's own bone marrow bounces back, "the idea is that these cells can
40 come in and take over that job," says Colleen Delaney, the company's chief medical officer and director of the Cord Blood Program at Seattle's Fred Hutchinson Cancer Research Center. Unlike bone marrow from adult donors, cord blood
45 transplants don't require a close match of genetic identification tags between donor and recipient cells, potentially allowing Nohla to produce vials of universal donor cells that could be frozen, thawed, and used on demand.
50   Delaney says that the work is part of a larger plan to use cord-blood-derived cells to fight a wide range of diseases, disorders, and injuries that can disrupt bone marrow's function. The anti-terrorism potential has attracted considerable
55 support; in 2009, Delaney won a multimillion-dollar grant from the Biomedical Advanced Research and Development Authority, part of the US Department of Health and Human Services. The authority's Project BioShield backs medical
60 measures that counter biological, chemical, radiological, and nuclear agents.
    John Wagner, Director of the Blood and Marrow Transplantation Program at the University of Minnesota, says Delaney's strategy could help
65 a large number of victims by providing a safety net until their damaged bone marrow recovers or they receive full transplants. "It's something that you could do immediately," he says, "and so I think it is a very important strategy."
70   Other researchers are more sceptical. Robert Peter Gale, now a visiting professor of haematology at Imperial College London, was among the experts who treated the scores of individuals exposed to radiation after Chernobyl.
75 Those who died in hospital, he says, did so not from severe bone marrow damage but from other bodily harm caused by the radiation.
    Other reports suggest that bone marrow failure contributed to the deaths, though Gale says that
80 his experience suggests that "very, very, very few people" would benefit from a post-disaster transplant of blood-forming cells. "It's a Pyrrhic

*See Page 171 for the citation for this text.

CONTINUE ➡

victory if we rescue them from dying from bone
marrow failure, if they are going to die three
85 weeks later or three months later from pulmonary
failure," he says.

Delaney and Wagner, however, note that cord
blood research is both progressing rapidly and
revealing an increasing number of benefits for
90 individuals with damaged bone marrow, whether
from radiation or other causes. In a recent study,
for instance, Delaney and her colleague Filippo
Milano showed that cord-blood-derived stem
cells reduced the risk of infection among people
95 with leukaemia who had received high-dose
chemotherapy.

Regardless of what the research ultimately
shows, Gale suggests that officials should
prioritize efforts to educate the public about the
100 true risks of radiation and to prevent nuclear
attacks or accidents from ever occurring.
"Prevention," he says, "will always trump
intervention."

1

The main purpose of the passage is to

A) cast doubt on the ability of cord blood cells to
   erase harmful radiation effects.

B) provide an overview of attempts to raise public
   awareness of the dangers of radiation.

C) analyze why cord blood cells offer some promise
   in treating exposure to radiation.

D) promote prevention as opposed to therapies such
   as the use of cord blood cells as the best means of
   handling the dangers of radiation.

2

Over the course of the passage, the author's focus
shifts from

A) describing a health liability to recording
   contrasting opinions that concern a possible
   treatment.

B) evoking the human cost of a health crisis to
   urging a more logical and clinical approach to the
   same problem.

C) summarizing the measures taken by governments
   to advocating for intensified cooperation between
   politicians and scientists.

D) presenting differing schools of thought to
   highlighting the importance of consensus in
   addressing a dilemma.

3

Which choice indicates that exposure to radiation
derived from nuclear power has had adverse effects
on public health in the past?

A) Lines 5-10 ("The journal's . . . act")

B) Lines 10-13 ("Less . . . plant")

C) Lines 22-24 ("Around 30 . . . 1986")

D) Lines 25-27 ("Radiation . . . cells")

4

As used in line 39, "bounces back" most nearly
means

A) resurfaces.

B) recovers.

C) retaliates.

D) recoils.

CONTINUE

5

Within the passage, Colleen Delaney characterizes her research endeavor involving cord blood as

A) a response to a single catastrophe.

B) an imperfect measure meant to galvanize other researchers.

C) an attempt to render bone marrow transplants obsolete.

D) a meaningful early stage in an initiative.

6

Which choice provides the best evidence for the answer to the previous question?

A) Lines 31-33 ("Seattle . . . countermeasure")

B) Lines 38-43 ("Until . . . center")

C) Lines 50-53 ("Delaney . . . function")

D) Lines 62-67 ("John Wagner . . . transplants")

7

In contrast to bone marrow transplants, cord blood transplants have the advantage of

A) reversing the effects of pulmonary diseases.

B) less restrictive genetic requirements for effective donor and recipient matches.

C) creating an above-average volume of blood-forming cells.

D) significant cost savings for both hospitals and patients.

8

As used in lines 64 and 69, "strategy" most nearly means

A) approach.

B) persuasion.

C) supervision.

D) cleverness.

9

Which of the following findings would contradict the ideas set forward by Robert Peter Gale in lines 70-86 ("Other . . . says")?

A) Pulmonary failure is a common cause of death even among patients who have not been exposed to radiation.

B) Transplants involving cord blood are limited in utility due to stringent genetic requirements for patients and donors.

C) Survival rates for patients exposed to radiation improve significantly if measures are taken to prevent pulmonary failure.

D) Most fatalities that are due to radiation exposure can be connected entirely to bone marrow damage.

10

The final sentence of the passage serves to

A) promote an unexpected initiative.

B) encapsulate a broad rule of action.

C) suggest one drawback of a research method.

D) criticize the shortsightedness of a single group.

CONTINUE

Reading 17

Questions 1-10 are based on the following passage.

This passage is adapted from Felicia Chou and Dewayne Washington, "NASA's Fermi Traces Source of Cosmic Neutrino to Monster Black Hole," a 2018 news release* from NASA.

For the first time ever, scientists using NASA's Fermi Gamma-ray Space Telescope have found the source of a high-energy neutrino from outside our galaxy. This neutrino traveled 3.7 billion years
Line
5   at almost the speed of light before being detected on Earth. This is farther than any other neutrino whose origin scientists can identify.
High-energy neutrinos are hard-to-catch particles that scientists think are created by
10   the most powerful events in the cosmos, such as galaxy mergers and material falling onto supermassive black holes. They travel at speeds just shy of the speed of light and rarely interact with other matter, allowing them to
15   travel unimpeded across distances of billions of light-years. The neutrino was discovered by an international team of scientists using the National Science Foundation's IceCube Neutrino Observatory at the Amundsen–Scott South Pole
20   Station. Fermi found the source of the neutrino by tracing its path back to a blast of gamma-ray light from a distant supermassive black hole in the constellation Orion.
"Again, Fermi has helped make another giant
25   leap in a growing field we call multimessenger astronomy," said Paul Hertz, director of the Astrophysics Division at NASA Headquarters in Washington. "Neutrinos and gravitational waves deliver new kinds of information about the most
30   extreme environments in the universe. But to best understand what they're telling us, we need to connect them to what the 'messenger' astronomers know best—light."
Scientists study neutrinos, as well as cosmic
35   rays and gamma rays, to understand what is going on in turbulent cosmic environments such

as supernovas, black holes, and stars. Neutrinos show the complex processes that occur inside the environment, and cosmic rays show the force
40   and speed of violent activity. Still, scientists rely on gamma rays, the most energetic form of light, to brightly flag what cosmic source is producing these neutrinos and cosmic rays.
"The most extreme cosmic explosions produce
45   gravitational waves, and the most extreme cosmic accelerators produce high-energy neutrinos and cosmic rays," says Regina Caputo of NASA's Goddard Space Flight Center in Greenbelt, Maryland, the analysis coordinator for the Fermi
50   Large Area Telescope Collaboration. "Through Fermi, gamma rays are providing a bridge to each of these new cosmic signals."
. . . On Sept. 22, 2017, scientists using IceCube detected signs of a neutrino striking the Antarctic
55   ice with energy of about 300 trillion electron volts—more than 45 times the energy achievable in the most powerful particle accelerator on Earth. This high energy strongly suggested that the neutrino had to be from beyond our solar system.
60   Backtracking the path through IceCube indicated where in the sky the neutrino came from, and automated alerts notified astronomers around the globe to search this region for flares or outbursts that could be associated with the event.
65   Data from Fermi's Large Area Telescope revealed enhanced gamma-ray emission from a well-known active galaxy at the time the neutrino arrived. This is a type of active galaxy called a blazar, with a supermassive black hole
70   with millions to billions of times the Sun's mass that blasts jets of particles outward in opposite directions at nearly the speed of light. Blazars are especially bright and active because one of these jets happens to point almost directly toward Earth.
75   Fermi scientist Yasuyuki Tanaka at Hiroshima University in Japan was the first to associate the neutrino event with the blazar designated TXS 0506+056 (TXS 0506 for short).
"Fermi's LAT monitors the entire sky in
80   gamma rays and keeps tabs on the activity of some 2,000 blazars, yet TXS 0506 really stood out," said Sara Buson, a NASA Postdoctoral

*See Page 171 for the citation for this text.

CONTINUE ➡

Part 2: Science, Single

Fellow at Goddard who performed the data analysis with Anna Franckowiak, a scientist at the Deutsches Elektronen-Synchrotron research center in Zeuthen, Germany. "This blazar is located near the center of the sky position determined by IceCube and, at the time of the neutrino detection, was the most active Fermi had seen it in a decade."

1

Which choice best summarizes the passage?

A) Scientists at the Neutrino Observatory at the Amundsen–Scott South Pole Station have gathered new data that contradicts previous findings.

B) Astronomers from all over the world are using powerful telescopes to study neutrinos and black holes.

C) High-energy neutrinos are used at the Amundsen–Scott South Pole Station to enhance the technology used to produce particle accelerators.

D) A newly-detected neutrino confirms previous scientific knowledge about blazars and is believed to provide information about another galaxy.

2

The authors' main purpose in including the information about blazars is to

A) establish a link between the appearance of neutrinos and the activity of a blazar.

B) provide an in-depth overview of the data gathered concerning the constellation Orion.

C) elaborate on the scientific importance of multimessenger astronomy.

D) confirm the fact that the explosions of supernovas create black holes.

3

The first paragraph serves mainly to

A) elaborate on the scientific importance of neutrinos.

B) describe how neutrinos are formed.

C) present an important scientific breakthrough.

D) analyze the various methods used to study neutrinos.

4

It can reasonably be inferred that NASA's Fermi Gamma-ray Space Telescope was used to "catch" neutrinos because

A) gamma rays can best detect the source of the neutrinos.

B) the device itself the most advanced telescope ever to be deployed by NASA.

C) a method developed by NASA scientists can provoke gravitational waves.

D) the technology triggered enhanced gamma-ray emission.

5

As used in line 13, "shy of" most nearly means

A) wary of.

B) reticent towards.

C) below.

D) against.

CONTINUE

6

Based on the information in the passage, it can reasonably be inferred that neutrinos are of great scientific importance because they

A) can move at the speed of light.

B) provide data about violent processes in the universe.

C) at present initiate massive explosions in our own galaxy.

D) inevitably are drawn into massive black holes outside our galaxy.

7

Which choice provides the best evidence for the answer to the previous question?

A) Lines 4-6 ("This . . . Earth")

B) Lines 28-30 ("Neutrinos . . . universe")

C) Lines 60-61 ("Backtracking . . . from")

D) Lines 86-88 ("This . . . detection")

8

As used in line 14, "interact with" most nearly means

A) consort with.

B) communicate with.

C) link to.

D) affect.

9

The text most strongly suggests that one specific branch of astronomy is

A) becoming less appealing to scientists as the result of an ideological realignment.

B) being disregarded due to budget cuts.

C) rapidly developing due to important discoveries.

D) no longer stirring international interest among specialists.

10

Which choice provides the best evidence for the answer to the previous question?

A) Lines 1-4 ("For . . . galaxy")

B) Lines 24-26 ("Again . . . astronomy")

C) Lines 34-37 ("Scientists . . . stars")

D) Lines 65-68 ("Data . . . arrived")

CONTINUE

Reading 18

Questions 1-10 are based on the following passage.

This passage is an excerpt from Jason Gilchrist, "Have scientists finally killed off the Loch Ness Monster?" an article published* by The Conversation in partnership with Edinburgh Napier University in 2019.

Scientists claim to have finally found a "plausible theory" for sightings of the Loch Ness Monster. She's not an aquatic reptile left over
Line from the Jurassic era or a circus elephant that got
5 in the water to bathe with her trunk aloft. If Nessie ever existed at all, she was most likely a giant eel, according to a new scientific survey of the loch.

Starting with an Irish missionary's report of a monster in the River Ness in 565AD, repeated
10 sightings in the modern era have kept Scotland's greatest myth alive. The most famous of these involves a grainy photo from 1934 which appears to show the shadowy outline of a long-necked creature, bobbing on the water's surface.

15 Until now, such glimpses were all people had to go on. But a new technique allows scientists to sample all the life contained within Loch Ness by gathering environmental DNA, or e-DNA as it's known. This is genetic material that's present
20 in the cells of organisms and shed into their surrounding environment. Finding and identifying e-DNA can tell scientists what organisms are living in a habitat without scientists having to observe or capture these lifeforms.

25 Speaking from Drumnadrochit, a village on the loch's western shore, scientists announced the results of their e-DNA survey of Loch Ness. The team took well over 200 one-litre samples of water from throughout the loch—including the
30 surface and deep water—and compared them with 36 samples from five "monster-free" lochs nearby. Their census provides a list of all the species that call Loch Ness home—from bacteria to plants and animals.

35 The study detected over 500 million individual organisms and 3,000 species. According to Neil Gemmill of University of Otago in New Zealand, who led the study, there are no DNA sequence matches for shark, catfish, or sturgeon. That rules
40 out a large exotic fish in the loch.

There are DNA matches for various land-living species that you would expect to see around Loch Ness, including badgers, deer, rabbits, voles, and different birds. Sheep, cattle and dogs appear on
45 the record alongside humans too. This suggests that the sampling is pretty good at picking up species that would only rarely visit the water— so it should be able to detect a monster living permanently in the loch.

50 The most popular representation of Nessie is as a plesiosaur—an ancient long-necked marine reptile that died out alongside the dinosaurs in the last great mass extinction 65m years ago. Scottish geologist Hugh Miller discovered the first British
55 plesiosaur bones on the Scottish Isle of Eigg in 1844. But according to Gemmill, there's "not a single reptile in our vertebrate data, and nothing that sat in the expected place that a plesiosaur [DNA] sequence might be predicted to lie—
60 somewhere between birds and crocodilians."

The most likely candidate for Nessie that has surfaced in media reporting of the research is a giant eel. This appears to be based simply on the fact that eel DNA was detected at "pretty much
65 every location sampled" in Loch Ness. Plenty of eel DNA doesn't confirm that Nessie is a giant eel—only that there are lots of eels. Scientists don't have monster DNA to compare with anything they found in the loch and so no one can
70 say for sure if there is or isn't a monster there. But the absence of anything unusual in the DNA record of Loch Ness suggests that there's nothing to get excited about—and that includes a giant eel.

If Nessie doesn't exist, why do eyewitness
75 accounts of the Loch Ness Monster persist? The answer is likely to be a psychological phenomenon called "expectant attention." This happens when people who expect or want to see something are more likely to misinterpret visual

---

*See Page 171 for the citation for this text.

CONTINUE ▶

80 cues as the thing that they expect or want to see.
This likely also happens with recently extinct
animals. The last known tasmanian tiger died in
1936 and exhaustive scientific surveys have failed
to turn up any evidence that they're still out there.
85 Even so, people often still report seeing them.

1

What is the main idea of the passage?

A) Scientific advancements have led to an instance
   of demystification.

B) People with vivid imaginations will pursue
   science even if some mysteries are resolved.

C) E-DNA testing has confirmed that people lived by
   Loch Ness in a distant era.

D) Giant eels live in only a few parts of Loch Ness
   despite the prevalence of a local legend.

2

The author mentions the circus elephant (line 4)
primarily to

A) satirize people's claims about seeing a mysterious
   animal in Loch Ness.

B) indicate that it is plausible that people have been
   seeing elephants in the lake.

C) give a general description of Nessie throughout
   the centuries.

D) depict the actual physical appearance of the
   monster living in Loch Ness.

3

The purpose of the first paragraph is to

A) confirm the reptilian nature of Nessie.

B) provide an alternative explanation of Nessie's
   existence.

C) convince people that the Loch Ness monster is
   real but harmless.

D) establish a connection between dinosaurs and
   Nessie.

4

The passage indicates that, in terms of inquiries
surrounding Loch Ness, e-DNA testing

A) is experimental and used exclusively for
   establishing endangered species.

B) yields inconclusive results about the origins of
   animal species.

C) can detect the presence of species that rarely
   approach the lake.

D) is widely subjected to dispute by the scientific
   world and should regarded with skepticism.

5

As used in line 59, "lie" most nearly means

A) accept.

B) rest.

C) surface.

D) stand.

CONTINUE

6

In describing recent examinations of the wildlife in Loch Ness, the author indicates that scientists

A) have reached a unanimous conclusion about psychological responses to monstrous creatures.

B) rely on a certain psychological phenomenon to explain the existence of large animals.

C) suspect that abnormal DNA exists in the lake, despite the scarcity of hard evidence.

D) cannot provide a definitive answer about the size of the eels in Loch Ness.

7

Which choice provides the best evidence for the answer to the previous question?

A) Lines 41-44 ("There . . . birds")

B) Lines 50-53 ("The most . . . ago")

C) Lines 65-67 ("Plenty . . . eels")

D) Lines 74-77 ("If Nessie . . . attention")

8

As used in line 80, "cues" most nearly means

A) signals.

B) reminders.

C) inspirations.

D) prompts.

9

The author uses the phrase "expectant attention" primarily to

A) describe a way in which the brain may be tricked into believing something unreal.

B) refer to the attentiveness of people who managed to actually spot Nessie in the past.

C) depict the scientists' eagerness to locate the monster living in Loch Ness.

D) support the claims made by eyewitness who have spotted Nessie in the lake.

10

Which choice provides the best evidence for the answer to the previous question?

A) Lines 8-11 ("Starting . . . alive")

B) Lines 54-56 ("Hugh . . . 1844")

C) Lines 70-73 ("But . . . about")

D) Lines 82-85 ("The last . . . them")

CONTINUE

Reading 19

Questions 1-10 are based on the following passage.

This passage is adapted from "'Wildling' mice could help translate results in animal models to results in humans," an article published* in 2019 by the National Institutes of Health.

Researchers at the National Institutes of Health developed a new mouse model that could improve the translation of research in mice into advances
Line in human health. The mouse model, which the
5 scientists called "wildling," acquired the microbes and pathogens of wild mice while maintaining the laboratory mice's genetics that make them more useful for research. In two preclinical studies, wildlings mirrored human immune responses,
10 whereas lab mice failed to do so. Led by scientists at the NIH's National Institute of Diabetes and Digestive and Kidney Diseases (NIDDK), the study was published online in *Science*.

"We wanted to create a mouse model that
15 better resembles a mouse you'd find in the wild," said Barbara Rehermann, M.D., chief of the Immunology Section in NIDDK's Liver Diseases Branch and senior author on the study. "Our rationale was that the immune responses and
20 microbiota of wild mice and humans are likely shaped in a similar way—through contact with diverse microbes out in the real world."

"Microbiota" refers to the trillions of tiny microbes, such as bacteria, fungi, and viruses, that
25 live in and on the bodies of people and animals and play a critical role in keeping immune systems healthy. Unlike squeaky clean lab mice raised in artificial settings, wild mice have developed symbiotic relationships with microbes they have
30 encountered in the outside world—just as people have done.

Rehermann and Stephan Rosshart, M.D., the study's lead author and NIDDK postdoctoral fellow, have long sought to improve animal
35 models of complex diseases in humans. In 2017,

they led research showing that transferring wild mice gut microbiota into lab mice helped the mice survive an otherwise lethal flu virus infection and fight colorectal cancer.
40 In the current study, they transplanted embryos of the most commonly used strain of laboratory mice for immune system research into female wild mice, who then gave birth to and raised wildlings. The researchers and their collaborators compared
45 the microbiota of the wildlings, wild mice, and lab mice. They found that the wildlings acquired the microbes and pathogens of wild mice and closely resembled wild mice in their bacterial microbes present at the gut, skin, and vagina, as well as in
50 the number and kinds of fungi and viruses present.

"A healthy microbiome is important not only for the immune system, but also for digestion, metabolism, even the brain," said Rosshart, who recently completed his fellowship in NIDDK and
55 will open a new lab in Germany. "The wildling model could help us better understand what causes diseases, and what can protect us from them, thus benefitting many areas of biomedical research."

The researchers also tested the stability
60 and resilience of the wildlings' microbiota and found that the microbiota were stable across five generations and resilient when faced with environmental challenges. For example, when the mice were given antibiotics for seven days,
65 the lab mice's gut microbiota changed and did not recover, while the wildlings' microbiota fully recovered. Further, when the mice were fed a 10-week high-fat diet, the microbiota of the lab mice changed significantly and never returned
70 to baseline. The wildlings' microbiota changed only mildly and recovered shortly after the diet ended. The authors suggest that the stability and resilience of wildlings, if the model were to be used widely, could improve the validity and
75 reproducibility of biomedical studies.

Finally, the researchers tested how well the wildlings could predict human immune responses. To do so, they drew from two studies in which drugs used to target immune responses were
80 successful in treating lab mice in preclinical trials

---

*See Page 171 for the citation for this text.

CONTINUE

but consequently failed to have therapeutic effects in humans. In the current study, the researchers treated wildlings and lab mice with the same drugs. The wildlings, but not the lab mice,
85 mimicked the human responses seen in clinical trials.

"We always strive for effective ways to shorten the gap between early lab findings and health advances in people, and the wildling model has
90 the potential to do just that," said NIDDK Director Griffin P. Rodgers, M.D. "By helping to predict immune responses of humans, the wildling model could lead to important discoveries to help treat and prevent disease, and ultimately improve
95 human health."

1

Which choice best describes the structure of the passage as a whole?

A) A group of researchers is profiled, their goals are considered, and a constant challenge is analyzed.

B) A pursuit is explained, its shortcomings are acknowledged, and corrective measures are endorsed.

C) An endeavor is praised, its theoretical importance is briefly discussed, and a resulting practical application is emphasized.

D) An objective is set forward, various inquiries are described, and potential benefits are noted.

2

The author explains that a "wildling" mouse is identifiable as an animal that

A) has unusually high levels of microbiota also found in humans.

B) is sturdier and healthier than a laboratory mouse.

C) is raised in a laboratory but exhibits a natural relationship to microbiota.

D) does not display significant changes in microbiota over its lifetime.

3

One of the central aims of Rehermann and Rosshart's research was to

A) reduce the frequency of procedural errors in medical research involving mice.

B) unearth new similarities between the immune systems of humans and mice.

C) better understand human health through more refined animal-based trials.

D) promote the replacement of standard laboratory mice with wildling mice.

4

Which choice provides the best evidence for the answer to the previous question?

A) Lines 32-33 ("Rehrmann . . . humans")

B) Lines 44-46 ("The researchers . . . mice")

C) Lines 51-53 ("A healthy . . . Rosshart")

D) Lines 70-72 ("The wildlings' . . . ended")

5

The main effect of the phrase "squeaky clean" in line 27 is to emphasize

A) the unnatural situation of lab mice in terms of microbe exposure.

B) the rigor and precision required in order to successfully produce wildling mice.

C) the primary source of inaccuracy in current clinical trails involving mice.

D) the desirable absence of microbes in laboratory settings.

CONTINUE

6

On the basis of the passage, all of the following would be classified as microbiota EXCEPT

A) the bacteria on the surface of a person's tongue.

B) non-lethal viruses that can be found in a reptile's stomach.

C) a thin coating of fungus on a mammal's foot.

D) tiny mold spores that proliferate on the bark of a tree.

7

In order to produce the wildling mice described in the passage, the NIKKD researchers used which process?

A) Multi-generational cross-breeding of wild mice and laboratory mice

B) Modification of the microbiota of mature laboratory mice

C) Artificial hybridization of wild mice and laboratory mice

D) Domestication of wild mice over several generations

8

In terms of medical treatment, which choice best explains the relationship between wildling mouse responses and human responses as described in the passage?

A) Wildling mice are most threatened by the same diseases that are most prevalent among humans.

B) Wildling mice exhibit immune system responses that closely approximate those of humans.

C) Wildling mice possess more resilient microbiota cultures than humans do.

D) Wildling mice more closely resemble humans in terms of virus and fungus microbiota than in terms of bacterial microbiota.

9

Which choice provides the best evidence for the answer to the previous question?

A) Lines 46-50 ("They . . . present")

B) Lines 63-66 ("For example . . . recovered")

C) Lines 76-77 ("Finally . . . responses")

D) Lines 91-95 ("By helping . . . health")

10

As used in line 87, "shorten" most nearly means

A) simplify.

B) diminish.

C) summarize.

D) dismiss.

Reading 20

Questions 1-10 are based on the following passage and supplementary material.

This passage is adapted from "Big Sagebrush Recovery After Fire Inhibited by Its Own Biology," a 2019 news release* from the United States Geological Survey.

Recovery of big sagebrush populations after fire is inhibited by the loss of adult plants and the limited ability of new seedlings to survive or
Line reproduce—a limitation with negative population
5 consequences that last for years to decades after post-fire seeding restoration efforts, according to a recently published study by the U.S. Geological Survey.

"The recovery of big sagebrush habitat is
10 one of the largest, if not the largest, ecosystem restoration challenges in the U.S. right now. Hundreds of thousands of acres burn each year, and millions of dollars are invested in trying to restore big sagebrush in these areas," said USGS
15 scientist and lead author of the study Robert Shriver. "This study could lead to new and more cost-effective strategies for land managers trying to restore big sagebrush populations after fire."

Big sagebrush is one of the most iconic plants
20 of the American West, and more than 300 species of conservation concern, like the sage-grouse and pygmy rabbit, rely on big sagebrush ecosystems. Wildlife like mule deer, elk, pronghorn, sage sparrows, and sagebrush voles also use sagebrush
25 for food and habitat.

Although big sagebrush is found throughout the Intermountain West—from Montana south to Arizona—human activity, non-native plant species invasions, and wildfire have resulted in widespread
30 loss of big sagebrush. To complicate matters, active attempts to restore big sagebrush after fires have had mixed results, even at locations that previously supported healthy populations.

To better understand why it is so difficult
35 for big sagebrush to recover, USGS scientists studied 531 burned sites in the Great Basin. Following fire, these sites were reseeded with big

sagebrush by the Bureau of Land Management. Using data collected on the re-established big
40 sagebrush individuals, combined with statistical and mathematical modeling, USGS scientists were able to reconstruct the rates of survival, growth and reproduction of big sagebrush at each of the 531 sites since these areas were seeded.

45 "One of the biggest challenges we face in trying to understand what controls big sagebrush recovery after fire is that there isn't a lot of long-term monitoring data available. This was a great opportunity to partner with the Bureau of Land
50 Management to return to areas seeded decades ago and assess what drove post-fire dynamics of big sagebrush," said Shriver.

The USGS scientists found that even though many sites originally supported healthy, mature
55 big sagebrush populations before they burned, and those sites are still capable of doing so, big sagebrush populations may not necessarily recover after seeding. This is because newly established big sagebrush populations are mostly
60 composed of small, young plants that have low survival and reproduction rates, resulting in rapid population decline and the potential for local extinction.

"What we find is that rather than recovering,
65 most populations decline for years or decades after seeding, leading some to completely die out at individual sites. A big driver of this is the biology of big sagebrush itself; without some larger plants to anchor the population by surviving
70 and reproducing, recovery becomes really difficult," said Shriver.

For example, smaller plants (6 inches or shorter) had only an 8% chance of surviving from year to year whereas plants greater than 30
75 inches tall had nearly a 100% chance of surviving from year to year. Likewise, older, larger plants are much more reproductively successful than younger, smaller plants.

However, there may be strategies that could
80 work to re-establish big sagebrush.

"This work suggests some good options for improving restoration going forward," said Shriver. "First, at high elevations, restoring

*See Page 171 for the citation for this text.

CONTINUE ➡

populations through seeding is often successful
85 because plants grow faster and reproduce more
than at lower elevations. But at low-elevation
sites where conditions are warmer and drier,
planting nursery-raised seedlings of sagebrush
may be a more effective strategy than seeding
90 to increase survival and reproduction and speed
up recovery." This approach would be similar to
wildlife conservation programs that rear animals
to a certain age before releasing them into nature:
applying this general strategy to big sagebrush
95 may help it survive those early years when it is
most vulnerable.

1

One of the author's main purposes in the passage is to

A) depict a presumably bleak future for sagebrush in Montana.

B) portray Robert Shriver as a well-meaning but ultimately indifferent scientist.

C) offer a tested solution to a problem affiliated with sagebrush.

D) emphasize the fact that humans are disrupting the North American ecosystem.

2

Which choice best summarizes the passage?

A) There is strong scientific evidence that the population of sagebrush is slowly disappearing.

B) Collaboration between scientists and organizations led to a solution to an ecological problem.

C) A large area populated with sagebrush has been destroyed by non-native plant invasions.

D) The recovery of big sagebrush populations is impossible without young plants.

3

It can reasonably be inferred that the recovery of big sagebrush populations

A) has been undertaken exclusively by USGS scientists after devastating fires.

B) has not been an easy task due to natural factors.

C) has only an 8% success rate despite new initiatives.

D) has not been taken seriously by the American government.

4

Which choice provides the best evidence for the answer to the previous question?

A) Lines 12-14 ("Hundreds . . . areas")

B) Lines 20-22 ("more than . . . ecosystems")

C) Lines 58-62 ("This . . . decline")

D) Lines 79-80 ("However . . . sagebrush")

5

As used in line 19, "iconic" most nearly means

A) popular.

B) religious.

C) successful.

D) classic.

CONTINUE

6

The scientist Robert Shriver most strongly suggests that research into the recovery of sagebrush populations is likely to

A) make the recovery process less expensive.

B) create strains of hybrid plants.

C) prevent fires from destroying sagebrush.

D) hinder the spread of non-native plants.

7

Which choice provides the best evidence for the answer to the previous question?

A) Lines 16-18 ("This . . . fire")

B) Lines 19-20 ("Big . . . American West")

C) Lines 28-30 ("non-native . . . sagebrush")

D) Lines 45-48 ("One . . . available")

8

According to the author, the role of the Bureau of Land Management is to

A) provide significant data about the rates of survival of sagebrush.

B) sponsor the re-population of sagebrush through long-established seeding practices.

C) maintain control over the fires and the human activity that often destroy sagebrush.

D) create a genetically modified sagebrush variant that could survive more easily.

9

As used in line 92, "rear" most nearly means

A) capture.

B) mentor.

C) nourish.

D) challenge.

10

The purpose of the final paragraph is to

A) gesture towards a relatively optimistic future for the sagebrush ecosystem.

B) elaborate on the dangers of burning sagebrush.

C) provide an unsupported yet intriguing claim about the loss of sagebrush.

D) emphasize the importance of facilitating sagebrush recovery in the United States.

106

CONTINUE

Reading 21

Questions 1-10 are based on the following passage and supplementary material.

This passage is adapted from Kayla Graham, "Fossilized Footprints Lead Scientists Down a Prehistoric Path," an article originally published by EveryONE, the community blog of the research journal PLOS ONE.

Whether tromping alone or running in a pack, all prehistoric creatures got around somehow. Paleontologists can use fossilized bones to learn
Line more about what dinosaurs ate, what they looked
5 like, and even how they might have moved, but bones are only part of the "rocky" story. We can study fossils of all shapes, sizes, and sources to piece together missing information about how these creatures moved, interacted, and lived. Trace
10 fossils, which include fossilized impressions like footprints and belly drag marks left in the ground, can tell us a surprising amount about how animals of the past lived and moved. They are more common than you might think, but typically
15 aren't studied as often as fossilized bones. PLOS ONE recently published two separate studies in which authors used trace fossils to provide insight on tyrannosaur social life and to illuminate the slow and slithering movements of an ancient
20 temnospondyl, bringing two prehistoric creatures to "life."

Many tyrannosaur bones have been collected and documented, but few scientists have studied tyrannosaur footprints. In a new PLOS ONE
25 study, researchers found three 75 million-year-old three-toed tyrannosaurid footprint with claw mark tracks heading southeast within an 8.5 meter-wide corridor in British Columbia, Canada. Scientists took molds and measurements of the
30 prints to understand the track-makers' behavior. These scientists aren't sure exactly which species of tyrannosaur made the prints, but similarities in depth and preservation of the tracks indicate that these three trackways were made by dinosaurs

35 walking alongside each other in the same direction at a normal pace, around 8.50 kilometers per hour.

These trackways add to previous research about tyrannasaurid social behavior and locomotion, but the authors acknowledge that
40 there is the possibility, although unlikely, that three dinosaurs could have passed through the same spot separately within a short period of time. Either way, the tracks make up the first record of the walking gait of tyrannosaurids and provide
45 insight about how they moved across Western Canada.

A 200 million-year-old mysterious trackway, called *Episcopopus ventrosus*, in southern Africa may have been made by a dinosaur, or
50 maybe by an early ancestor of the crocodile. Researchers who mapped, cast, and laser-scanned the best-preserved part of the *Episcopopus ventrosus* trackway found that the track belongs to a primitive amphibian-like animal from one
55 of the earliest groups of limbed vertebrates, temnospondyls. The authors estimate that the track-maker was 3.5 meters long and dragged the hind portion of its body along a wet sand bar on the bank of a river bend, using only the claw-less
60 tips of its digits.

The movements were likely made by a large-headed, slithering, and slow-moving amphibian-like animal. Researchers usually use hind-limb-driven salamanders as a model for temnospondyl
65 locomotion, but this discovery is causing researchers to re-examine their use of salamander models for this front-limb-driven temnospondyl.

From signs of dinosaurs moving in packs to amphibian-like animals slithering across river
70 banks, trace fossils can support what we already know about prehistoric creatures, but they can moreover shake up the assumptions we've made and, in the case of the tetrapod, potentially change the way we study them. Fossilized bones may still
75 be the better known field of study, but footprints and other trace fossils may help shape our understanding of patterns, reconstructing of past lives, and bringing of prehistoric animals back to "life."

---

*See Page 171 for the citation for this text.

CONTINUE ▶

Part 2: Science, Single

1

Which choice indicates a clear difference between the tyrannosaur and temnospondyl tracks described in the passage?

A) The tyrannosaur tracks were most likely produced by multiple animals; the temnospondyl tracks were attributed to a single specimen.

B) The tyrannosaur tracks were readily discernible; the temnospondyl tracks had been obscured and required careful reconstruction.

C) The tyrannosaur tracks were the result of purposeful hunting activity; the temnospondyl tracks have not been linked to a single clear goal.

D) The tyrannosaur tracks were generated by multiple known species; the themnospondyl tracks remain unclassified in terms of exact species.

2

What purpose is served by the word "life" as placed between quotation marks in line 21 and line 79?

A) To call into question the significance of a few research outcomes

B) To signal that the author's phrasing should be understood figuratively

C) To explain why a current consensus is appealing

D) To indulge in an easygoing and humorous tone

3

Which of the following statements does NOT directly support the idea that researchers prioritize the study of bone fossils?

A) Lines 6-9 ("We . . . lived")

B) Lines 13-15 ("They . . . bones")

C) Lines 22-24 ("Many . . . footprints")

D) Lines 74-77 ("Fossilized . . . patterns")

4

As used in lines 32 and 34, "made" most nearly means

A) left behind.

B) thought up.

C) organized.

D) pioneered.

5

Which additional piece of information, if true, would best support the "possibility" mentioned in line 40?

A) Tyrannosaurs tended to be most successful at hunting prey when operating alone.

B) Tracks of tyrannosaurs walking single-file, rather than side-by-side, have recently been discovered.

C) Adult tyrannosaurs rarely gathered in groups larger than individual male-female mating pairs.

D) Multiple species of tyrannosaurs were known to hunt prey in a cooperative manner.

6

The author's description of the temnospondyl suggests that this prehistoric animal

A) could not have used claws for either aggression of self-defense.

B) is larger than most modern salamanders but otherwise anatomically similar.

C) had trouble escaping fast-moving predators.

D) displayed some unexpected resemblances to a modern crocodile.

CONTINUE

Three Sets of Dinosaur Tracks

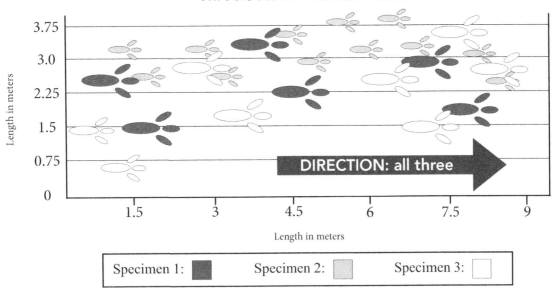

Specimen 1: ■   Specimen 2: ▨   Specimen 3: □

7

One significant outcome of recent investigation of dinosaur tracks is

A) a decline in the popularity of bone fossils in terms of the priorities of paleontological study.

B) reassessment of ideas about animals that are not themselves prehistoric.

C) more coherent sets of anatomical terms for both tyrannosaurid and temnospondyl samples.

D) creation of new software programs that consider large numbers of data points.

8

Which choice provides the best evidence for the answer to the previous question?

A) Lines 38-20 ("Scientists . . . behavior")

B) Lines 43-46 ("Either . . . Canada")

C) Lines 63-67 ("Researchers . . . temnospondyl")

D) Lines 68-74 ("From . . . them")

9

Without further information, the tracks represented in the figure could be traced to all of the following EXCEPT

A) one dinosaur covering the same ground at different stages of its growth.

B) three dinosaurs walking together side-by-side.

C) three dinosaurs walking together single-file.

D) three dinosaurs covering the same ground in different years.

10

Could one of the sets of tracks portrayed in the visual be the tracks of a temnospondyl?

A) Yes, because the sets of tracks indicate that at least some of the movement was labored.

B) Yes, because the tracks were not produced by dinosaurs that possessed claws

C) No, because all of the dinosaur tracks were apparently produced by four-footed animals.

D) No, because no set of tracks centers on a trailing length of body that leaves its own impression.

CONTINUE ▶

Reading 22

Questions 1-10 are based on the following passage and supplementary material.

This passage is adapted from Ivy F. Kupec, "Precious Time," an article published in 2015 by the National Science Foundation.

Prior to the mid 18th century, it was tough to be a sailor. If your voyage required east-west travel, you couldn't set out to a specific *Line* destination and have any real hope of finding it
5 efficiently.

At the time, sailors had no reliable method for measuring longitude, the coordinates that measure a point's east-west position on the globe. To find longitude, you need to know the time
10 in two places—the ship you're on, and the port you departed from. By calculating the difference between those times, sailors got a rough estimate of their position. The problem: the clocks back then just couldn't keep time that well. They lost
15 their home port's time almost immediately after departing.

Today, time is just as important to navigation, only instead of calculating positioning with margins of errors measured in miles and leagues,
20 we have GPS systems that are accurate within meters. And instead of springs and gears, our best timepieces rely on cesium atoms and lasers. But given the history, it's fitting that scientists like Clayton Simien, a National Science Foundation
25 (NSF)-funded physicist at the University of Alabama at Birmingham who works on atomic clocks, was inspired by the story of John Harrison, an English watchmaker who toiled in the 1700s to come up with the first compact marine
30 chronometer. This device marked the beginning of the end for the "longitude problem" that had plagued sailors for centuries.

"If you want to measure distances well, you really need an accurate clock," Simien said.
35 Despite the massive leaps navigation technology has made since Harrison's time,

scientists—many NSF-funded—are looking for new ways to make clocks more accurate, diminishing any variables that might distort
40 precise timekeeping. Some, for example, are looking for ways to better synchronize atomic clocks on earth with GPS satellites in orbit, where atmospheric distortion can limit signal accuracy to degrees that seem minute but are profound for
45 the precise computer systems that govern modern navigation.

The National Institute of Standards and Technology (Department of Commerce) joins NSF in the search for even better atomic clocks.
50 But today's research isn't just about building a more accurate timepiece. It's about foundational science that has other ramifications.

Atomic clocks precisely measure the ticks of atoms, essentially tossing cesium atoms upward,
55 much like a fountain. Laser-beam photons "cool down" the atoms to very low temperatures, so that the atoms can transfer back and forth between a ground state and an excited state.

The trick to this process is finding just the right
60 frequency to move directly between the two states and overcome Doppler shifts that distort rhythm. (Doppler shifts are increases or decreases in wave frequency as the waves move closer or further away—much like the way a siren's sound changes
65 depending on its distance.) Laser improvements have helped scientists to control atoms better and to address the Doppler issue. In fact, lasers helped to facilitate something known as an optical lattice, which can layer atoms into "egg cartons"
70 to immobilize them, helping to eliminate Doppler shifts altogether.

That shift between ground state and excited state (better known as the atomic transition frequency) yields something equivalent to the
75 official definition of a second: 9,192,631,770 cycles of the radiation that gets a cesium atom to vibrate between those two energy states. Today's atomic clocks mostly still use cesium.

NSF-funded physicist Kurt Gibble,
80 of Pennsylvania State University, has an international reputation for assessing accuracy and improving atomic clocks, including some of

---

CONTINUE ➡

the most accurate ones in the world: the cesium clocks at the United Kingdom's National Physical
85 Laboratory and the Observatory of Paris in France. But accurate as those are, Gibble says that the biggest advance in atomic clocks will be a move from current-generation microwave frequency clocks—the only kind commonly in
90 operation—to optical frequency clocks.

Accuracy* (Best Fit Line) of Atomic and Optical Clocks

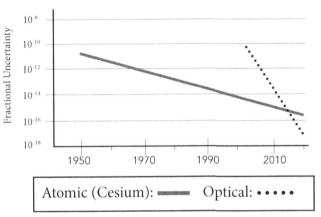

NOTE: lower marginal uncertainty for both clock types correlates with higher accuracy

---

1

The main purpose of the passage is to

A) provide an overview of the history of nautical timekeeping.

B) map out a debate among timepiece researchers.

C) chart various advances in timekeeping technology.

D) point out similarities between cesium clocks and earlier timepieces.

2

The first two paragraphs of the passage serve primarily to

A) relate the technical content of the passage to the reader's own personal experiences.

B) underscore the pivotal role of cesium clocks in the development of modern navigation systems.

C) create a tone of urgency while anticipating the technical discussion that follows.

D) present a scenario that is no longer applicable under modern conditions.

3

Which choice best indicates that the "problem" mentioned in line 13 has been resolved?

A) Lines 30-32 ("This device . . . centuries")

B) Lines 33-34 ("If you . . . said")

C) Lines 40-46 ("Some . . . navigation")

D) Lines 50-52 ("But . . . ramifications")

4

As used in line 35, "massive" most nearly means

A) fortified.

B) cumbersome.

C) impressive.

D) severe.

CONTINUE

Part 2: Science, Single

5

As used in line 59, "trick" most nearly means

A) key.

B) deception.

C) pleasure.

D) habit.

6

The author indicates that cesium is particularly useful in atomic clocks because

A) it is compatible with simple and elegant clock engineering designs.

B) its material properties can be used to clarify a core concept in timekeeping.

C) it can be used to eliminate Doppler shift disruptions more effectively than lasers can.

D) its widespread availability has made it especially cost-efficient.

7

Which choice provides the best evidence for the answer to the previous question?

A) Lines 21-22 ("And . . . lasers")

B) Lines 65-67 ("Laser . . . issue")

C) Lines 72-77 ("That . . . states")

D) Lines 77-78 ("Today's . . . cesium")

8

Which of the following could, on the basis of the passage, be one of Kurt Gibble's past research projects?

A) Construction of the world's first optical frequency clock

B) Comparative analysis of five different atomic clocks to determine which one is most reliable

C) Redefinition of the concept of a single second based on observation of cesium clocks

D) Reduction of the Doppler shifts that are common in optical frequency clocks

9

If the trend lines in the graph hold true for most atomic and optical clocks, which of the following would most likely be most the accurate clock?

A) Atomic clock, 2000

B) Atomic clock, 2020

C) Optical clock, 2000

D) Optical clock, 2020

10

In relation to the passage, the graph features information relevant to

A) the role of Doppler shifts in the operations of two kinds of clock.

B) a recent timekeeping technology that is briefly mentioned in the passage.

C) the origins of Kurt Gibble's work with traditional clock technology.

D) a long-lived timekeeping convention that has been updated in recent years.

CONTINUE ▶

Reading 23

Questions 1-10 are based on the following passage and supplementary material.

This passage is an excerpt from Samantha Mascuch and Julia Kubanek, "Seaweed and sea slugs rely on toxic bacteria to defend against predators," an article originally published by The Conversation in 2019.

Plants, animals, and even microbes that live on coral reefs have evolved a rich variety of defense strategies to protect themselves from predators.

Line Some have physical defenses like spines and
5 camouflage. Others have specialized behaviors—like a squid expelling ink—that allow them to escape. Soft-bodied or immobile organisms—like sponges, algae, and sea squirts—often defend themselves with noxious chemicals that taste bad
10 or are toxic.

Some animals that can't manufacture their own chemical weapons feed on toxic organisms and steal their chemical defenses, having evolved resistance to toxins. One animal that does this
15 is a sea slug that lives on the reefs surrounding Hawaii and dines on toxic Bryopsis algae. Marine scientists suspected that the toxin is made by a bacterium that lives within the alga but have only just discovered the species responsible and teased
20 apart the complex relationship between slug, seaweed, and microbe.

Ultimately, noxious chemicals allow predators and prey to coexist on coral reefs, increasing their diversity. This is important because diverse
25 ecosystems are more stable and resilient. A greater understanding of the drivers of diversity will aid in reef management and conservation.

As marine scientists, we too study chemical defenses in the ocean. Our laboratory group at
30 the Georgia Institute of Technology explores how marine organisms use chemical signaling to solve critical problems of competition, disease, predation, and reproduction. That's why we were particularly excited by the discovery of this new
35 bacterial species.

In a report published in the journal *Science*, researchers at Princeton University and the University of Maryland discovered that a group of well-studied toxic defense chemicals, the
40 kahalalides, are actually produced by a bacterium that lives inside the cells of a particular species of seaweed. The scientific community had long speculated that a bacterium might be responsible for producing the kahalalides. So the discovery
45 of the kahalalide-producing bacteria—belonging to the class *Flavobacteria*—has solved a long-standing scientific mystery.

Bryopsis provides the bacteria with a safe environment and the chemical building blocks
50 necessary for life and for manufacturing the kahalalides. In return, the bacterium produces the toxins for the algae, which protect them from hungry fish scouring the reefs. But the seaweed isn't the only organism that benefits from this
55 arrangement.

The kahalalides, originally discovered in the early 1990s, also protect a sea slug, *Elysia rufescens*, that consumes them. The sea slugs accumulate the toxins from the algae, which then
60 protects them from predators. The discovery of a symbiosis between a bacterium and a seaweed to produce a chemical defense is noteworthy. There are many examples of bacteria living inside the cells of invertebrate animals (like sponges) and
65 manufacturing toxic chemicals, but a partnership involving a bacterium living in the cells of a marine seaweed to produce a toxin is unusual.

This finding adds a new dimension to our understanding of the types of ecological
70 relationships that produce the chemicals shaping coral reef ecosystems. Our lab is home to an enthusiastic multidisciplinary team of marine chemists, microbiologists, and ecologists who strive to understand how chemicals facilitate
75 interactions between species in the marine environment. We also use ecological insights to guide discovery of novel pharmaceuticals from marine organisms. Chemicals used by marine organisms to interact with their environment,
80 including toxins which protect them from predators, often show promising medical

*See Page 171 for the citation for this text.

CONTINUE ➡

applications. In fact, the most toxic kahalalide, kahalalide F, has been the focus of clinical trials for the treatment of cancer and psoriasis.

85   Currently, we conduct our fieldwork in Fiji and the Solomon Islands in collaboration with a research group led by Katy Soapi at the University of the South Pacific. There you can find us scuba diving to conduct ecological experiments or to
90 collect algae and coral microbes to bring back for study in the laboratory. During the course of our field work we have had the opportunity to observe Bryopsis and have been struck by how lovely it is, standing out with its bright green color against the
95 pinks, grays, browns and blues of a coral reef.

1

As used in line 2, "a rich" most nearly means

A) an expressive.

B) a cloying.

C) a considerable.

D) an extravagant.

2

Which of the following most nearly resembles the "sea slug" mentioned in line 15?

A) The "microbes" (line 1)

B) "Some" animals (line 4)

C) The "Others" (line 5)

D) The "organisms" (line 7)

3

As used in line 26, "drivers of" most nearly means

A) reasons developed by.

B) influences behind.

C) inspirations of.

D) advocates for.

4

Which of the following, according to the authors of the passage, was a relatively recent finding?

A) The fact that the toxins that occur in reef ecosystems are directly produced by sea slugs such as *Elysia rufescens.*

B) The discovery that healthy reef ecosystems require a balance of prey and predator species.

C) The unearthing of the first bacterial species that produce toxins that harm predators but not bacteria host organisms.

D) The realization that *Flavobacteria* are responsible for producing the kahalalide toxins found in algae.

5

Which choice provides the best evidence for the answer to the previous question?

A) Lines 16-21 ("Marine . . . microbe")

B) Lines 22-25 ("Ultimately . . . resilient")

C) Lines 42-44 ("The scientific . . . kahalalides")

D) Lines 51-53 ("In return . . . reefs")

6

The authors of the passage argue that kahalalides

A) commonly serve defensive purposes for various seaweed species.

B) were deemed inexplicable by researchers when these toxins were first discovered.

C) have been traced to bacteria found in more than one kind of host organism.

D) are central components of a few of the life-saving pharmaceuticals currently in use.

CONTINUE

Part 2: Science, Single

Predators and Biodiversity in Five Coral Reef Ecosystems

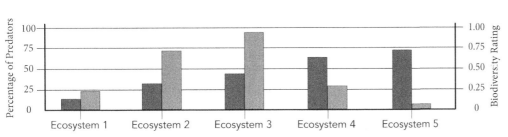

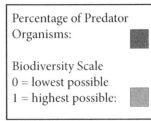

7

Which choice provides the best evidence for the answer to the previous question?

A) Lines 44-47 ("So . . . mystery")

B) Lines 56-58 ("The kahalalides . . . it")

C) Lines 62-67 ("There . . . unusual")

D) Lines 76-78 ("We . . . organisms")

8

In the final paragraph, the authors mention various colors in order to convey a sense of

A) skepticism about the role of personal experience in scientific discovery.

B) supportiveness for those who are engaged in preserving marine ecosystems.

C) enthusiasm about specific firsthand observations of the natural world.

D) fascination with aspects of marine life that remain mysterious.

9

Based on the graph, high biodiversity would be expected in a reef ecosystem with a predator population that is

A) slightly larger than the prey population.

B) considerably larger than the prey population.

C) equivalent to the prey population.

D) noticeably smaller than the prey population.

10

The authors of the passage would most likely argue that Ecosystem 3, as presented in the graph, is

A) home to a greater variety of prey species than any other ecosystem pictured.

B) bound to increasingly resemble Ecosystem 1 over time.

C) less inherently vulnerable than some of the other ecosystems depicted.

D) likely to be the single largest ecosystem of the five depicted.

CONTINUE

Reading 24

Questions 1-10 are based on the following passage and supplementary material.

This passage is an excerpt from Jason Dorrier, "Writing the First Human Genome by 2026 Is Synthetic Biology's Grand Challenge," an article that was originally published by SingularityHub in 2016.

A "top secret" meeting of scientists was held at the Langone Medical Center on Halloween 2015. Their aim? To kickstart a new Human Genome
Line Project and build a functional human genome
5   from the base pairs up by 2026.

"There's only one grand challenge in synthetic biology. Only one. And it's to write a human genome. And we have to do that," said Autodesk Fellow Andrew Hessel at Singularity University's
10   Exponential Medicine 2016 conference.

Like the first Human Genome Project before it—which resulted in the first fully-sequenced human genome—writing a human genome from scratch is an audacious goal. Hessel said a number
15   of organizations are already writing DNA, and we can fabricate million-pair DNA constructs. But the human genome contains three billion base pairs.

We're a long way from writing DNA on that scale. "It took a year to design the yeast genome,
20   even though there were barely any changes made to [it]. So, we need better design tools," Hessel said.

Work on the yeast genome is the most advanced thing going on in synthetic biology.
25   It's been pushing the field forward, but not as fast as Hessel would like. His career was hugely influenced by the race to map the first human genome in the 90s and early 2000s, and he thought to himself—now we need something like
30   that for synthetic biology.

That's why Hessel and fellow scientists are pushing for a new Human Genome Project focused on synthetic biology—something to spark people's imaginations. That "top secret" meeting

35   and a subsequent white paper made just the splash they were looking for.

"Two hundred news organizations picked up the story, and we got ninety-two million page impressions in the first week," Hessel said.
40   "Everybody suddenly knew about the secret meeting to synthesize the human genome."

Though interest in the project is high, it's just the beginning. "This is really hard work . . . trying to go from DNA to packaged chromosome put
45   into a cell and functional is hard. I don't want to gloss over the technical challenges," Hessel said.

Hessel's work at Autodesk is focused on making more effective design tools. He started writing viruses two years back, and it took
50   weeks to get the DNA. Now, he's writing more complicated viruses to fight cancer. The larger the amount of DNA, the longer it takes to assemble.

But there are a number of fields, from health and medicine to electronics (DNA is an excellent
55   medium for long-term information storage), creating big incentives to speed development. Hessel is excited at the prospects. Though it's still early, he thinks 2026 for a fully engineered human genome is realistic if synthetic biology follows an
60   exponential pace like genome sequencing did.

"So, a new genome race is starting, ladies and gentlemen," Hessel said. "It's starting now. It's still in the organizational phase, but it is going to accelerate and, guaranteed, by 2026, we're going
65   to succeed."

As for the more controversial aspects of the project, like the worry that the work may result in synthetic humans? The intentions behind this project are not to produce synthetic babies.
70   "We couldn't advocate that," Hessel said. It's more about pushing the science and technology necessary to build a whole human genome—but no more. And he has a personal motivation too.

"I'm doing this because I want my daughter
75   to literally have the best nanomedicine in the future, the best diagnostics, the best treatments," Hessel said. "I hope you realize that by 2026, it's a completely different game."

*See Page 171 for the citation for this text.

CONTINUE

1

The "grand challenge in synthetic biology" mentioned in lines 6-7 can best be characterized as

A) linked to a well-regarded moral imperative embraced by researchers.

B) dependent on scientific breakthroughs that have not yet arrived.

C) reliant on methodologies that are interchangeable with those that facilitated an earlier project.

D) premised on a theoretical construct once perceived as illogical.

2

Which choice provides the best evidence for the answer to the previous question?

A) Lines 8-10 ("And . . . conference")

B) Lines 11-14 ("Like . . . goal")

C) Lines 16-17 ("But . . . pairs")

D) Lines 19-22 ("It took . . . said")

3

Which of the following would NOT be a desired outcome of the research described in the passage?

A) The appearance of several new breakthroughs in nanomedicine

B) The emergence of viable synthetic genomes for non-human organisms

C) The creation of humans who have unnatural genetic traits

D) The intensification of joint ventures in DNA mapping and electronics engineering

4

Within the passage, Andrew Hessel is presented as a researcher who

A) has an stake in genomics that extends beyond purely academic interest.

B) hopes that the public will actively participate in creating a synthetic human genome.

C) sees current predictions about technological advances as overly optimistic.

D) is working to correct the misconceptions that surround the Human Genome Project.

5

Which choice provides the best evidence for the answer to the previous question?

A) Lines 31-34 ("That's . . . imagination")

B) Lines 37-41 ("Two hundred . . . genome")

C) Lines 57-60 ("Hessel . . . did")

D) Lines 74-77 ("I'm . . . said")

6

As used in line 46, "gloss over" most nearly means

A) downplay.

B) excuse.

C) embellish.

D) discredit.

CONTINUE

Part 2: Science, Single

7

How do the words "early" (line 58) and "starting" (lines 61 and 62) influence the tone of the passage?

A) They establish a concerned tone by suggesting that various conclusions were ultimately premature.

B) They establish an easygoing tone by addressing and alleviating possible doubts about the validity of recent evidence.

C) They establish an accessible tone through impartial description of a particular stage of a research endeavor.

D) They establish an urgent tone by alluding to the humanitarian importance of an inquiry that would otherwise seem to be purely technical.

8

In the final paragraphs of the passage (lines 61-78), Hessel delivers a series of remarks in a manner that is best understood as

A) skeptical and mystified.

B) cautious and meditative.

C) confident and assertive.

D) idealistic and combative.

9

Which choice best summarizes the information presented in the graph?

A) Researchers cannot achieve perfect accuracy in modeling the human genome.

B) The accuracy of models of the human genome improved considerably due to advances in biomedical technology.

C) Models of the human genome have experienced exponential improvements in accuracy in the recent past.

D) A mostly-accurate model of the human genome was present for all five years depicted.

10

For Andrew Hessel, the data presented in the graph would be most directly related to

A) the creation of new diagnostic tools based on genetic analysis.

B) the development of a project that will reach its culmination in 2026.

C) a formative stage of his own scientific career.

D) an instance of surprisingly intense publicity.

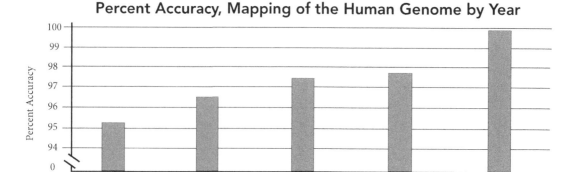

Percent Accuracy, Mapping of the Human Genome by Year

CONTINUE

Reading 25

Questions 1-10 are based on the following passage and supplementary material.

This passage is adapted from Jared Sagoff, "Scientists devise catalyst that uses light to turn carbon dioxide to fuel," a press release originally issued in 2019 by the Argonne National Laboratory.

The concentration of carbon dioxide in our atmosphere is steadily increasing, and many scientists believe that it is causing impacts in our environment. Recently, scientists have sought
5 ways to recapture some of the carbon in the atmosphere and potentially turn it into usable fuel—which would be a holy grail for sustainable energy production.

In a recent study from the U.S. Department of
10 Energy's (DOE) Argonne National Laboratory, scientists have used sunlight and a catalyst largely made of copper to transform carbon dioxide to methanol. A liquid fuel, methanol offers the potential for industry to find an additional source
15 to meet America's energy needs. The study describes a photocatalyst made of cuprous oxide (Cu_2O), a semiconductor that when exposed to light can produce electrons that become available to react with, or reduce, many compounds. After
20 being excited, electrons leave a positive hole in the catalyst's lower-energy valence band that, in turn, can oxidize water.

"This photocatalyst is particularly exciting because it has one of the most negative conduction
25 bands that we've used, which means that the electrons have more potential energy available to do reactions," said Argonne Distinguished Fellow Tijana Rajh, an author of the study.

Previous attempts to use photocatalysts, such
30 as titanium dioxide, to reduce carbon dioxide tended to produce a whole mish-mash of various products, ranging from aldehydes to methane. The lack of selectivity of these reactions made it difficult to segregate a usable fuel stream, Rajh
35 explained.

"Carbon dioxide is such a stable molecule and it results from the burning of basically everything, so the question is how do we fight nature and go from a really stable end product to something
40 useful and energy rich," Rajh said.

The idea for transforming carbon dioxide into useful energy comes from the one place in nature where this happens regularly. "We had this idea of copying photosynthesis, which uses carbon
45 dioxide to make food, so why couldn't we use it to make fuel?" Rajh said. "It turns out to be a complex problem, because to make methanol, you need not just one electron but six." By switching from titanium dioxide to cuprous oxide, scientists
50 developed a catalyst that not only had a more negative conduction band but that would also be dramatically more selective in terms of its products. This selectivity results not only from the chemistry of cuprous oxide but also from the
55 geometry of the catalyst itself. "With nanoscience, we start having the ability to meddle with the surfaces to induce certain hotspots or change the surface structure, cause strain or certain surface sites to expose differently than they are in the
60 bulk," Rajh said.

Because of this "meddling," Rajh and Argonne postdoctoral researcher Yimin Wu, now an assistant professor at the University of Waterloo, managed to create a catalyst with a bit of a split
65 personality. The cuprous oxide microparticles they developed have different facets, much like a diamond has different facets. Many of the facets of the microparticle are inert, but one is very active in driving the reduction of carbon dioxide
70 to methanol.

According to Rajh, the reason that this facet is so active lies in two unique aspects. First, the carbon dioxide molecule bonds to it in such a way that the structure of the molecule actually bends
75 slightly, diminishing the amount of energy it takes to reduce. Second, water molecules are also absorbed very near to where the carbon dioxide molecules are absorbed.

"In order to make fuel, you don't simply need
80 to have carbon dioxide to be reduced; you need to have water to be oxidized," Rajh said. "Also,

*See Page 171 for the citation for this text.

CONTINUE ➡

absorption conformation in photocatalysis is extremely important—if you have one molecule of carbon dioxide absorbed in one way, it might be
85 completely useless. But if it is in a bent structure, it lowers the energy to be reduced."

1

The main point of the passage is that

A) carbon dioxide is so useful as a fuel that the presence of this substance is not a global ecological dilemma.

B) selectivity in catalysts is a problem that must be addressed through new research.

C) the concentration of carbon dioxide in the atmosphere is contributing to climate change.

D) a novel photocatalyst shows promise in addressing a global environmental concern.

2

Which of the following best supports the notion that the negativity of the conduction band is directly related to reducing carbon dioxide in the atmosphere?

A) Lines 19-22 ("After . . . water")

B) Lines 23-28 ("This photocatalyst . . . the study")

C) Lines 29-32 ("Previous . . . methane")

D) Lines 33-35 ("The lack . . . explained")

3

As used in line 34, "segregate" most nearly means

A) isolate.

B) stigmatize.

C) discern.

D) differentiate.

4

The passage states that cuprous oxide is a better catalyst than titanium dioxide for reducing carbon dioxide for all of the following reasons EXCEPT that

A) it decreases the amount of energy needed.

B) it is less expensive.

C) it has a more negative conduction band.

D) it absorbs water near carbon dioxide.

5

According to the passage, stable molecules are NOT

A) abundant.

B) sustainable.

C) energy-rich.

D) liquid-based.

6

Which choice provides the best evidence for the answer to the previous question?

A) Lines 4-8 ("Recently . . . production")

B) Lines 13-15 ("A liquid . . . energy needs")

C) Lines 36-37 ("Carbon dioxide . . . everything")

D) Lines 38-40 ("so the question . . . Rajh said")

7

As used in line 69, "driving" most nearly means

A) transporting.

B) blocking.

C) inspiring.

D) catalyzing.

CONTINUE

Figure 1: Concentration of Carbon Dioxide in Earth's Atmosphere

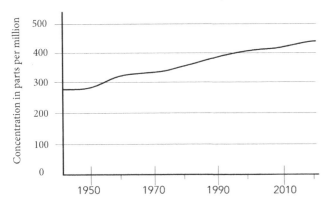

Figure 2: Sources of Carbon Dioxide in Earth's Atmosphere (2020)

Human-Produced

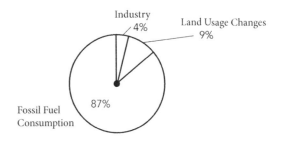

Natural

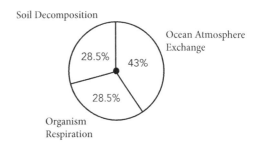

8

The purpose of lines 79-81 ("In order . . . Rajh said") is to

A) explain the content of a previous sentence.

B) define a term.

C) refute a contention.

D) question claims present in the sentence that follows.

9

On the basis of figure 2, it can be reasonably concluded that most of the carbon dioxide in the atmosphere

A) comes directly from the burning of fossil fuels.

B) was already present in some form before 1950.

C) is not the direct result of natural causes.

D) cannot be traced to human land usage change.

10

Which choice properly pairs a claim from the passage with the figure that supports this claim?

A) Lines 1-2 ("The concentration . . . increasing"); figure 1

B) Lines 1-2 ("The concentration . . . increasing"); figure 2

C) Lines 2-4 ("many . . . environment"); figure 1

D) Lines 2-4 ("many . . . environment"); figure 2

CONTINUE ➡

Reading 26

Questions 1-10 are based on the following passage and supplementary material.

This passage is adapted from Marlene Cimons, "Researcher studies unsolved problem of interacting objects," an article published* in 2014 by the National Science Foundation.

One of science's biggest puzzles is figuring out how interacting objects behave collectively. Take water, for example. "It's a molecule, but it's also a liquid with specific properties," says Daniel Sheehy, an assistant professor of physics at Louisiana State University. "How does the liquid come from the microscopic action of these water molecules?"

Sheehy doesn't study water, but he likes to use it to describe what he does study, which is many-particle quantum mechanics, that is, how atoms organize themselves at very low temperatures when they become trapped in beams of laser light, and whether they reach a superfluid state, a phenomenon that occurs only when it is extremely cold.

In a superconductor, the electrons form a superfluid which "is like a liquid, but better," Sheehy says. "It never slows down and the electrical resistance is zero, meaning none of the energy is lost." The down side, however, is that this requires very cold temperatures to achieve, on the order of 10 kelvins (minus 263 C, minus 442 F), for conventional superconductors, which is why they generally only are used in special applications, such as in MRI machines, where they are kept cold with liquid helium.

"This is why they are not used in power lines," he says. "You would need refrigerators, which isn't very practical."

Sheehy's goal is to gain further insights that could enable more widespread uses for superconducting materials. "Might it be possible to make material that is a superconductor at ambient temperatures?" he asks. "No one knows. It is a very difficult goal, a very big goal. But

we would like to use superconductors in places where they are not used now." He is performing theoretical calculations regarding clouds of extremely cold atoms—imagine very dilute particles of gases trapped in a laser field—to see how they behave and whether they show superconducting properties. "All I want to know is if I put a million atoms in a small region and watch them interact, what can they do?" he says.

Sheehy is examining the activities of different alkali gases—those in the first column of the Periodic Table—because "they have only one outermost electron, making them easier to control," he says. "First, let's understand the simplest system we can think of so we can develop the theory. Let's fundamentally understand nature and this unsolved problem of interacting objects." He does not conduct actual physical experiments, but is a theorist "who uses a computer, as well as paper and pencil calculations," to determine the properties of these clouds of atoms. "I am interested in the superfluid states of these atoms, which is where the particles don't have any viscosity; they flow without resistance," he says.

Sheehy is conducting his research under a National Science Foundation (NSF) Faculty Early Career Development (CAREER) award, which he received in 2012. The award supports junior faculty who exemplify the role of teacher-scholars through outstanding research, excellent education, and the integration of education and research within the context of the mission of their organization. NSF is funding his work with $428,200 over five years. The grant's educational component includes developing more interactive materials in large-size physics classes so that students go beyond the "lecture" format, "with more hands-on activities that get them thinking," he says. "We will be trying to use Internet applications with certain computer programs that demonstrate the principles of quantum mechanics. This, hopefully, will get them to better learn physics, and get them excited about a future in science." He also plans an outreach project to the public, and to high school and middle school

*See Page 171 for the citation for this text.

CONTINUE ▶

students, including an in-school demonstration program aimed at inspiring the interest of minority
85 students in science, and in pursuing science careers.

"The field of cold atoms is growing rapidly, fueled by numerous recent experimental breakthroughs, making it an ideal area for
90 students to work in," he says. "We're working on fundamental problems that are conceptually simple but yet still intellectually stimulating and experimentally relevant."

1

The purpose of the discussion in lines 3-8 (Take . . . molecules?") is to

A) provide a contrast to the prior sentence.

B) set forth an analogy for Sheehy's area of study.

C) offer an example of one of Sheehy's experiments.

D) establish Sheehy's research credentials.

2

As used in line 7, "action" most nearly means

A) properties.

B) steps.

C) responses.

D) energy.

3

According to the passage, the energy loss of non-superconductors can be attributed to

A) valence electrons.

B) very low temperatures.

C) electrical resistance.

D) liquid flow.

4

Which choice provides the best evidence for the answer to the previous question?

A) Lines 14-16 ("and whether . . . cold")

B) Lines 17-18 ("In a . . . but better")

C) Lines 19-21 ("the electrical . . . is lost")

D) Lines 46-49 ("Sheehy . . . electron")

5

According to the passage, Sheehy's goal is to

A) develop a viable way to employ water as a superconductor.

B) transition from mathematical models to physical experiments.

C) learn more about superconductors that are currently in use.

D) create superconductors that could be deployed more broadly than those in use today.

6

As used in line 35, "ambient" most nearly means

A) incidental.

B) pervasive.

C) controlled.

D) moderate.

CONTINUE

Part 2: Science, Single

7

Which of the following choices best supports the notion that Sheehy is working on more interactive methods to teach physics?

A) Lines 71-76 ("The grant's . . . he says")

B) Lines 76-78 ("We will . . . mechanics")

C) Lines 79-81 ("This, hopefully . . . science")

D) Lines 90-93 ("We're working . . . relevant")

8

The tone of the last paragraph (lines 87-93) can best be described as

A) hesitant.

B) optimistic.

C) ambivalent.

D) curious.

9

Which of the superconductors represented in the graph could fit the passage's definition of a superfluid?

A) Superconductor 1 only

B) Superconductor 2 only

C) Both superconductor 1 and superconductor 2

D) Neither superconductor 1 nor superconductor 2

10

One similarity between the graph and the commentary from Daniel Sheehy is that both address

A) water as a standard for evaluating other substances.

B) helium as a means of creating artificially low temperatures.

C) the practical applications of different types of superconductors.

D) the composition of superconductors at an atomic level.

Fluid Properties of Three Substances, Varying Temperatures

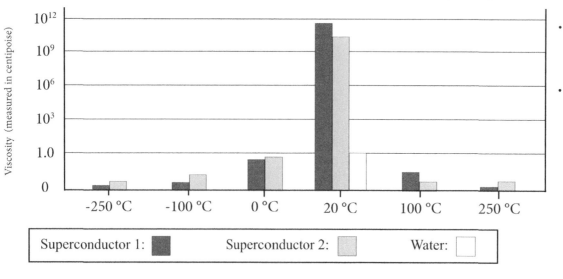

- Higher centipoise quantities indicate lower fluidity for a given substance

- Water freezes at 0 °C and evaporates at 100 °C (so that viscosities for water cannot be measured under 0 °C or above 100 °C)

CONTINUE

Reading 27

Questions 1-10 are based on the following passage and supplementary material.

This passage is adapted from Ed Yong, "The Mosquito Breeder," an article originally published by Mosaic in 2014.

The worst thing about feeding hundreds of mosquitoes on your own blood is not the itching—if you do it enough times, your body gets
Line used to the bites. It's not even the pain, although
5 it is always painful since the mosquitoes will use their snouts to root about your flesh in search of a blood vessel.

It is more that, sometimes, the little suckers take their time.

10 "They just walk around on your arm. You're sitting there and thinking, 'Seriously? I have things to do'," says Chiara Andolina.

Andolina is an infectious disease researcher who works at the Shoklo Malaria Research
15 Unit, a world-renowned laboratory nestled in an unassuming town near the Thai-Myanmar border. She runs the Unit's insectory, where mosquitoes are bred, reared, infected with the Plasmodium parasites that cause malaria, and dissected.
20 There are only five or six such facilities in Thailand, largely because the malarial mosquitoes of South-east Asia are delicate, wilting flowers. In Africa, malaria is transmitted by Anopheles gambiae—hardy insects with catholic tastes.
25 They will go without food for days. They will endure through tough environmental conditions. They will suck blood from rabbits, cows— basically anything that they can get their probosces into.
30 Their Asian cousins, Anopheles dirus, are very different. "You blow on them a little bit and they're like: 'No. I'm not mating today. I'm upset.'" They also refuse to eat anything except human blood, which is why Andolina has to feed
35 them herself.

She does this simply by sticking her arm through a muslin sock and into their cages. It takes half an hour and she does it every four days. "They're very spoiled," she says.

40 Andolina fed around 600 mosquitoes yesterday and you wouldn't be able to tell—her arm is free of any marks because she has built up resistance to the allergens in the mosquito saliva. Her boss, François Nosten, had to fill in for her two weeks
45 ago and his arm is still covered in welts. This is why there is no feeding rota. It's just Andolina. She has tried to convince her research assistants to help but, for some strange reason, they aren't keen.

50 The boxes contain two closely related species of mosquito: Anopheles dirus B and C. The two colonies have to be kept apart. If someone mixes them by mistake, it would be nigh impossible to fix the error. B and C look identical, even under
55 the microscope, and only their genes reveal them to be distinct species. They also transmit very different malarial parasites: B carries Plasmodium falciparum, the main cause of malaria in these parts, while C transmits P. vivax. Andolina once
60 spent a few years on an experiment that just wouldn't work, because she was trying to infect one of the species with the wrong parasite.

Only female mosquitoes drink blood, and they use proteins in their meals to make the shells of
65 their eggs. But they also need mating partners, and A. dirus are as finicky about sex as they are about food. Andolina used to have to force-mate them. . . . It takes another two weeks for them to turn into adults. Now, they're ready for experiments.
70 Typically, this involves infecting them with malaria.

Andolina loads a feeding pump with blood samples from people with malaria. The pump delivers the blood into a grey cylinder, with a
75 membrane stretched across it. She places this on top of a sheet of muslin, draped over an empty noodle cup containing dozens of mosquitoes. The cylinder is like an upside-down feeding trough. The mosquitoes dangle upside-down from the
80 muslin, pierce the adjacent membrane, and suck up the blood.

Once they are infected, security is paramount. The law dictates that there must be four doors

CONTINUE ▶

between them and the outside world, so they're
85 kept inside an incubator within one of three
adjoining rooms. Andolina counts them every day
to make sure that none have escaped. If she ever
misses one—and that hasn't happened yet—she
won't be allowed to leave the lab until she has
90 found and killed it.

"I don't do it because I love mosquitoes," says
Andolina. Her work creates a ready supply of
parasites. She provides these to collaborators in
Paris and Singapore, who are trying to develop
95 new drugs that target malarial parasites holding
out in a patient's liver.

1

What bothers Andolina the most about her mosquito
research is

A) the pain of getting bitten by mosquitoes.

B) the itching that results from the mosquito bites.

C) the time that it takes to feed the mosquitoes.

D) the fear of catching malaria.

2

As explained in the passage, only female mosquitoes
drink blood because

A) they use blood proteins to feed their young.

B) they use blood proteins to generate their eggs.

C) the malarial parasite only infects male
mosquitoes.

D) female larvae use the blood to mature into adults.

3

According to the passage, the goal of Andolina's
work is to

A) breed mosquitoes that do not harbor Plasmodium.

B) find a way to desensitize people to mosquito
allergens.

C) find ways to better contain infected mosquitoes.

D) generate Plasmodium for other researchers.

Mosquito Species and Malaria Transmission

Species	Geographic Range	Human	Pig	Cow	Rabbit
A	Throughout Asia, eastern Europe	Yes	No	No	No
B	North America, western Europe	Yes	Yes	No	No
C	Southeast Asia, various Pacific islands	No	Yes	Yes	No
D	Throughout Africa, southern Europe	Yes	Yes	Yes	Yes

Blood sources accepted by each mosquito species

4

Which choice provides the best evidence for the answer to the previous question?

A) Lines 43-45 ("Her boss . . . in welts")

B) Lines 52-54 ("If someone . . . error")

C) Lines 82-86 ("Once they . . . rooms")

D) Lines 92-96 ("Her work . . . liver")

5

As used in line 24, "catholic" most nearly means

A) religious.

B) wide-ranging.

C) strict.

D) eclectic.

6

The purpose of lines 43-45 ("Her . . . welts") is to

A) contrast Andolina's experience of getting bitten with that of someone who is not resistant to the mosquitoes' allergens.

B) elicit sympathy from the reader.

C) illustrate the negative effects that mosquitoes have on humans and emphasize the need to overcome these effects with research.

D) defend the research facility's decision not to use a feeding rota.

7

As used in line 48, the word "strange" conveys

A) humor.

B) fear.

C) ridicule.

D) distrust.

8

Which of the following choices offers the best support for the statement in lines 54-56 ("B and C . . . distinct species")?

A) Lines 20-22 ("There . . . flowers")

B) Lines 50-52 ("The boxes . . . kept apart")

C) Lines 56-59 ("They . . . P. vivax")

D) Lines 59-62 ("Andolina . . . wrong parasite")

9

Which of the mosquitoes represented in the table would one expect to find near a farm in California?

A) Mosquito A

B) Mosquito B

C) Mosquito C

D) Mosquito D

10

On the basis of the table, which mosquitoes are most likely Anopheles gambiae and Anopheles dirus, respectively?

A) Mosquito A; Mosquito D

B) Mosquito D; Mosquito A

C) Mosquito C; Mosquito D

D) Mosquito D; Mosquito C

CONTINUE

Reading 28

Questions 1-10 are based on the following passage and supplementary material.

This passage is adapted from "Variants in Three Genes Account for Most Dog Coat Differences," a 2009 news release* from the National Institutes of Health.

Variants in just three genes acting in different combinations account for the wide range of coat textures seen in dogs—from the poodle's tight
Line curls to the beagle's stick-straight fur. A team led
5 by researchers from the National Human Genome Research Institute (NHGRI), part of the National Institutes of Health, reports these findings today in the advance online issue of the journal *Science*. "This study is an elegant example of using
10 genomic techniques to unravel the genetic basis of biological diversity," said NHGRI Scientific Director Eric Green, M.D., Ph.D. "Genomics continues to gain new insights from the amazing morphological differences seen across the canine
15 species, including many that give clues about human biology and disease."

Until now, relatively little was known about the genes influencing the length, growth pattern, and texture of the coats of dogs. The researchers
20 performed a genome-wide scan of specific signposts of DNA variation, called single-nucleotide polymorphisms, in 1,000 individual dogs representing 80 breeds. These data were compared with descriptions of various coat types.
25 Three distinct genetic variants emerged to explain, in combination, virtually all dog hair types.

"What's important for human health is the way we found the genes involved in dog coats and figured out how they work together, rather than
30 the genes themselves," said Elaine A. Ostrander, Ph.D., chief of the Cancer Genetics Branch in NHGRI's Division of Intramural Research. "We think this approach will help to pinpoint multiple genes involved in complex human conditions,
35 such as cancer, heart disease, diabetes and obesity."

Artificial selection, at the heart of breeding for desirable traits in domesticated animals, has yielded rapid change in a short span of canine
40 history. While researchers estimate that modern dog breeds diverged from wolves some 15,000 years ago, the genetic changes in the dog genome that create multiple coat types are more likely to have been pursued by breeders in just the past
45 200 years. In fact, short-haired breeds, such as the beagle, display the original, more wolf-like versions of the three genes identified in the study.

Modern dog breeds are part of a unique population structure, having been selectively
50 bred for many years. Based on this structure, the researchers were able to break down a complex phenotype—coat—into possible genetic variations. "When we put these genetic variants back together in different combinations, we found
55 that we could create most of the coat varieties seen in what is among the most diverse species in the world—the dog," Dr. Ostrander said. "If we can decipher the genetic basis for a complex trait such as the dog's coat, we believe that we can do
60 it as well with complex diseases."

Specifically, the researchers found an alteration in the RSPO2 gene that results in wiry hair that grows in a pattern that gives the dogs a mustachioed look with long details
65 called furnishings. Examples of dog breeds with wiry coats are Scottish terrier, Irish terriers, and schnauzers. Long hair that is silky or fluffy was linked to a variant in the FGF5 gene. Cocker spaniels, Pomeranians, and long-haired
70 Chihuahuas are examples of dogs with long coats. A variant in the KRT71 gene produces curly coated dogs, such as the Irish water spaniel. Finally, if all three variants are present, a dog has a long and curly coat with furnishings. Examples
75 of this type of breed include poodles and Portuguese water dogs.

"We don't yet know the precise roles, if any, of these three genes in the variety of hair textures seen among humans," Dr. Ostrander said. The
80 FGF5 (long hair) gene and KRT71 (curly hair) gene have been found to affect hair in mice and cats in addition to dogs, so humans may be

---

*See Page 171 for the citation for this text.

CONTINUE

included as well. The RSPO2 gene has not been previously identified to influence hair texture in
85 mammals, but it does belong to a pathway that has been associated with a coarse hair type found in some people of East Asian ancestry.

The study's lead author, Edouard Cadieu, a graduate student in NHGRI's Cancer Genetics
90 Branch, added, "The carefully controlled breeding of dogs offers advantages in pinpointing the genes that determine particular traits, which may have immediate application to the study of diseases, like cancer, that are common to both dogs and
95 humans."

1

As used in line 2, "range" most nearly means

A) size.

B) diversity.

C) selection.

D) field.

2

Which of the following choices best supports the notion that genetic variation is correlated with phenotype variation in dogs?

A) Lines 19-22 ("The researchers . . . polymorphisms")

B) Lines 23-24 ("These data . . . coat types")

C) Lines 50-53 ("Based on . . . variations")

D) Lines 73-75 ("Examples . . . water dogs")

3

Which of the following, as related to dogs, was NOT studied by the researchers described in the passage?

A) Coat color

B) Coat texture

C) Coat length

D) Coat growth pattern

4

According to the passage, complex human diseases

A) can be addressed with genetically-derived vaccines.

B) have been accelerated by artificial breeding of animal species.

C) originated in dogs and canine ancestors.

D) involve multiple genes.

5

Which choice provides the best evidence for the answer to the previous question?

A) Lines 13-16 ("Genomics . . . disease")

B) Lines 27-30 ("What's . . . themselves")

C) Lines 37-40 ("Artificial . . . history")

D) Lines 90-95 ("The carefully . . . humans")

6

The seventh paragraph (lines 77-87) functions to

A) imply that RSPO2 doesn't affect human hair.

B) explore geographic differences among humans.

C) show the evolutionary relationships between humans, dogs, cats, and mice.

D) explain the relationship between animal fur genetics and human hair genetics.

CONTINUE

DNA Profiles of Different Organisms

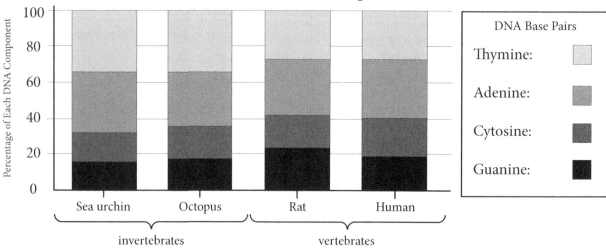

7

According to the passage, a potential application of the research regarding coat phenotypes is a better understanding of

A) how to increase the average lifespan of dogs.

B) selective breeding of dogs.

C) complex diseases in humans.

D) how to alter dogs' coats.

8

As used in line 92, "determine" most nearly means

A) discover.

B) conclude.

C) produce.

D) calculate.

9

Which of the following conclusions CANNOT be drawn from the information in the graph?

A) Thymine constitutes a smaller portion of human DNA than it does of octopus DNA.

B) Guanine constitutes a greater portion of rat DNA than it does of human DNA.

C) Thymine and adenine are more abundant than cytosine and guanine in the DNA profiles of some vertebrates.

D) Most vertebrates have DNA profiles that are comprised mostly of thymine and adenine.

10

Which choice best describes the graph as it relates to the passage as a whole?

A) The graph offers additional information about the basic composition of DNA.

B) The graph portrays the composition of DNA in a more simplistic manner than the passage does.

C) The graph challenges a central assumption made by the researchers described in the passage.

D) The graph indicates the roles of genes that are briefly mentioned in the passage.

CONTINUE ➡

Reading 29

Questions 1-10 are based on the following passage and supplementary material.

This passage is adapted from Andrew Good and Alana Johnson, "Global Storms on Mars Launch Dust Towers Into the Sky," an article published* in 2019 by NASA.

Dust storms are common on Mars. But every decade or so, something unpredictable happens: a series of runaway storms breaks out, covering the entire planet in a dusty haze.

Line

5   Last year, a fleet of NASA spacecraft got a detailed look at the life cycle of the 2018 global dust storm that ended the Opportunity rover's mission. And while scientists are still puzzling over the data, two papers recently shed new light

10   on a phenomenon observed within the storm: dust towers, or concentrated clouds of dust that warm in sunlight and rise high into the air. Scientists think that dust-trapped water vapor may be riding them like an elevator to space, where solar

15   radiation breaks apart their molecules. This might help explain how Mars' water disappeared over billions of years.

      Dust towers are massive, churning clouds that are denser and climb much higher than the normal

20   background dust in the thin Martian atmosphere. While they also occur under normal conditions, the towers appear to form in greater numbers during global storms. A tower starts at the planet's surface as an area of rapidly lifted dust about

25   as wide as the state of Rhode Island. By the time a tower reaches a height of 50 miles (80 kilometers), as seen during the 2018 global dust storm, it may be as wide as Nevada. As the tower decays, it can form a layer of dust 35 miles (56

30   kilometers) above the surface that can be wider than the continental United States.

      The recent findings on dust towers come courtesy of NASA's Mars Reconnaissance Orbiter (MRO), which is led by the agency's Jet

35   Propulsion Laboratory in Pasadena, California. Though global dust storms cloak the planet's

surface, MRO can use its heat-sensing Mars Climate Sounder instrument to peer through the haze. The instrument is designed specifically

40   for measuring dust levels. Its data, coupled with images from a camera aboard the orbiter called the Mars Context Imager (MARCI), enabled scientists to detect numerous swelling dust towers.

      Dust towers appear throughout the Martian

45   year, but MRO observed something different during the 2018 global dust storm. "Normally the dust would fall down in a day or so," said the paper's lead author, Nicholas Heavens of Hampton University in Hampton, Virginia. "But

50   during a global storm, dust towers are renewed continuously for weeks." In some cases, multiple towers were seen for as long as 3.5 weeks.

      The rate of dust activity surprised Heavens and other scientists. But especially intriguing

55   is the possibility that dust towers act as "space elevators" for other material, transporting matter through the atmosphere. When airborne dust heats up, it creates updrafts that carry gases along with it, including the small quantity of water vapor

60   sometimes seen as wispy clouds on Mars.

      A previous paper led by Heavens showed that during a 2007 global dust storm on Mars, water molecules were lofted into the upper atmosphere, where solar radiation could break them down into

65   particles that escape into space. That might be a clue to how the Red Planet lost its lakes and rivers over billions of years, becoming the freezing desert it is today.

      Scientists can't say with certainty what causes

70   global dust storms; they've studied fewer than a dozen to date. "Global dust storms are really unusual," said Mars Climate Sounder scientist David Kass of JPL. "We really don't have anything like this on the Earth, where the entire

75   planet's weather changes for several months."

      With time and more data, the MRO team hopes to better understand the dust towers created within global storms and what role they may play in removing water from the Red Planet's

80   atmosphere.

---

*See Page 171 for the citation for this text.

CONTINUE ➡

Part 2: Science, Single

1

The main purpose of the passage is to

A) cite deficiencies in an experiment that was at one point thought to be definitive.

B) present competing accounts of how dust towers form on Mars in order to refute a common misconception.

C) describe how scientists have examined but not fully elucidated the properties of dust towers on Mars.

D) question the utility of technological advancement in garnering new knowledge about the solar system.

2

Under what conditions would researchers typically expect to observe dust towers on Mars?

A) Year-round, under both normal circumstances and during large dust storms

B) Year-round, only during large dust storms

C) Only in select seasons, under both normal circumstances and during large dust storms

D) Only in select seasons, only during large dust storms

3

In lines 23-31, the authors' references to the geography of the United States serve to

A) suggest how long a typical dust tower will last before it decays.

B) underscore the fact that dust towers are prominent on Mars but not unique to this planet.

C) clarify ideas about a few different stages of dust tower formation.

D) explain how the dust tower models developed in 2018 departed from earlier simulations.

4

As used in line 36, "cloak" most nearly means

A) excuse.

B) exaggerate.

C) embellish.

D) envelop.

5

Which of the following assumptions about the history of Mars is present in the passage?

A) Mars was at one point home to substantial bodies of water that eventually disappeared.

B) The basic properties of the geography of Mars were misunderstood before the MRO was deployed.

C) Mars featured conditions necessary to sustain simple lifeforms at some point in the distant past.

D) The duration and intensity of dust towers on Mars have both increased as the composition of the planet's surface has changed.

6

Which choice provides the best evidence for the answer to the previous question?

A) Lines 36-39 ("Though . . . haze")

B) Lines 44-46 ("Dust . . . storm")

C) Lines 54-57 ("But . . . atmosphere")

D) Lines 65-67 ("That . . . today")

CONTINUE

Part 2: Science, Single

Possible Heights and Widths of a Dust Tower on Mars

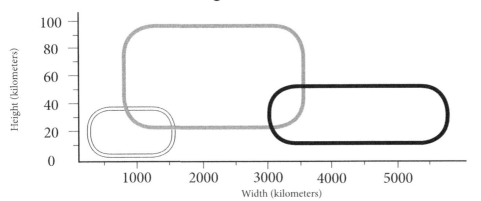

On the basis of the passage, scientists interested in studying dust storms on Mars would NOT have an evident use for

A) space probe images that could lead to a definitive explanation of how global dust storms arise on Mars.

B) a simulation that accurately indicates whether dust towers act as "space elevators."

C) a computer-based model that would predict the size of a global dust storm on Earth.

D) new data that suggest how Martian waterways disappeared.

Which choice provides the best evidence for the answer to the previous question?

A) Lines 61-65 ("A previous . . . space")

B) Lines 69-71 ("Scientists . . . date")

C) Lines 71-75 ("Global . . . months")

D) Lines 76-80 ("With . . . atmosphere")

9

It can be reasonably concluded from the information in the graph that dust towers on Mars

A) are most stable during their middle stages.

B) do not reach heights of over 100 kilometers.

C) expand rapidly and contract slowly.

D) do not change in height for the duration of a given dust storm.

Researchers discover a dust tower on Mars that is 30 kilometers high. Which of the following statements is best supported by the information in the graph and the passage?

A) The dust tower is part of an early-stage storm.

B) The dust tower is part of a middle-stage storm.

C) The dust tower is part of a late-stage storm.

D) The researchers cannot draw a conclusion without more data about the duration of the storm.

CONTINUE

Reading 30

Questions 1-10 are based on the following passage and supplementary material.

This passage is an excerpt from Jason Dorrier, "Robotic Exoskeletons, Like This One, Are Getting More Practical," an article originally published* by SinguarityHub in 2019.

When you imagine an exoskeleton, chances are it might look a bit like the Guardian XO from Sarcos Robotics. The XO is literally a robot you
Line wear (or maybe, it wears you). The suit's powered
5 limbs sense your movements and match their position to yours with little latency to give you effortless superstrength and endurance—so that lifting 200 pounds will feel like lifting 10.

A vision of robots and humankind working
10 together in harmony. Now, isn't that nice?

Of course, there isn't anything terribly novel about an exoskeleton. We've seen plenty of concepts and demonstrations in the last decade. These include light exoskeletons tailored to
15 industrial settings—some of which are being tested out by the likes of Honda—and healthcare exoskeletons that support the elderly or folks with disabilities. Full-body powered robotic exoskeletons are a bit rarer, which makes the
20 Sarcos suit pretty cool to look at. But like all things in robotics, practicality matters as much as vision. It's worth asking: Will anyone buy and use the thing? Is it more than a concept video?

Sarcos thinks so, and they're excited about it.
25 "If you were to ask the question, what does 30 years and $300 million look like," Sarcos CEO Ben Wolff told IEEE Spectrum, "you're going to see it downstairs."

The XO appears to check a few key boxes.
30 For one, it's user friendly. According to Sarcos, it only takes a few minutes for the uninitiated to strap in and get up to speed. Feeling comfortable doing work with the suit takes a few hours. This is thanks to a high degree of sensor-based
35 automation that allows the robot to seamlessly match its user's movements.

The XO can also operate for more than a few minutes. It has two hours of battery life, and with spares on hand, it can go all day. The batteries are
40 hot-swappable, meaning you can replace a drained battery with a new one without shutting the system down. The suit is aimed at manufacturing, where workers are regularly moving heavy stuff around. Additionally, Wolff told CNET, the suit
45 could see military use. But that doesn't mean *Avatar*-style combat. The XO, Wolff said, is primarily about logistics (lifting and moving heavy loads) and isn't designed to be armored, so it won't likely see the front lines.
50 The system will set customers back $100,000 a year to rent, which sounds like a lot, but for industrial or military purposes, the six-figure rental may not deter would-be customers if the suit proves itself a useful bit of equipment. (And
55 it's reasonable to imagine the price coming down as the technology becomes more commonplace and competitors arrive.)

Sarcos got into exoskeletons a couple decades ago and was originally funded by the military (like
60 many robotics endeavors). Videos hit YouTube as long ago as 2008, but after announcing that the company was taking orders for the XO earlier this year, Sarcos says they'll deliver the first alpha units in January, which is a notable milestone.
65 Broadly, robotics has advanced a lot in recent years. YouTube sensations like Boston Dynamics have regularly earned millions of views (and, inevitably, headlines stoking robot fear). They went from tethered treadmill sessions
70 to untethered backflips off boxes. While today's robots really are vastly superior to their ancestors, they've struggled to prove themselves useful. A counterpoint to flashy YouTube videos, the DARPA Robotics Challenge gave birth to another
75 meme altogether. Robots falling over. Often and awkwardly.

This year marks some of the first commercial fruits of a few decades' research. Boston Dynamics recently started offering its robot dog,
80 Spot, to select customers in 2019. Whether this proves to be a headline-worthy flash in the pan or something sustainable remains to be seen.

---

*See Page 171 for the citation for this text.

CONTINUE ➡

But between robots with more autonomy and exoskeletons like the XO, the exoskeleton variety
85 will likely be easier to make more practical for various uses.

Whereas autonomous robots require highly advanced automation to navigate uncertain and ever-changing conditions—automation which,
90 at the moment, remains largely elusive (though the likes of Google are pairing the latest AI with robots to tackle the problem)—an exoskeleton mainly requires physical automation. The really hard bits, like navigating and recognizing and
95 interacting with objects, are outsourced to its human operator.

1

A central idea of the passage is that

A) technological advancement is not self-justifying and that inventions must be useful.

B) robots in their current form are not cost-effective or susceptible to mass production.

C) the military is an important source of funding for robotics development.

D) exoskeleton robots are superior to autonomous robots in addressing utilitarian tasks.

2

The tone of lines 9-10 ("A vision . . . that nice?") can best be described as

A) hopeful.

B) sarcastic.

C) fearful.

D) relieved.

3

As used in line 11, "terribly" most nearly means

A) sadly.

B) dangerously.

C) oddly.

D) particularly.

CONTINUE

4

The passage suggests that exoskeleton robots have the potential to

A) perform heavy lifting less expensively than an unaided workforce could.

B) injure the workers who are wearing them.

C) replace human workers because robots are cheaper than human labor.

D) incorporate artificial intelligence.

5

Which choice provides the best evidence for the answer to the previous question?

A) Lines 34-36 ("This is . . . movements")

B) Lines 37-39 ("The XO . . . all day")

C) Lines 50-54 ("The system . . . equipment")

D) Lines 87-93 ("Whereas . . . automation")

6

According to the passage, a difference between autonomous robots and exoskeleton robots is that

A) autonomous robots are more expensive than exoskeleton robots are.

B) autonomous robots can identify objects, while exoskeleton robots cannot.

C) autonomous robots can be used in changing environments, while exoskeleton robots cannot.

D) autonomous robots have been around for longer than exoskeleton robots have.

7

Which of the following choices best supports the notion that robots have wide-ranging applications?

A) Lines 4-8 ("The suit's . . . like 10")

B) Lines 14-18 ("These . . . disabilities")

C) Lines 30-32 ("For one . . . to speed")

D) Lines 58-59 ("Sarcos got . . . the military")

8

As used in line 78, "fruits" most nearly means

A) produce.

B) profits.

C) descendants.

D) results.

CONTINUE

Properties of Various Exoskeletons

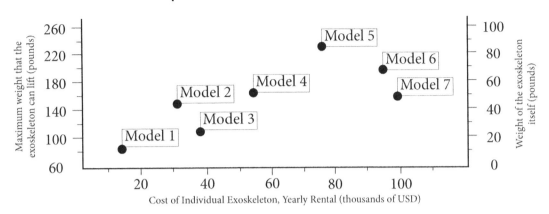

9

A construction company wants to buy an exoskeleton that can lift 150 pounds but that does not cost more than $70,000. Which model, on the basis of the graph, would be most appropriate for the company?

A) Model 3

B) Model 4

C) Model 5

D) Model 6

10

On the basis of the information presented in the graph, the exoskeleton described in the first paragraph of the passage could be

A) Model 2.

B) Model 3.

C) Model 4.

D) Model 5.

STOP
If you have finished this section, consult the relevant answers and explanations.
Do not turn to any other section.

Answer Key
Part 2: Science, Single

Reading 16
1. C
2. A
3. C
4. B
5. D
6. C
7. B
8. A
9. D
10. B

Reading 17
1. D
2. A
3. C
4. A
5. C
6. B
7. B
8. D
9. C
10. B

Reading 18
1. A
2. A
3. B
4. C
5. D
6. D
7. C
8. A
9. A
10. D

Reading 19
1. D
2. C
3. C
4. A
5. A
6. D
7. C
8. B
9. D
10. B

Reading 20
1. C
2. B
3. B
4. C
5. D
6. A
7. A
8. A
9. C
10. A

Reading 21
1. A
2. B
3. A
4. A
5. C
6. A
7. B
8. C
9. B
10. D

Reading 22
1. C
2. D
3. A
4. C
5. A
6. B
7. C
8. B
9. D
10. B

Reading 23
1. C
2. D
3. B
4. D
5. A
6. C
7. B
8. C
9. D
10. C

Reading 24
1. B
2. D
3. C
4. A
5. D
6. A
7. C
8. C
9. D
10. C

Reading 25
1. D
2. B
3. A
4. B
5. C
6. C
7. D
8. A
9. D
10. A

Reading 26		Reading 27		Reading 28		Reading 29		Reading 30	
1.	B	1.	C	1.	B	1.	C	1.	A
2.	A	2.	B	2.	B	2.	A	2.	B
3.	C	3.	D	3.	A	3.	C	3.	D
4.	C	4.	D	4.	D	4.	D	4.	A
5.	D	5.	B	5.	B	5.	A	5.	C
6.	D	6.	A	6.	D	6.	D	6.	B
7.	A	7.	A	7.	C	7.	C	7.	B
8.	B	8.	D	8.	C	8.	C	8.	D
9.	C	9.	B	9.	D	9.	B	9.	B
10.	A	10.	B	10.	A	10.	D	10.	D

Answer Explanations

Passage 16, Pages 92-94

1. C is the correct answer.

The passage states that "a handful of research groups are exploring if treatments based on umbilical cord blood could provide a temporary lifeline in the immediate aftermath of an accidental or deliberate release of radiation" (lines 15-19) and then goes on to provide more detailed explanations of some of this research. Choose C to reflect this content. A and B can be eliminated since the passage explicitly engages with the idea that cord blood cells can be beneficial in the case of radiation exposure, and since the focus of the passage is on one possible response to radiation, NOT on providing information about the dangers of radiation overall. D can also be eliminated since the importance of prevention is stressed at the end of the passage, but is NOT one of the central ideas articulated throughout (since the passage also has an emphasis on recent research).

2. A is the correct answer.

The passage begins with the author describing the potential health risks associated with an accidental or deliberate release of radiation and then moves to describe the debate about whether or not cord blood cells could be helpful for individuals who have been exposed to radiation. Choose A to reflect this content. B can be eliminated because there is no current existing health crisis around radiation exposure, (despite the past catastrophic events mentioned early in the passage), while C can be eliminated because the passage summarizes competing research findings but does NOT advocate for collaboration between scientists and politicians (since debate among scientists remains the main focus). D can be eliminated because, while different schools of thought are addressed in the passage, the passage concludes by emphasizing the need for prevention (NOT the need for consensus) and often presents different quotations without strong bias.

3. <u>C</u> is the correct answer.

Lines 22-24 state that "Around 30 people died from [acute radiation syndrome] in the first few months after the Chernobyl meltdown in 1986." This content cites a specific example of an instance when radiation exposure has had adverse health effects; choose C as appropriate. A describes a POTENTIAL military threat, while B identifies a site where radiation levels were found to be high. D identifies one specific way in which radiation damages human bodies. None of these other answers identifies a specific situation in which radiation exposure is known to have caused adverse health effects (despite raising hypotheticals or possibilities in some cases), and therefore they should all be eliminated.

4. <u>B</u> is the correct answer.

In line 39, "bounces back" refers to how bone marrow will eventually return to normal function. Choose B to reflect this meaning. A (inappropriately implying something becoming apparent after a period of being hidden), C (inappropriately implying responding to aggression in a similarly aggressive way) and D (inappropriately implying responding with horror and disgust) all introduce improper meanings and should therefore be eliminated.

5. <u>D</u> is the correct answer.

Lines 50-53 state that "Delaney says that the work is part of a larger plan to use cord-blood-derived cells to fight a wide range of diseases, disorders, and injuries that can disrupt bone marrow's function." This content indicates that Delaney's current research is one aspect of a "larger," long-term research initiative; choose D to reflect this idea. A and B can be eliminated since Delaney's research has possible implications in the case that a catastrophe occurs but was NOT itself developed as a crisis response, and since nothing in the passage shows Delaney positioning the research as a call to action for other researchers (despite the possible utility of the research). C can be eliminated since Delaney's research is designed to develop technologies which could complement but NOT necessarily replace bone marrow transplants.

6. <u>C</u> is the correct answer.

See the previous answer explanation for analysis of the correct line reference. A describes one research project, and the topic that it is designed to explore, while B quotes an expert describing one potential implication of the research study. D quotes an expert describing some potential benefits associated with a new therapeutic strategy. None of the other answers situate Delaney's research study in the context of larger research goals (despite referencing relevant research areas generally), and therefore they should all be eliminated.

7. <u>B</u> is the correct answer.

The passage explains that "cord blood transplants don't require a close match of genetic identification tags between donor and recipient cells" (lines 44-47); choose B as the answer that properly introduces a contrast between bone marrow transplants and cord blood transplants. A and C can be eliminated since there is no evidence that cord blood can reverse pulmonary diseases (a NEW liability mentioned late in the passage); moreover, while the transplanted cord blood cells would themselves be multiplied prior to transplantation, but this feature is part of a method of production, NOT part of the advantage that they offer. D can readily be eliminated since the relative costs of bone marrow and cord blood transplants are NOT discussed in the passage, which focuses mainly on health outcomes.

8. A is the correct answer.

In lines 64 and 69, "strategy" refers to the therapeutic process developed by Delaney and her team. Choose A to reflect this meaning. B (inappropriately implying a personal inclination or tendency), C (inappropriately implying someone providing guidance or feedback to someone else), and D (inappropriately implying intelligence or wit) all introduce improper contexts and should therefore be eliminated.

9. D is the correct answer.

In lines 70-86, Gale argues that bone marrow failure has not been shown to be a frequent cause of death among individuals who have been exposed to high levels of radiation. Therefore, his claim would be contradicted by a finding that most deaths associated with radiation exposure can be linked to bone marrow damage. Choose D as appropriate. A can be eliminated since findings that pulmonary failure is a common cause of death among individuals who have not been exposed to radiation would supplement, NOT undermine, Gale's argument. B can be eliminated since this statement is mostly relevant to content (lines 44-47) that is situated BEFORE Gale's argument is introduced, and C can be eliminated since it would further support Gale's argument by indicating that pulmonary failure is a leading cause of death for individuals exposed to radiation.

10. B is the correct answer.

The final sentence of the passage pivots away from an analysis of how to treat individuals exposed to radiation and suggests an overall strategy of working to ensure that individuals are not exposed to radiation in the first place. Choose B to reflect this content. A and C can be eliminated since the notion that preventing exposure to radiation is more important than finding ways to treat it does NOT represent a focused initiative or a methodological critique; the passage indicates that both treatment and prevention are priorities. D can also be eliminated since the focus on prevention represents an important alternative perspective and a useful method, NOT a critique of any particular group.

Passage 17, Pages 95-97

1. D is the correct answer.

The passage focuses on a particular neutrino, which was first detected in September 2017 by scientists at an Antarctic research station. After the neutrino was detected, scientists "Backtracked the path through IceCube indicat[ing] where in the sky the neutrino came from" (lines 60-61), and this analysis led to confirmation of existing knowledge about blazars. Choose D to reflect this sequence of events and discovery. Be careful not to choose A or B, since scientists at the Amundsen–Scott South Pole Station did make a new discovery, but this discovery confirms rather than challenges existing theories. B is also incorrect because only one team of researchers is cited as focusing on neutrinos; the other research teams mentioned are focusing on other aspects of astronomy. C can also be eliminated since scientists study neutrinos for what they can reveal about different galaxies, NOT in order to harness them to refine particle accelerators.

2. <u>A</u> is the correct answer.

The passage describes how, after detecting the neutrino, scientists worked to find its origins and were eventually able to connect it to a type of active galaxy known as a blazar. Blazars are introduced into the passage because of this connection between their activity and the appearance of the neutrino; choose A as appropriate. B can be readily eliminated, since the focus on a specific neutrino is not as broad as the focus on Orion overall that this answer indicates, and C can be eliminated since the connection between the neutrino and the blazar is an example of multi-messenger astronomy, NOT evidence used to argue for why this field of study is important. D can also be eliminated since black holes are mentioned as a feature of blazars, but the passage does not discuss how black holes are formed.

3. <u>C</u> is the correct answer.

The first paragraph summarizes a significant new discovery: "For the first time ever, scientists . . . have found the source of a high-energy neutrino from outside our galaxy." The paragraph then goes on to establish some context for this discovery by providing details about the neutrino. Choose C to reflect this content. A can be eliminated since the first paragraph only presents a new discovery related to neutrinos and does NOT offer analysis of why neutrinos are scientifically important. B and D can also be eliminated since they refer to information which appears later in the passage but is not addressed in the first paragraph.

4. <u>A</u> is the correct answer.

In describing the study of neutrinos, the author explains that "scientists rely on gamma rays . . . to brightly flag what cosmic source is producing these neutrinos and cosmic rays" (lines 40-43). Because gamma rays can detect the source of neutrinos, and Fermi is a gamma-ray telescope, it is reasonable to assume that this relationship is why Fermi allows scientists to study neutrinos. Choose A as appropriate. B can be eliminated since nothing in the passage specifies that Fermi (though useful) is more advanced than other telescopes (which are not discussed at length). C and D can also be eliminated since Fermi can detect gravitational waves and gamma ray emissions but does NOT itself enhance or provoke these astronomical events.

5. <u>C</u> is the correct answer.

In line 13, "shy of" refers to how neutrinos travel at speeds approaching, but not quite equaling, the speed of light. Choose C to reflect this context. A (inappropriately implying fear or another emotional response), B (inappropriately implying an adopted attitude or behavior), and D (inappropriately implying tension or conflict) all introduce improper contexts and should be eliminated.

6. <u>B</u> is the correct answer.

In lines 28-30, the author states that "Neutrinos and gravitational waves deliver new kinds of information about the most extreme environments in the universe." This content indicates that the scientific value of neutrinos is linked to the information that they can provide about volatile and violent processes; choose B as the best answer. A can be eliminated since neutrinos move at slightly under the speed of light, and C can be eliminated since neutrinos may result from massive explosions but do NOT cause these explosions. D can be ruled out since the passage does not present a consistent theory of neutrinos behaving in this way; in fact, neutrinos may RESULT from black hole activity (lines 20-23).

7. <u>B</u> is the correct answer.

See the previous answer explanation for analysis of the correct line reference. A describes the history of the neutrino in the period before it was detected, while C describes how scientists worked to locate the point of origin for the neutrino. D clarifies the behavior of the blazar which appears to be linked to the newly-detected neutrino. None of these other answers clarify what types of scientific knowledge neutrinos can provide (although some refer to the discovery of neutrinos), and therefore they should all be eliminated.

8. <u>D</u> is the correct answer.

In line 14, "interact with" refers to how neutrinos rarely influence or create altered behaviors in other matter. Choose D to reflect this meaning. A (inappropriately implying a romantic or flirtatious relationship), B (inappropriately implying using language or signs to convey a message), and C (inappropriately implying a connection between two distinct entities) all introduce improper contexts and should be eliminated.

9. <u>C</u> is the correct answer.

Lines 24-26 quote an expert who explains that "Again, Fermi has helped make another giant leap in a growing field we call multimessenger astronomy." This content suggests that a specific field of scientific research (multimessenger astronomy) is growing as new discoveries allow scientists to expand their knowledge. Choose C as appropriate. A, B, and D can all be eliminated since all of these answers indicate that, for varying reasons, a scientific field is in decline, whereas the passage argues that the field of multimessenger astronomy is growing and expanding.

10. <u>B</u> is the correct answer.

See the previous answer explanation for analysis of the correct line reference. A summarizes a recent scientific breakthrough, while C explains why scientists are interested in studying neutrinos. D describes another discovery identified as scientists explored the neutrino further. None of these other answers describe the expansion of a specific branch of astronomy (although some reference astronomy inquiries WITHOUT raising the idea of expansion), and therefore they should all be eliminated.

Passage 18, Pages 98-100

1. <u>A</u> is the correct answer.

The passage describes how scientists have arrived at a plausible theory to explain the myth of the Loch Ness monster: by analyzing environmental DNA, they have concluded that sightings of the monster were most likely sightings of eels. Choose A to reflect this content. Be careful not to choose C or D, since e-DNA testing did NOT attempt to date records of human settling or show the existence of eels in any particular location (since, in fact, eel DNA was found everywhere). B can also be ruled out because it is too broad of a claim to be fully addressed by the passage; the role of imagination is described MAINLY in lines 74-85, not in the entirety of the passage, and B also omits any clear reference to the Loch Ness monster.

2. <u>A</u> is the correct answer.

In lines 4-5, the author refers to a circus elephant as a way to poke fun at the claims people have made about seeing strange creatures in the waters of the lake. Since it would be unlikely for a circus elephant to escape and show up in the lake, this comparison indicates that the author is not convinced by claims of a strange and unknown species (which are critiqued throughout the passage) and is making fun of that idea. Choose A to reflect this content. B can be eliminated, since the author is NOT positively inclined towards the elephant claims and since given the lake's location in Scotland it is clearly not plausible for there to be frequent sightings of elephants. C and D can also be eliminated since the image of an elephant is designed to poke fun at an alternative explanation but does NOT (in THIS specific line reference, despite later content) provide context for what an actual sea monster might look like.

3. <u>B</u> is the correct answer.

The first paragraph of the passage references the longstanding idea that a strange creature may live in the Loch Ness lake, and then provides a current scientific explanation ("most likely a giant eel," line 6) which would provide an answer to this misconception. Choose B to reflect this content. A and D should both be eliminated because, at this point in the passage, details about the description of Nessie and a resemblance to other species have not yet been established. C can also be eliminated since the first paragraph clearly debunks the notion of a Loch Ness monster as understood in popular lore.

4. <u>C</u> is the correct answer.

The passage indicates that e-DNA testing can identify both species which make their home in the lake and species which might only occasionally visit it, such as sheep, cattle, and dogs (lines 35-49). Choose C to reflect this content. A and D can be eliminated since nothing in the passage indicates that e-DNA testing (an established and useful method) is emerging or unreliable. B can also be eliminated since e-DNA testing is NOT used to study the origins of animal species but to identify what types of organism live in a given habitat.

5. <u>D</u> is the correct answer.

In line 59, "lie" refers to the position in a dataset at which a scientist would expect to see information about a particular species, if samples from that species were present. Choose D to reflect this meaning. A (inappropriately implying agreement or consent), B (inappropriately implying coming to a position of stillness or calm), and C (implying rising to the top of a given environment) all introduce inappropriate meanings and therefore should be eliminated.

6. <u>D</u> is the correct answer.

In lines 65-67, the author qualifies the conclusion of the scientists by noting that e-DNA testing indicates the presence of an eel population in the lake, but NOT the respective size of those eels. Choose D to reflect this content. A can be eliminated since the primary goal of the scientists in this study was to examine which species might live in the lake, NOT to examine the psychological response to monstrous creatures (a consideration that interests the AUTHOR instead). B and C can also be eliminated since both of these answers imply that scientists seek to validate belief in strange creatures, whereas the passage clearly shows researchers debunking this perspective.

7. <u>C</u> is the correct answer.

See the previous answer explanation for analysis of the correct line reference. A references some of the species whose DNA turned up in the sampling, while B offers a description of Nessie which has taken hold in the popular imagination. D asks a rhetorical question in order to introduce a new scientific theory into the passage. None of these other answers address the information that scientists have and have not been able to establish about eels in the lake, and therefore all should be eliminated.

8. <u>A</u> is the correct answer.

In line 80, "cues" refers to what individuals see or perceive when they believe that they are likely to observe a specific occurrence. Choose A to reflect this context. B (inappropriately implying triggering a memory or recollection), C (inappropriately implying triggering a creative impulse), and D (inappropriately implying something which instigates action) all introduce improper contexts and should be eliminated.

9. <u>A</u> is the correct answer.

In lines 82-85, the author describes how a particular species has been conclusively determined to be extinct, yet people still report seeing specimens of this species. The author uses this example as evidence of "expectant attention" and to indicate that the mind of an observer can be fooled into drawing inaccurate conclusions. Choose A to reflect this content. B and D can be eliminated since they indicate that the author is endorsing the claims of individuals who believe that they have seen Nessie, whereas the author wants to explain why these individuals were mistaken. C can also be eliminated because scientists were aiming to find an alternative explanation for Nessie, NOT to validate her existence.

10. <u>D</u> is the correct answer.

See the previous answer explanation for analysis of the correct line reference. A describes the history of the myth of the Loch Ness monster, while B describes an archaeological discovery which might be related to the myth of the monster. C summarizes one way of interpreting the findings of the study. None of these other answers describe how expectant attention can lead to individuals being mistaken about what they are observing (and some avoid "expectant attention" altogether), and therefore they should all be eliminated.

Passage 19, Pages 101-103

1. <u>D</u> is the correct answer.

The passage describes how scientists are developing wildling mice and the ways in which these mice are different from both lab mice and wild mice (lines 1-8). This passage then concludes by suggesting some of the potential scientific developments which can be advanced due to research featuring wildling mice (lines 87-95). Choose D as appropriate. A and B can be eliminated since the passage focuses on a scientific innovation (wilding mice) but NOT on an ongoing challenge (since the mice apparently offer promising possibilities), and since the mostly positive passage does NOT provide extensive analysis of the shortcomings of working with wilding mice. C can be eliminated since the passage does NOT have a major focus on any specific practical application of wilding mice, but alludes in more general terms to how they might advance scientific research.

2. C is the correct answer.

The passage explains that wildling mice "acquired the microbes and pathogens of wild mice, while maintaining the laboratory mice's genetics that make them more useful for research" (lines 5-8). Choose C to reflect this content. Be careful not to choose A or D, since a wildling mouse's microbiota is one of its defining features, but a wildling's microbiota does NOT entirely resemble that of a human (beyond roughly similar origins, lines 18-22) and does NOT necessarily remain stable over a lifetime. B can be eliminated since the relative health of a wildling and lab mouse is NOT explicitly discussed in the passage; this topic should not be confused with the idea that wilding mice are superior to lab mice in clinical studies.

3. C is the correct answer.

The passage states that "Rehermann and Stephan Rosshart . . . have long sought to improve animal models of complex diseases in humans." This content indicates that their research was motivated by a desire to develop more refined techniques and to improve human health outcomes; choose C as appropriate. A and B can be eliminated because the initial intention was NOT to show similarities in human and animal immune systems (a side feature of developing useful wilding mice) and since there is no evidence in the passage that existing mouse research was plagued by procedural errors. D can be eliminated because the refinement and popularization of wilding mice were attractive outcomes of the research, NOT motivating goals.

4. A is the correct answer.

See the previous answer explanation for analysis of the correct line reference. B describes one characteristic which was compared across different types of mice, while C quotes an expert explaining the importance of the microbiome. D provides an example of how the microbiota of wilding mice seem to be resilient and support the health of the organism. None of these other answers (which focus on facts and procedures) explain the underlying GOAL motivating the research, and therefore they should all be eliminated.

5. A is the correct answer.

In line 27, "squeaky clean" is used to describe how lab mice have not developed microbiota due to a lack of natural exposure, and therefore they do not possess bacteria, fungi, and viruses in the expected quantities. Choose A to reflect this meaning. B can be eliminated because the description is directly relevant to lab mice, NOT wilding mice, while C can be eliminated since there is no evidence in the passage that traditional mouse trials tend to experience high levels of inaccuracy (despite the desirability of wilding mice). Be careful not to choose D since, in the case of laboratory mice, a lack of microbes is actually NOT desirable.

6. D is the correct answer.

The passage specifies that the microbiome refers to microbiota "that live in and on the bodies of people and animals" (lines 23-27). As a result, organisms living on the surface of a tree would not qualify because a tree is a plant, NOT a person or an animal. Choose D as appropriate. All of the other answers can be eliminated because they represent cases in which the direct criteria for microbiota have been adequately met.

7. C is the correct answer.

The passage explains that wildling mice were produced by transplanting the embryos of laboratory mice into wild mice (lines 40-43). This process required two different kinds of mice to be artificially combined to create a hybrid mouse; choose C as appropriate. A and B can both be eliminated wild and laboratory mice did not reproduce together, and since mature mice were not altered to produce this hybrid species. D can also be eliminated since wild mice were genetically altered, not simply tamed, in order to produce wildling mice.

8. B is the correct answer.

Lines 91-95 state that "By helping to predict immune responses of humans, the wildling model could lead to important discoveries to help treat and prevent disease, and ultimately, improve human health." This content implies that wildling mice approximate the immune responses displayed by humans; choose B to reflect this content. A can be eliminated since wildling mice were used to study specific clinical responses relevant to humans, NOT to see what diseases humans were naturally susceptible to. C and D can be eliminated since the respective resilience of human and mouse microbiota is NOT compared at length in the passage (despite indications of general similarities), nor is the presence of different types of microbiota (despite the author's broad definition of "microbiota") evaluated in the passage.

9. D is the correct answer.

See the previous answer explanation for analysis of the correct line reference. A describes the similarities that wildling mice displayed in relation to wild mice, and B provides an example of how wildling mice displayed greater resilience than laboratory mice. C describes another feature which makes wildling mice useful for scientific research. None of the other answers state that wildling mice show immune responses similar to those of humans (and some answers do not present clear connections between humans and wildling mice in any way), and therefore they should all be eliminated.

10. B is the correct answer.

In line 87, "shorten" refers to a desire to reduce the time required for medical research to become clinically viable for human use. Choose B to reflect this meaning. A (inappropriately implying an ability to make a process more streamlined or less complex), C (inappropriately implying capturing only the most important points of information), and D (inappropriately implying rejection of someone or something) all introduce improper contexts and should therefore be eliminated.

Passage 20, Pages 104-106

1. C is the correct answer.

The author spends the majority of the passage explaining the challenges of the American big sagebrush population (lines 9-71) but concludes by describing a potential strategy which has been successfully employed to support populations of vulnerable animal species (lines 79-96). Choose C to reflect this content. Be careful not to choose A, since while the author does describe many challenges facing big sagebrush, the passage also highlights the commitment of researchers trying to solve this problem and ends on a hopeful note. B and D can also be eliminated since the portrayal of Shriver and the effects of human disruption on the environment are NOT the main topics of the passage, which mostly deals with ecological problems and solutions.

2. B is the correct answer.

Towards the end of the passage, the author points to a potential solution: growing young sagebrush plants under controlled conditions before introducing them into the wild. This solution represents a collaboration between scientists and organizations; choose B as appropriate. A can be eliminated since the passage provides evidence that the big sagebrush population is threatened but avoids the central topic of solution-based research. C and D can be eliminated since invasive plant species is one challenge faced by big sagebrush, but not the ONLY one, and since the focus on young plants is only one aspect of the passage.

3. B is the correct answer.

In lines 58-62, the author explains that "because newly established big sagebrush populations are mostly composed of small, young plants that have low survival and reproduction rates," it is not easy to recover and restore a population. Choose B to reflect this content. A can be eliminated since fires are one, but NOT the only, reason that populations may need to be restored, while C can be eliminated since such a precise rate for the odds of a population being restored is not provided in the article. D can be eliminated since the author cites meaningful examples of government efforts to support and restore sagebrush populations.

4. C is the correct answer.

See the previous answer explanation for analysis of the correct line reference. A describes a threat to sagebrush populations and the expense used to counter that threat, while B describes other organisms which rely on the sagebrush for survival. D marks a shift away from describing the problems facing sagebrush towards presenting a possible solution. None of these other answers explain why it can often be challenging to restore sagebrush populations (although solutions are mentioned), and therefore they should all be eliminated.

5. D is the correct answer.

In line 19, "iconic" refers to an archetypal and long-held image: the visual presentation of the sagebrush that tends to evoke ideas of the American West. Choose D to reflect this meaning. A (inappropriately implying something which many individuals like or enjoy), B (inappropriately implying something affiliated with a particular spiritual tradition), and C (inappropriately implying someone who typically meets exact goals) all introduce improper contexts and should be eliminated.

6. <u>A</u> is the correct answer.

In lines 16-18, Shriver explains the two goals of the study: to make sagebrush recovery efforts more successful, and to make such undertakings less expensive. Choose A to reflect this content. Be careful not to choose C or D, since the study and Shriver's comments focus on restoration efforts after a plant population has already been damaged, not on efforts to safeguard it in the first place. B can also be eliminated since restoring populations, not developing new and "hybrid" plants, is the focus of the research efforts.

7. <u>A</u> is the correct answer.

See the previous answer explanation for analysis of the correct line reference. B describes why sagebrush is a well-known plant species, while C describes some of the threats which sagebrush faces. D explains a gap in scientific information which has hindered progress in researching sagebrush recovery. None of these other answers reflect the exact goal of using research to make recovery programs less expensive (despite the broad relevance of these answers to research endeavors), and therefore they should all be eliminated.

8. <u>A</u> is the correct answer.

In the study described in the passage, the Bureau of Land Management provided the opportunity for scientists to return to areas where attempts had been made to restore a post-fire population and calculate how successful these attempts had been (lines 45-52). Choose A to reflect this content. Be careful not to choose B, since while the reseeding of sagebrush is occurring with the assistance of the Bureau of Land Management, it is unclear whether the practices utilized are traditional or (as may be more likely) innovative. C and D can be eliminated since the research discussed in the passage does NOT discuss attempts to safeguard sagebrush populations or to breed hybrid species; the Bureau simply oversees and promotes rehabilitation through seeding.

9. <u>C</u> is the correct answer.

In line 92, "rear" refers to how conservationists will sometimes nurture juvenile animals under controlled conditions in order to increase their odds of survival. Choose C to reflect this meaning. A (inappropriately implying forcibly seizing something), B (inappropriately implying preparation for a particular role or career path), and D (inappropriately implying purposefully creating obstacles for someone or something) all introduce improper contexts and should therefore be eliminated.

10. <u>A</u> is the correct answer.

In the final paragraph, the focus of the passage shifts to a hopeful and optimistic perspective, as the author argues that strategies used to help other vulnerable species might help sagebrush restoration efforts. Choose A to reflect this content. B and C can be eliminated since there is no discussion of burning sagebrush (an earlier possibility that DESTROYED sagebrush populations) and since the paragraph centers on solutions that the author in a positive manner. Be careful not to choose D, since the importance of recovering sagebrush has been established elsewhere in the passage but is NOT the primary focus of the final paragraph, which mostly explains one promising method.

Passage 21, Pages 107-109

1. A is the correct answer.

The passage discusses two specific examples of studies relying on trace fossils. In the first example, trace fossils left by a tyrannosaurid species resulted from several dinosaurs walking next to each other (lines 22-36), while in the second example, trace fossils left by a temnospondyl seem to result from the movement of a single individual (lines 47-60). Choose A to reflect this content. B and C can be eliminated since there is no discussion of whether either fossil was easy or difficult to detect, and since there is no indication that the tyrannosaurid tracks were associated with hunting activity, especially since the tracks seem to have been made by multiple dinosaurs together without a single defined purpose. D can also be eliminated since the tyrannosaurid tracks were made by multiple individuals from the same loosely-defined species.

2. B is the correct answer.

In lines 21 and 79, "life" refers to creating a more vivid portrait and detailed understanding of prehistoric creatures through the study of fossils. It does NOT signal an actual attempt to resuscitate long-extinct species, and the quotes thus function to signal this distinction. Choose B to reflect this meaning. A and C can readily be eliminated since in neither example is there discussion of consensus or a research outcome (despite the use of specific research perspectives ELSEWHERE in the passage). Be careful not to choose D, since the expression is somewhat informal and non-scientific, but NOT necessarily intended to be humorous or unusual.

3. A is the correct answer.

A identifies the connection between fossils and an understanding of prehistoric creatures. B highlights a difference in how frequently trace fossils and fossilized bones are studied, while C distinguishes between how tyrannosaurids have been studied based on bones and footprints (a form of trace fossil). D acknowledges that studying fossilized bones remains more popular than studying trace fossils. B, C, and D all indicate that scientists tend to focus on the study of fossilized bones more frequently than on the study of trace fossils. Therefore, all of these answers can be eliminated. A is the only answer which does NOT distinguish between different types of fossil, and therefore it should be selected as the correct answer.

4. A is the correct answer.

In lines 32 and 34, "made" refers to how dinosaurs left impressions of their feet in the ground when they walked. Choose A to reflect this meaning. B (inappropriately implying developing a scheme or plan), C (inappropriately implying generating a planned series of steps or actions), and D (inappropriately implying innovating or developing a new technique) all introduce improper contexts and should therefore be eliminated.

5. C is the correct answer.

In lines 39-42, the author states that while the likely scenario is that three tyrannosaurids were walking side by side, it is also possible that three animals walked by the same spot separately in a short time frame. If it were true that tyrannosaurids rarely gathered in groups of more than two dinosaurs, this fact would make the possibility of the tracks being caused by solitary animals more likely. Choose C to reflect this scenario. A and

D can be eliminated since the dinosaurs being more effective when hunting alone would NOT necessarily mean that they never congregated in groups, and since a tendency to hunt in groups would actually make it more likely that the tracks were caused by a group of animals walking together. B can also be eliminated since evidence of how this species walked when walking together would NOT make it more likely that the tracks were caused by solitary animals.

6. <u>A</u> is the correct answer.

The passage specifies that the temnospondyl did not have claws on its digits (lines 56-60); choose A to reflect this content. B and C can be eliminated because the animal displayed important anatomical differences from modern salamander (front-limb driven rather than hind-leg driven) and since there is no evidence that it struggled to escape from predators. D can be eliminated since, because this organism was possibly a distant ancestor of a crocodile, similarities between the two organisms could be plausible.

7. <u>B</u> is the correct answer.

Lines 63-67 state that "Researchers usually use hind-limb-driven salamanders as a model for temnospondyl locomotion, but this discovery is causing researchers to re-examine their use of salamander models for this front-limb-driven temnospondyl." This content indicates that discoveries made because of the study of trace fossils has provided insight into non-prehistoric animals (like salamanders). Choose B as appropriate. A and C can be eliminated since studying bone fossils remains more popular than studying trace fossils, and since anatomical terms have not been developed as an outcome of trace fossil research (which has mostly indicated new facts about animals WITHOUT requiring new terminology). D can be eliminated since there is no discussion of whether software (as opposed to modeling generally) was used in the analysis of trace fossils.

8. <u>C</u> is the correct answer.

See the previous answer explanation for analysis of the correct line reference. A describes how the scientists engaged with the tyrannosaurid tracks, while B demonstrates the significance of information provided by the study of the track marks. D summarizes the impact and importance of what researchers can learn by studying trace fossils. None of these other answers provide information about non-extinct species (though some answers do broadly indicate that the research was important) and therefore they should all be eliminated.

9. <u>B</u> is the correct answer.

The figure shows three sets of tracks of different sizes spaced out, with some tracks appearing in front of others. The tracks could reflect one dinosaur at different stages of growth (showing why the tracks are of varying sizes), three dinosaurs walking single-file (explaining the different sizes and the positioning of the tracks), or three dinosaurs walking over the same territory at different points in time (explaining the different sizes, and possible since there is no indication that the tracks were created at the same time). The tracks could NOT reflect three dinosaurs walking side by side because the tracks are not positioned appropriately. Choose B and eliminate all other answers.

10. <u>D</u> is the correct answer.

The temnospondyl moved by dragging its body along the ground, rather than by walking on entirely on its feet. As presented in the figure, various feet-only tracks were left by a three-toed animal that did NOT leave a dragging trail from its body. Therefore, these tracks could not have been left by a temnospondyl; choose D as appropriate. A and B can both be eliminated since the tracks as represented in the figure do NOT reveal whether the animal moved in a labored way or whether it had claws or not; it is only clear that the animal walked along and left three-toed tracks. C can be eliminated because only direction and footprint shape (NOT how many feet the animal possessed) are specified.

Passage 22, Pages 110-112

1. C is the correct answer.

The passage provides an overview of how timekeeping technology has progressed with significant developments between the 1700s and the present day; then, the author discusses how scientific research is continuously striving to make time keeping more accurate. Choose C as the best answer. A and B can be eliminated since nautical timekeeping is discussed briefly in the passage, but other more modern timekeeping methods (particularly those related to cesium clocks) are given attention; moreover, different developments are discussed, but no particular debates or conflicts are highlighted. D can also be eliminated since, while cesium atomic clocks are discussed in the passage, they are NOT compared to earlier timekeeping technology in any extended way (a topic addressed only in the early stages of the passage).

2. D is the correct answer.

The first two paragraphs discuss how longitude was calculated in an earlier era when modern technology was not yet available; choose D to reflect this content. A and B can be eliminated since a distant historical example is used, NOT a personal one from the author's own life, and cesium clocks (a later topic) are NOT discussed in this section of the passage. C can be eliminated since the paragraphs discuss a process which occurred in the distant past and which is clearly no longer applicable; therefore, no urgency is created by these paragraphs.

3. A is the correct answer.

Line 13 describes the problem of seafaring clocks being unable to keep time effectively. Lines 30-32 state that the development of the compact marine chronometer "marked the beginning of the end for the "longitude problem"." Thus, choose A as appropriate. B quotes an expert explaining in simple terms why effective time keeping is necessary, while C identifies a research challenge which modern scientists are currently looking for ways to address. D pivots to describing how researching accurate timekeeping can have broader scientific implications. None of these other answers reflect a solution to difficulties that early sailors experienced with keeping time at sea, and therefore they should all be eliminated.

4. C is the correct answer.

In line 35, "massive" refers to how significantly and powerfully navigation technology has progressed. Choose C to reflect this meaning. A (inappropriately implying something being protected against military aggression), B (inappropriately implying something heavy and unwieldy), and D (inappropriately implying a serious and grave situation) all introduce improper contexts and should therefore be eliminated.

5. <u>A</u> is the correct answer.

In line 59, "trick" refers to a crucial factor which determines success or failure. Choose A to reflect this meaning. B (inappropriately implying something being concealed or passed off as something else), C (inappropriately implying something which triggers pleasant sensations), and D (inappropriately implying something which is repeated on a routine basis) all introduce improper contexts and should therefore be eliminated.

6. <u>B</u> is the correct answer.

Lines 72-77 explain that "That shift between ground state and excited state (better known as the atomic transition frequency) yields something equivalent to the official definition of a second: 9,192,631,770 cycles of the radiation that gets a cesium atom to vibrate between those two energy states." This content indicates that a property of cesium clarifies the concept of a second; choose B as the best answer. A and D can be eliminated because there is no association made in the passage between cesium and clock design or cost effectiveness (though the use of cesium to define a second is essential to timekeeping as a whole). Be careful not to choose C because cesium atoms are potentially impacted by Doppler shifts, NOT used to combat them.

7. <u>C</u> is the correct answer.

See the previous answer explanation for analysis of the correct line reference. A identifies the technology that is most frequently used in modern timekeeping research, while B describes how lasers are used to make cesium clocks more effective and accurate. D describes how pervasive the use of cesium is in atomic clocks is. None of these answers explains the connection between cesium and the concept of a second (though some refer to cesium clocks in OTHER respects), and therefore they should all be eliminated.

8. <u>B</u> is the correct answer.

Kurt Gibble is described in the passage as someone possessing "an international reputation for assessing accuracy and improving atomic clocks" (lines 80-82). Based on this content, it is logical that Gibble might contribute to a project focused on comparing the accuracy of different atomic clocks; choose B as the best answer. A and C can be eliminated because Gibble's research focus does not necessarily align with constructing an optical resolution clock or revising the standard definition of a second: both optical clocks and the definition of a second are mentioned in the passage but NOT in relation to Gibble's interest in clock accuracy. D can also be eliminated since nothing in the passage necessarily suggests that Gibble could work effectively on reducing Doppler shifts; such shifts are at most mentioned (lines 67-71) BEFORE Gibble is introduced.

9. <u>D</u> is the correct answer.

The graph indicates that both optical and atomic clocks are becoming steadily more accurate; however, after 2010, optical clocks surpassed atomic clocks in accuracy (displaying a lower rate of fractional uncertainty). Since these trends continue to 2020, an atomic clock would display a very low rate of uncertainty and therefore be highly accurate. Choose D to reflect this content. A and B can be eliminated since, in 2000, the atomic clock still displayed a level of uncertainty which continued to decrease, and the level of uncertainty in the atomic clock is decreasing at a slower rate. C can be eliminated because the uncertainty level around the optimal clock declined sharply after 2000, indicating a significant rise in accuracy.

10. <u>B</u> is the correct answer.

The passage briefly mentions that optical frequency clocks represent an exciting innovation in atomic timekeeping (lines 86-90), and the graph reveals further information about the relative accuracy of this technology. Choose B to accurately reflect this relationship. A and C can be eliminated since the graph only provides information about the relative accuracy of optical and atomic clocks, NOT about Doppler shifts or traditional clock technology. D, much like C, can also be eliminated because the graph only shows information about technologies which were developed fairly recently.

Passage 23, Pages 113-115

1. <u>C</u> is the correct answer.

In line 2, "rich" is used to refer to how organisms living in a coral reef have numerous and diverse defense strategies. Choose C to reflect this meaning. A (inappropriately implying revealing emotions or an inner state), B (inappropriately implying smothering or being overbearing), and D (inappropriately implying something excessive or overindulgent) all introduce improper contexts and therefore should be eliminated.

2. <u>D</u> is the correct answer.

The sea slug described in line 15 eats toxic algae in order to make use of toxic chemicals. This makes it similar to the organisms described in line 7, which use noxious chemicals to protect themselves. Choose D as appropriate. A can be eliminated because a sea slug is not a microbe, and B can be eliminated because there is no mention of the sea slug having physical defense mechanisms. C can also be eliminated because the sea slug does not use specialized evasive movement which is comparable to the behavior described in line 5.

3. <u>B</u> is the correct answer.

In line 26, "drivers of" refers to factors which lead to the existence of diversity. Choose B to reflect this meaning. A (inappropriately implying that something is caused by, rather than being a cause of, something else), C (inappropriately implying an emotional or uplifting experience), and D (inappropriately implying someone encouraging support for a person or a cause) all introduce improper contexts and should be eliminated.

4. <u>D</u> is the correct answer.

Lines 16-21 state that "Marine scientists suspected that the toxin is made by a bacterium that lives within the alga but have only just discovered the species responsible and teased apart the complex relationship between slug, seaweed, and microbe." This content foreshadows the information revealed later in the passage that scientists now know that *Flavobacteria* are responsible for producing the kahalalide toxins found in algae. Choose D as appropriate. A and B can be eliminated since sea slugs do not produce toxins directly themselves, and since the balance between predators and prey (lines 22-24) has long been understood as vital for a healthy ecosystem. C can be eliminated because, while a specific bacterium has been discovered in connection to a host, this instance is not defined as the FIRST such case of such a survival mechanism.

5. A is the correct answer.

See the previous answer explanation for analysis of the correct line reference. B describes how noxious chemicals benefit the coral reef ecosystem, while C identifies a scientific hypothesis that has now been validated. D describes how the bacterium benefits the algae. None of these other answers identify a RECENT finding as required by the previous question (or, in terms of topic, explain the relationship between the slug, seaweed, and the microbe), and therefore they should all be eliminated.

6. C is the correct answer.

Lines 56-58 state that "kahalalides, originally discovered in the early 1990s, also protect a sea slug, *Elysia rufescens*, that consumes it." While the initial description of kahalalides describes how they serve to protect seaweed, this content also shows that they protect another organism as well (the sea slug). Choose C to reflect this content. A and B can be eliminated because the passage focuses on one specific species of seaweed and does NOT indicate that kahalalides protect many species; moreover, the passage suggests that researchers had devised a hypothesis well before they were finally able to prove it. D can be eliminated because, while there is the possibility of using kahalalides in medical applications, these toxins are NOT currently in use in any life-saving pharmaceuticals.

7. B is the correct answer.

See the previous answer explanation for analysis of the correct line reference. A describes how a scientific discovery has resolved a long-standing question, while C explains why this discovery is notable. D connects coral reef research to human health applications. None of these answers show that kahalalides function to protect multiple species of organisms, and therefore they should all be eliminated.

8. C is the correct answer.

In the final portions of the passage, the authors move from objective reporting of scientific findings to personal reflection. This shift is used to signal their feeling about observing a feature of the natural world while completing fieldwork; choose C as the best answer. A and B can be eliminated because the tone of the relevant lines is positive and not skeptical, yet the enthusiasm of the authors (which relates mostly to sensory descriptions) is not connected to advocating for protecting the natural world. D can also be eliminated because the relevant species are the subjects of significant discovery which advances understanding of them and therefore cannot be considered entirely mysterious.

9. D is the correct answer.

The graph shows that, in Ecosystems 2 and 3, the biodiversity of the habitat is relatively high (approaching 0.75 or greater of the total possible biodiversity). In these same Ecosystems, the percentage of predators is relatively low (between 25% and 50% of the total species). In Ecosystems 4 and 5, the biodiversity is much lower (less than 0.50 of the total possible biodiversity), and the percentage of predators is much higher (between 50% and 75% of the total species). The data indicate that high biodiversity seems to be correlated with a low percentage of predators; choose D as the best answer. A and B can be eliminated because both of these answers wrongly suggest that a higher percentage of predators would be correlated with greater biodiversity. C can be eliminated because none of the ecosystems depicted in the graph show an example where predator and prey numbers are equal (EXACTLY 50% predator).

10. <u>C</u> is the correct answer.

The graph reveals that Ecosystem 3 has a very high biodiversity rating, and since the authors of the passage connect biodiversity and resilience (lines 24-27), they would most likely see Ecosystem 3 as less vulnerable than the other ecosystems. Choose C as appropriate. A and B can be eliminated because Ecosystems 4 and 5 have a higher percentage of prey organisms, and since nothing in the graph (which mostly gives figures from one point in time) indicates that ANY ecosystem will become more similar to Ecosystem 1 over time. D can also be eliminated because the graph does not provide any data about the relative size of the ecosystems, a factor which should NOT be confused with biodiversity or range of organism types.

Passage 24, Pages 116-118

1. <u>B</u> is the correct answer.

Lines 19-22 state that, in relation to past research, ""It took a year to design the yeast genome, even though there were barely any changes made to [the genome]. So, [researchers] need better design tools." Since the "grand challenge in synthetic biology" refers to the writing of a human genome, this content indicates that the successful writing of a human genome requires technology which is not currently available. Choose B as appropriate. A and D can be dismissed since there is no moral imperative attached to the need to write the human genome (despite its worthwhile nature as a research endeavor), and since the passage does not describe any theoretical construct underlying the writing of the human genome (which is considered mostly in terms of practice and results). Be careful not to choose C, since an earlier project (fully sequencing the human genome) has been completed, but WRITING the human genome requires different methodology and tools.

2. <u>D</u> is the correct answer.

See the previous answer explanation for analysis of the correct line reference. A mentions an expert bluntly stating the need to write the human genome, while B draws a parallel between the scope of ambition in this project and in the earlier project to sequence the human genome. C states a fact about the human genome which implies the scope and difficulty of the proposed project. Since none of these other answers imply that writing the genome requires yet-to-be-developed technology (despite broadly referencing the effort and the human genome), they can all be eliminated.

3. <u>C</u> is the correct answer.

The passage states that a wide variety of fields could potentially benefit from advancing research in synthetic genomics. Since those fields range "from health and medicine to electronics" (lines 53-54), A, B, and D all represent desirable outcomes which could result from research. Eliminate these answers since they DO all represent desirable research outcomes. The passage quotes researchers explicitly stating that they are not aiming to use these findings to produce "synthetic" or "artificial" humans. Therefore, C represents a research outcome that would NOT be considered desirable and should be selected.

4. <u>A</u> is the correct answer.

In lines 74-77, Hessel is quoted as stating: "I'm doing this because I want my daughter to literally have the best nanomedicine in the future, the best diagnostics, the best treatments." This content indicates that Hessel has an investment in the research which is personal and not purely theoretical. Choose A as appropriate. B and C can be eliminated since Hessel advocates for public interest, but NOT direct public participation in the genome project, and is cautious but hopeful about the possibility of technological advancements which could support the research goals. D can be eliminated since Hessel responds to one potential critique of the project but does NOT actively address misconceptions about the project.

5. <u>D</u> is the correct answer.

See the previous answer explanation for analysis of the correct line reference. A describes a strategy which scientists are currently advocating for, while B describes some initial outcomes of that strategy. C describes one possible timeline for the research project. None of these other answers shed light on Hessel's personal investment in the genomics research (though some do mention efforts that would be of deep interest to him), and therefore they should all be eliminated.

6. <u>A</u> is the correct answer.

In line 46, "gloss over" refers to Hessel's refusal to minimize the real challenges presented by a line of research. Choose A to reflect this meaning. B (inappropriately implying forgiveness or justification for inappropriate or uncouth behavior), C (inappropriately implying fabricating or overstating), and D (inappropriately implying proving something to be inaccurate or false) all introduce improper contexts and should therefore be eliminated.

7. <u>C</u> is the correct answer.

The words "early" and "starting" indicate that the author of the passage acknowledges that the research project being described is in an early stage; the author is committed to describing the research objectively without exaggerating or sensationalizing it, despite the fact that the research is often presented as intriguing. Choose C to reflect this content of straightforward description. A and B can be eliminated since conclusions have NOT yet been reached around the writing of the human genome, and since the passage focuses on research which will hopefully yield results soon, NOT research which has already provided decisive evidence. D should be eliminated since the passage indicates that genomics research can benefit human health and wellness, but NOT that there is a primarily humanitarian intention to a project that mostly has a scientific basis.

8. <u>C</u> is the correct answer.

In the final section of the passage, Hessel comments on his optimism that research into synthetic genomes is going to accelerate rapidly, predicts a date when this research goal may be achieved, and provides reassurance regarding the goals of this research. This content shows he that is clear in his beliefs and confident that his desired outcomes can be achieved; choose C as the best answer. A and B can be eliminated since Hessel has no doubts about the value of this research (and in fact has a personal stake in its results) and urges bold and committed action towards the research goal of producing a synthetic genome. D can be eliminated since nothing in the passage suggests that Hessel's goals are unrealistic or strongly challenged within the scientific community (which in fact seems to support genomic inquiry).

9. <u>D</u> is the correct answer.

Between 1999 and 2003, the degree of accuracy for human genome mapping ranged between 95% and nearly 100%. Since even at its lowest point, in 1999, the accuracy exceeded 95%, it is fair to say that a mostly-accurate model of the human genome was present in all years depicted in the graph. Choose D as appropriate. Be careful not to choose A, since the graph does show that no model has achieved perfect accuracy so far, but it does NOT necessarily follow that perfect accuracy will never be achieved in a LATER year. B can be eliminated since, while the graph does show increases in the accuracy of human genome modeling, there is no way to know whether that accuracy can be attributed to advancements in biomedical technology (since the graph on its own does not designate a CAUSE of increased accuracy). C can be eliminated since the graph does show improvements in the accuracy of modeling, but only by very small increments on a year-to-year basis.

10. <u>C</u> is the correct answer.

Hessel's career initially focused on mapping the human genome, and once that goal was achieved, he moved his research focus towards writing a synthetic human genome. The data displayed on the graph relate to the mapping of the human genome, and therefore it is reasonable to infer that, for Hessel, these data would represent a link to an earlier stage of his career. Choose C to properly reflect the content of the passage. A and B can be eliminated since nothing in the graph displays a link to diagnostic tools, and since the data in the graph are relevant to a project which has already been completed, not the ongoing project which is projected to be completed by 2026. D can be eliminated since the passage does not mention anything about the public attention received by increasingly accurate genomic modeling.

Passage 25, Pages 119-121

1. <u>D</u> is the correct answer.

The passage identifies a serious environmental concern (increasing concentrations of carbon dioxide in the atmosphere) and then discusses how a novel photocatalyst shows promise in addressing this problem because this photocatalyst can contribute to recapturing atmospheric carbon and converting it to usable fuel. Choose D as the best answer. A and B can be eliminated since the passage clearly states that the presence of carbon dioxide in the atmosphere is problematic and identifies that selectivity in catalysts in generally beneficial. C can be eliminated because the passage notes that increasing concentrations of atmospheric carbon dioxide may be impacting the environment but does NOT stipulate what those impacts are.

2. <u>B</u> is the correct answer.

Lines 23-28 explain that a specific "photocatalyst is particularly exciting because it has one of the most negative conduction bands that [researchers have] used, which means that the electrons have more potential energy available to do reactions." Choose B to indicate that the negativity of the conduction band is related to electrons possessing greater energy, and therefore being better suited to reducing atmospheric carbon dioxide. A explains why more highly excited electrons are valuable, while C describes the results of using other types of photocatalysts. D describes a negative consequence associated with using other photocatalysts. None of these other answers articulate the connection between the negativity of the conduction band and the reduction of atmospheric carbon dioxide.

3. A is the correct answer.

In line 34, "segregate" refers to attempts to separate usable fuel sources from other byproducts of a chemical reaction. Choose A to reflect this meaning. B (inappropriately implying creating a negative viewpoint towards someone or something), C (inappropriately implying making a thoughtful or well-researched choice), and D (inappropriately implying distinguishing one thing from another) all introduce improper contexts and should therefore be eliminated.

4. B is the correct answer.

The passage focuses on exploring the many benefits of using cuprous oxide as a photocatalyst. Moreover, the author establishes that cuprous oxide has a more negative conduction band than other catalysts, and therefore absorbs water near carbon dioxide. Also, because of the way in which cuprous oxide bonds with carbon dioxide, less energy is required for the reaction. Because of this content, A, C, and D should all be eliminated because they describe factors which make cuprous oxide a superior catalyst. B is the correct answer because the passage does NOT discuss the cost of using cuprous oxide as a catalyst.

5. C is the correct answer.

Lines 36-37 state that "Carbon dioxide is such a stable molecule and it results from the burning of basically everything" but the passage goes on to explain that a challenge exists around moving from a stable molecule to energy-rich products. This content indicates that stable molecules are typically not energy-rich; choose C as appropriate. A and B can be eliminated since the passage does NOT say anything about the relative abundance or sustainability of stable molecules (in contrast to the actual focus on the dynamics and activity of these molecules). D can also be eliminated since the passage does NOT discuss whether or not stable molecules are typically liquid-based.

6. C is the correct answer.

See the previous answer explanation for analysis of the correct line reference. A describes a current goal that scientists are working towards, while B describes some properties and advantages associated with methanol. D identifies a challenge which scientists are working to resolve. None of these other answers establish that stable molecules are typically not energy-rich (often avoiding questions of energy and classification to focus on research methods), and therefore they should all be eliminated.

7. D is the correct answer.

In line 69, "driving" refers to how one specific facet of cuprous oxide microparticles initiates and speeds up the transformation of carbon dioxide into methanol. Choose C to reflect this meaning. A (inappropriately implying moving something from one location to another), B (inappropriately implying obstructing access to someone or something), and C (inappropriately implying motivating a thought or idea) all introduce improper contexts and should therefore be eliminated.

8. A is the correct answer.

In lines 79-81, Rajh follows up on a statement from the previous sentence, which stated that it was advantageous when a facet of cuprous oxide microparticles leads to water molecules being absorbed. Rajh explains this statement by providing the information that "In order to make fuel, you [. . .] need to have water to be oxidized." Choose A to reflect the purpose of this sentence. B and C can be eliminated since the sentence explains a concept, but does NOT define a term or refute a claim. D can also be eliminated since the claim in the following sentence builds on Rajh's statement and is thus automatically NOT contradicted by it.

9. D is the correct answer.

Figure 2 shows that only about 9% of the carbon dioxide present in Earth's atmosphere can be attributed to land usage changes; choose D to reflect this information. A can be eliminated since the burning of fossil fuels accounts for the majority of human-produced carbon dioxide, but it is NOT clear based on the figure whether human-produced carbon dioxide accounts for more or less of the total carbon dioxide (including naturally-produced carbon dioxide). B can be eliminated because the figure 2 (in contrast to figure 1) only shows data about carbon dioxide in 2020, and C (much like A) can be eliminated because the figure does NOT distinguish between how much carbon dioxide comes from natural versus human-produced sources.

10. A is the correct answer.

Lines 1-2 state that "The concentration of carbon dioxide in our atmosphere is steadily increasing" and figure 1 shows that the concentration of atmospheric carbon dioxide has increased since 1950. Choose A to reflect that both the content from the passage and the content from the figure align. B can be eliminated since figure 2 (which focuses on one year) does NOT provide any data about changes in the concentration of atmospheric carbon dioxide over time. C and D can both be eliminated since lines 2-4 indicate that rising levels of carbon dioxide are impacting the environment, but no direct environmental data are available in either figure 1 or 2 to support this claim.

Passage 26, Pages 122-124

1. B is the correct answer.

Lines 3-8 present water as an example of a substance which is both a liquid and a molecule; specific properties of the molecule lead to water existing in a liquid state. This example acts as an analogy for Sheehy's study of many-particle quantum mechanics because it compares a familiar substance to a more obscure and complicated concept. Choose B as appropriate. A and C can be eliminated since the example in these lines extends the idea from the previous lines, and since, at this point, none of Sheehy's experiments have been discussed in the passage. D can be eliminated because the analogy helps to explain the focus of Sheehy's research but does NOT establish his research credentials (a matter of personal background, not of experimental concepts).

2. A is the correct answer.

In line 7, "action" refers to the behavior of water molecules. Choose A to reflect this content. B (inappropriately implying a series of actions leading towards a specific goal), C (inappropriately implying one action or thought formulated in reaction to another), and D (inappropriately implying power derived from the use of resources) all introduce improper contexts and should therefore be eliminated.

3. <u>C</u> is the correct answer.

Lines 19-21 feature Sheehy explaining that, for a given superconductor, "the electrical resistance is zero, meaning none of the energy is lost." Since superconductors reduce energy loss due to the absence of electrical resistance, it follows logically that non-superconductors allow energy loss due to their electrical resistance. Choose C as the best answer. A and B can be eliminated since valence electrons (a particle type NOT to be confused with electrical resistance) are not discussed in the passage, and since cold temperatures are required to make a superconductor possible but are NOT the reason why superconductors minimize energy loss. Be careful not to choose D, since in a superfluid no actual liquid exists, although the passage compares some of its properties to the properties of a liquid.

4. <u>C</u> is the correct answer.

See the previous answer explanation for analysis of the correct line reference. A describes the conditions required to achieve a superfluid state, while B compares a superfluid to a standard liquid. D describes the object of Sheehy's research focus and indicates why he focuses on this topic. None of these other answers connect energy loss to electrical resistance (despite references to superfluid activity), and therefore they should all be eliminated.

5. <u>D</u> is the correct answer.

In lines 37-38, Sheehy states that "we would like to use superconductors in places where they are not used now." This content indicates that one of his goals is to create superconductors that could be deployed more broadly than those in use today are deployed; choose D as appropriate. A and B can be eliminated since Sheehy does not research water and instead plans to continue working only with mathematical models. C can also be eliminated since Sheehy's research focuses largely developing new superconductors, NOT on gaining a deeper understanding of ones which already exist.

6. <u>D</u> is the correct answer.

In line 35, "ambient" refers to a typical temperature which is neither extremely hot nor extremely cold. Choose D to reflect this meaning. A (inappropriately implying something which is not intentionally created, but is produced regardless), B (inappropriately implying something which is very widespread and common), and C (inappropriately implying something which is structured and pre-determined) all introduce improper contexts and should therefore be eliminated.

7. <u>A</u> is the correct answer.

Lines 71-76 state, in reference to a grant that Sheehy received, that "The grant's educational component includes developing more interactive materials in large-size physics classes so that they go beyond the 'lecture' format, 'with more hands-on activities that get [students] thinking'." This content indicates that Sheehy is working on opportunities to teach physics in a more interactive way; choose A as the best answer. B and C can both be eliminated because they indicate a specific connection between the Internet and the study of physics and bring up a goal for this new educational initiative, but avoid the precise theme of interactive activity. D can be eliminated because, though broadly relevant to Sheehy, this answer mainly addresses Sheehy's summary of the nature of the research that he is performing. None of these other answers specifically highlight Sheehy's pursuit of more interactive methods to teach physics, and therefore they should all be eliminated.

8. B is the correct answer.

The final paragraph describes why Sheehy predicts that the field of cold atoms will grow and provide opportunities for future scientists. Because of its positive and future-focused outlook, the paragraph can best be described as optimistic. Choose B as appropriate. A and C can be eliminated since Sheehy's perspective is very positive in this paragraph, and both of these answers imply a tone that involves some doubt or negativity. D can also be eliminated because the paragraph is expressing an established perspective, NOT presenting future inquiries or analyzing what is unknown.

9. C is the correct answer.

The passage defines a superfluid as a substance which forms when a superconductor is exposed to extremely cold temperatures and achieves zero electrical resistance. While the graph does not indicate levels of electrical resistance, it indicates that both superconductors have discernible fluid properties (low viscosity signaled by low centipoise) when they reach a temperature of -250 degrees Centigrade. This data indicates that both superconductors could fit the passage's definition of a superfluid; therefore, choose C as the best answer and eliminate D as CONTRADICTED by the graph by the same logic. A and B can be eliminated since both superconductors display similar behaviors at extremely cold temperatures, and therefore both have equal chances of fitting the definition of a superfluid.

10. A is the correct answer.

The passage begins by introducing Sheehy's research via a comparison to water, and the graph also compares the properties of superconductors to the properties of water (specifically at 20 °C). Choose A to reflect the proper parallel. B and C can be eliminated since the graph does not communicate anything about how the extremely low temperatures were created or about the potential applications of superconductors; only the fluid properties of superconductors are assessed. The graph (in contrast to the passage) also does NOT communicate any information about the atomic composition of superconductors, so that D is problematic.

Passage 27, Pages 125-127

1. C is the correct answer.

The passage explains that Andolina sometimes feels frustration due to the amount of time it takes to feed the mosquitoes (lines 8-9). Choose C as appropriate. A and B can both be eliminated since Andolina has become immune to the itching response and is willing to tolerate the discomfort associated with the bites (lines 1-7). D can also be eliminated since there are strong safety protocols in place and minimal risk of her catching malaria.

2. <u>B</u> is the correct answer.

The passage states that "Only female mosquitoes drink blood, and they use proteins in their meals to make the shells of their eggs" (lines 63-65). Choose B to reflect this content. A and D can be eliminated since female mosquitoes do not provide food for their young after the eggs hatch, and it is adults, and not larvae, which consume blood. C can also be eliminated since female mosquitoes, which drink blood, can clearly be infected with malarial parasites as a side effect (lines 70-73).

3. <u>D</u> is the correct answer.

Lines 92-96 state that Andolina's "work creates a ready supply of parasites. She provides these to collaborators in Paris and Singapore, who are trying to develop new drugs that target malarial parasites holding out in a patient's liver." This content indicates that Andolina's work aims to generate parasites (*plasmodium falciparum*) which can be used in the research of others. Choose D as appropriate. A can be eliminated because Andolina deliberately infects her mosquitoes with plasmodium, while B can be eliminated because individuals already become desensitized to mosquito allergens if they build up enough exposure. C can also be eliminated because the containment of mosquitoes involved in research is a safety protocol, NOT an aim of the research itself.

4. <u>D</u> is the correct answer.

See the previous answer explanation for analysis of the correct line reference. A describes what happened when the mosquitoes were fed by someone who had not established an allergen tolerance, and B describes an error that is possible in the course of research (NOT a final goal). C describes the safety protocols used to ensure that the infected mosquitoes do not transmit disease. None of these others answers state the goal of Andolina's research (despite referring to the research itself in some respects), and therefore they should all be eliminated.

5. <u>B</u> is the correct answer.

In line 24, "catholic" refers to the mosquito's tendency to feed from a wide variety of sources. Choose B to reflect this meaning. A (inappropriately implying a belief in a particular philosophical or ethical system), C (inappropriately implying something which only occurs within well-defined parameters), and D (inappropriately implying eccentric or diverse aesthetic taste, NOT diversity in terms of food sources) all introduce improper meanings and therefore should be eliminated.

6. <u>A</u> is the correct answer.

Lines 43-45 describe how Andolina's arm is unmarked, even though she has been bitten by many mosquitoes. This detail establishes the contrast between her and someone who is not resistant to mosquito allergens; choose A as appropriate. B and C can be eliminated since the lines describe a lack of reaction and are therefore unlikely to elicit sympathy, and since the impact of the welts left by mosquito bites is not a serious concern for human health (while the different issue of malaria IS a concern). D can be eliminated since the decision to feed the mosquitoes directly from Andolina's arm is not subject to critique within the passage.

7. <u>A</u> is the correct answer.

In line 48, "strange" is used humorously and sarcastically: it is very obvious why research assistants do not want to continue with the project (because they do not enjoy being bitten by the mosquitoes). Moreover, on the basis of line 45, another participant emerged with an arm "covered in welts." The use of the word "strange" introduces an ironic tone into the passage; choose A as the best answer. B and C can be eliminated because there is nothing dangerous about the research situation (not to be confused with the dangers of malaria), and since the author (instead of mocking the research assistants) is sympathetic to objections. D can be eliminated because there is nothing to be suspicious or mistrustful of, as wrongly indicated by this overly negative answer.

8. <u>D</u> is the correct answer.

Lines 54-56 state that it is virtually impossible to tell the two species of mosquitoes apart unless their genes are inspected. This claim is further supported by the story in lines 59-62, which indicates that even Andolina once confused the two species and wasted time on an unsuccessful experiment as a result. Choose D as appropriate. A describes the fragility of South-eastern Asian mosquitoes, while B describes a feature of how Andolina's lab is set up. C describes the different malarial parasites which are transmitted by the two different species. None of these other answers support the idea of the extreme difficulty of telling the species apart, and therefore they should all be eliminated.

9. <u>B</u> is the correct answer.

Of all the mosquitoes described in the table, only species B has a range within North America (where California is located). Choose B as appropriate. All of the other answers can readily be eliminated since they represent species of mosquito whose home range (despite other factors) does NOT include North America.

10. <u>B</u> is the correct answer.

The passage explains that Anopheles gambiae is a species of mosquito found in Africa, while Anopheles dirus is found in Asia. Therefore, Anopheles gambiae is likely mosquito D (which has a home range including Africa), while Anopheles dirus is most likely mosquito C (which has a range throughout Asia, broadening the odds of it being Anopheles dirus). B represents a plausible scenario under which both mosquitoes would be classified in an appropriate way. Choose B as the best answer. A and C can be eliminated since Anopheles gambiae is NOT found in Asia, and D can be eliminated since mosquito C has a specific and localized range relevant to Anopheles dirus, NOT Anopheles gambiae.

Passage 28, Pages 128-130

1. <u>B</u> is the correct answer.

In line 2, "range" refers to the diverse and widespread types of coats observed in dogs. Choose B to reflect this content. A (inappropriately implying physical stature), C (inappropriately implying choices which are available for consumption), and D (inappropriately implying the scope of research or an area of study) all introduce improper contexts and should therefore be eliminated.

2. <u>B</u> is the correct answer.

Lines 23-24 state that data about genetic variants were compared with descriptions of different coat types. This comparison was conducted to validate the hypothesis that genetic variation is correlated with phenotype variation in dogs; choose B as the best answer. A describes how researchers analyzed genetic variation in 1000 dogs, while C describes the information which became available due to this research. D provides examples of some specific breeds which display a specific combination of genetic variants. None of these other answers support the idea that genetic variation is linked with phenotype variation (despite some references to genetic variation ALONE), and therefore they should all be eliminated.

3. <u>A</u> is the correct answer.

The researchers described in the passage were interested in investigating dog coats, which are made of a number of factors including length of fur, texture of fur, and the pattern of fur growth (lines 17-19). While color is seemingly relevant trait, it was NOT a trait which researchers in fact investigated. Choose A as appropriate. The other answers can be eliminated as representing traits which the researchers DID investigate.

4. <u>D</u> is the correct answer.

Lines 27-30 quote a researcher who explains that "What's important for human health is the way we found the genes involved in dog coats and figured out how they work together, rather than the genes themselves." This content indicates that if the value to human health relies on the interaction between multiple genes, then it follows that diseases typically involve multiple genes. Choose D as appropriate. A and B can be eliminated since the development of vaccines (as opposed to genetic solutions) is NOT discussed in the passage, and NO correlation is established between diseases in humans and the breeding (as opposed to study) of animals. C can be eliminated because the passage does NOT establish a connection between animals and the rise of human diseases; research involving dogs instead may promote greater understanding of human health in the PRESENT.

5. <u>B</u> is the correct answer.

See the previous answer explanation for analysis of the correct line reference. A describes how the study of genetic variance in dogs can contribute valuable insight into human health (but is too broad to justify the focus on genes in the correct answer to the previous question), while C describes the impact of artificial selection on canine genetics. D describes the connection between selective breeding of dogs and contributions to research into human health. None of these other answers imply that complex human diseases result from the interplay of multiple genes, and therefore they should all be eliminated.

6. <u>D</u> is the correct answer.

The seventh paragraph introduces a discussion of the genes associated with hair texture in humans and establishes the relationship between these genes and the genes associated with fur texture in animals. Choose D as the best answer. A and B can be eliminated since the RSP02 gene IS found to be associated with human hair, and since no geographic differences (as opposed to genetic properties) are discussed in the paragraph. C can be eliminated since the passage focuses on specific genes in different mammals, NOT on the evolutionary heritage of animals overall.

7. <u>C</u> is the correct answer.

The passage describes research into coat phenotypes in dogs and connects this research to possible advancements in the understanding of complex human diseases. Choose C to reflect this content. A and B can be eliminated since the aim of this research (which clearly connects to human health) is NOT specifically to benefit canine health or to optimize selective breeding. D can be eliminated because the research did NOT serve to advance strategies to alter dog coats (though the research DID explain present variations) and explores dog coats in order to gain deeper insight into human genetics and health.

8. <u>C</u> is the correct answer.

In line 92, "determine" refers to genes generating or triggering particular traits. Choose C to reflect this meaning. A (inappropriately implying encountering someone or something for the first time), B (inappropriately implying arriving at a final decision or perspective), and D (inappropriately implying performing analysis to arrive at information or insight) all introduce improper contexts and should be eliminated.

9. <u>D</u> is the correct answer.

The graph presents data about two particular vertebrate species (humans and rats) but NOT about a wider cross-section of vertebrate species. Based on the graph alone, it is NOT possible to arrive at generalizations which are true about MOST vertebrates, and therefore D should be identified as the correct answer. A can be eliminated because the relative percentages of thymine in human and octopus DNA are visible in the graph, while B can be eliminated because the relative percentages of guanine in human and rat DNA are visible in the graph. C can be eliminated because the graph shows that, in the case of the DNA profile of humans (one vertebrate species), thymine and adenine are more abundant than cytosine and guanine are.

10. <u>A</u> is the correct answer.

The passage provides information about how specific genes determine specific traits in mammals but does not explain the basic composition of DNA (which is referenced briefly in lines 19-26). The graph provides information about the make-up of DNA in different species, providing additional information beyond the scope of the passage. Choose A as appropriate. B and C can be eliminated since the passage does NOT explore the composition of DNA at all (despite noting that DNA is relevant to genetic research), and the graph (in offering further information) does NOT directly connect to any of the claims made in the passage. D can be eliminated because the graph provides information about DNA composition overall, but does NOT provide information about any specific genes.

Passage 29, Pages 131-133

1. <u>C</u> is the correct answer.

The passage focuses on two recent scientific studies examining dust towers. These studies presented additional insights into dust towers, but there are still significant questions about these towers which scientists have not yet answered (lines 69-80). Choose C as appropriate. A and B can both be eliminated since the scientists did

NOT perform any specific experiments but rather gathered data based on observation, and since these studies are among the first to provide information about how dust towers form and are therefore NOT meant to refute previous theories. D can be eliminated since the findings about dust towers were enabled by emerging scientific technology, which is presented positively in the passage.

2. A is the correct answer.

The passage states that dust towers "occur under normal conditions" and that "the towers appear to form in greater numbers during global storms" (lines 21-23). This content indicates that one could expect to observe dust towers year-round; choose A as appropriate. Be careful not choose B, since while the towers are more likely to occur during storms, they ALSO occur at other times. C and D can be eliminated since nothing in the passage indicates that dust towers only occur during specific seasons; in fact, lines 44-45 indicate that dust storms occur "throughout the Martian year."

3. C is the correct answer.

Lines 23-31 discuss the stages of dust tower formation, indicating increases in size by using references to American geography to provide a sense of scale. Choose C as the best answer. A and B can be eliminated since the references to American geography are mentioned only when the gradual formation of a dust tower is being discussed, and not in reference to its lifespan (which is not designated) or on which planets dust towers occur. D can be eliminated since the references are not used to distinguish findings from one study from another; instead, the different geographies offer different reference points within a SINGLE explanation.

4. D is the correct answer.

In line 36, "cloak" refers to how dust storms cover or blanket the surface of Mars. Choose D to reflect this meaning. A (inappropriately implying forgiving or rationalizing an error or flaw), B (inappropriately implying overstating or dramatizing the effects of something), and C (inappropriately implying adding adornments) all introduce improper contexts and should therefore be eliminated.

5. A is the correct answer.

Lines 65-67 state that "the Red Planet lost its lakes and rivers over billions of years, becoming the freezing desert it is today," thus indicating that Mars was once home to bodies of water which have now vanished. Choose A as appropriate. B can be eliminated since the passage implies that the MRO provided greater details about some features of Mars but NOT that the planet's terrain was previously totally unknown. Be careful not to choose C, since the passage states that Mars once had water on its surface, but NOT that it had all the necessary conditions to support life (despite arguably having ONE condition with liquid water). D can be eliminated since, although the passage explores the duration and intensity of dust towers, this relatively new data cannot be compared over time; scientists thus do not know how the behaviors of dust towers have changed over time.

6. D is the correct answer.

See the previous answer explanation for analysis of the correct line reference. A describes how the MRO has contributed to research into dust towers on Mars, while B describes an observation which scientists made for the first time in 2018. C describes one hypothesis about dust towers which has captured the imaginations of scientists. None of these other answers refer to Mars once having been home to bodies of water (despite some references to conditions on Mars), and therefore they should all be eliminated.

7. C is the correct answer.

Lines 71-75 quote an expert stating that "Global dust storms are really unusual . . . We really don't have anything like this on the Earth, where the entire planet's weather changes for several months." This content indicates that, because global dust storms don't occur on Earth, there would be little use for a computer program to model such storms. Choose C, while A and B can be eliminated since the passage indicates that scientists are eager to learn more about how global dust storms form on Mars and hope to understand additional properties of dust towers. D can be eliminated since, while scientists are aware that the water on Mars apparently vanished (lines 65-68), the passage does not indicate that this fact has been fully explained.

8. C is the correct answer.

See the previous answer explanation for analysis of the correct line reference. A describes previous research relevant to the impact of dust storms on Mars, while B describes a research question which has not yet been answered. D identifies areas for future research. None of these answers highlight why scientists would be unlikely to be interested in attempts to model global dust storms on planet Earth (although some answers reference facts relevant to Mars and possible areas of inquiry), and therefore they should all be eliminated as not aligned with the correct answer to the previous question.

9. B is the correct answer.

The graph indicates that, regardless of stage, none of the dust towers reached a height of greater than 100 km. Choose B to reflect this information. A can be eliminated since the graph indicates that dust towers in their middle stage displayed a wider range of heights and widths, while those in their early stage showed a smaller range. This fact indicates that towers display a greater range during their middle stages, but whether this range involves high or low stability is NOT clearly indicated by the graph. C can be eliminated because the graph does NOT provide any information about the rate at which dust towers change size, and D can be eliminated since the graph indicates that, due to the considerable height ranges for any given stage, a dust tower MAY change in height during its early, middle, or late stage.

10. D is the correct answer.

The graph indicates that the height range for all types of dust towers (early, middle, and late stage) includes towers of 30km in height. Therefore, based on height alone, researchers would not be able to determine what type of storm the dust tower emanated from. A, B, and C can all readily be eliminated since they all indicate that the type of storm associated with a dust tower could be determined based on a 30 km height, whereas the graph indicates that such a conclusion would not be possible.

Passage 30, Pages 134-137

1. A is the correct answer.

In lines 20-23, the author explains that "like all things in robotics, practicality matters as much as vision. It's worth asking: Will anyone buy and use the thing?" This content indicates that technological innovations must have a practical use value; choose A as the best answer. B and C can be eliminated since the passage states that robots COULD be mass-produced and cost-effective (since they are in demand for manufacturing) and since the passage states that robots may have military applications, but the military is NOT necessarily funding these developments. D can be eliminated because the passage describes how autonomous robots and exoskeletons handle utilitarian tasks differently (lines 65-76), but does NOT establish which approach is superior.

2. B is the correct answer.

Lines 9-10 establish contrast between what is literally being stated by the author (that collaboration between humans and robots would be nice) and what is implied (that this outcome is unlikely or unexpected if a robot "wears you," line 4). Due to this gap between the literal and implied meaning, a sarcastic tone is established. Choose B as appropriate. A and D can be eliminated because the tone of these lines might be hopeful or relieved if the stated words were intended to be taken in ANOTHER, literal context. C can be eliminated because the author's tone is skeptical about collaboration between humans and robots, but the author (who acknowledges that robots remain imperfect) is NOT necessarily afraid of what this relationship might look like.

3. D is the correct answer.

In line 11, "terribly" is used to imply that there is not anything special or notable about the development of an exoskeleton. Choose D to reflect this meaning. A (inappropriately implying regret or a feeling of loss), B (inappropriately implying risk or the threat of harm), and C (inappropriately implying something unusual or unexpected) all introduce improper and often strongly negative contexts and should therefore be eliminated.

4. A is the correct answer.

Lines 50-54 state, in describing one exoskeleton, that "The system will set customers back $100,000 a year to rent, which sounds like a lot, but for industrial or military purposes, the six-figure rental may not deter would-be customers if the suit proves itself a useful bit of equipment." This content indicates that while exoskeletons are expensive, they may actually be LESS expensive than unaided human work; choose A as appropriate. B and D can be eliminated since the passage does NOT mention exoskeletons injuring workers (despite some ironic and critical references elsewhere) and does NOT discuss combining exoskeletons with artificial intelligence. Be careful not to choose C, since the passage implies that combining exoskeletons with human labor may lead to cost-effective solutions but does NOT discuss the TOTAL replacement of human workers.

5. C is the correct answer.

See the previous answer explanation for analysis of the correct line reference. A describes the technology which allows an exoskeleton robot to be functional, while B describes how long the XO suit can remain functional. D describes how exoskeletons differ from other forms of robotics and automation. None of these

Answer Explanations, Part 2

other answers consider the cost difference between unaided labor and labor using an exoskeleton (although some do address features of exoskeletons), and therefore they should all be eliminated.

6. <u>B</u> is the correct answer.

The passage explains that, in the case of exoskeleton robots, "The really hard bits, like navigating and recognizing and interacting with objects, are outsourced to its human operator." This content indicates that exoskeleton robots are not capable of identifying objects, and thus differ from autonomous robots, which DO do have this capability. Choose B as the best answer. A and D can be eliminated because the passages does NOT contrast the relative costs of exoskeleton robots and autonomous robots (despite contrasting the capabilities of such robots), and since the passage explains that exoskeletons (NOT autonomous robots) have been available in various forms for a long time. Be careful not to choose C since, while autonomous robots have greater capacity to respond to change, it does NOT necessarily follow that exoskeleton robots cannot be used in changing environments at all.

7. <u>B</u> is the correct answer.

Lines 14-18 provide examples of different utilities associated with exoskeletons: "light exoskeletons tailored to industrial settings—some of which are being tested out by the likes of Honda—and healthcare exoskeletons that support the elderly or folks with disabilities." This content indicates that robots (such as exoskeleton robots) have a wide range of potential uses; choose B as appropriate. A describes how wearing the suit changes the experience of carrying out tasks, while C describes how it is easy for individuals to learn how to utilize the suit. D describes the history of an individual who is now active in robotics research. None of these other answers support the idea that robotics have wide-ranging applications (despite mentioning robotics as a broad topic), and therefore they should all be eliminated.

8. <u>D</u> is the correct answer.

In line 78, "fruits" refers to the products or results of early research into robotics. Choose D to reflect this meaning. A (inappropriately implying organic food items grown for human consumption), B (inappropriately implying the money received as a result of a business venture), and C (inappropriately implying individuals who belong to a particular family of origin) all introduce improper contexts and should therefore be eliminated.

9. <u>B</u> is the correct answer.

The graph reveals that Model 4 can lift approximately 160 pounds and costs slightly more than $50,000. As a result, Model 4 meets the stipulations of the construction company; choose B as appropriate. A can be eliminated because Model 3 can only lift between 100 and 120 pounds, while C can be eliminated because Model 5 costs more than $70,000. D can be eliminated because Model 6 costs more than $90,000 and is therefore outside of the stipulated price range.

10. <u>D</u> is the correct answer.

The first paragraph of the passage describes an exoskeleton which allows users to lift at least 200 pounds while wearing it. According to the graph, the only relevant model of exoskeleton which allows individuals to lift 200 pounds or more is Model 5. Choose D as the best answer. All other answers can readily be eliminated because they refer to models which only allow users to lift LESS then 200 pounds.

NOTES

- Passage 16, "Umbilical cord blood: a new lifeline after a nuclear disaster?" is adapted from the article of the same name by Bryn Nelson and published by Mosaic Science. 27 March 2017, Mosaic. https://mosaicscience.com/story/umbilical-cord-blood-new-lifeline-after-nuclear-disaster/. Accessed 9 April 2020.

- Passage 17, "NASA's Fermi Traces Source of Cosmic Neutrino to Monster Black Hole," is adapted from the article of the same name by Felicia Chou and Dewayne Washington and published by NASA. 12 July 2018, NASA. https://www.nasa.gov/press-release/nasa-s-fermi-traces-source-of-cosmic-neutrino-to-monster-black-hole. Accessed 9 April 2020.

- Passage 18, "Have scientists finally killed off the Loch Ness Monster?" is an excerpt from the article of the same name by Jason Gilchrist and published by The Conversation (in partnership with Edinburgh Napier University). 6 September 2019, The Conversation. https://theconversation.com/have-scientists-finally-killed-off-the-loch-ness-monster-123075. Accessed 9 April 2020.

- Passage 19, " 'Wildling' mice could help translate results in animal models to results in humans," is adapted from the article of the same name published by the National Institutes of Health. 1 August 2019, NIH. https://www.nih.gov/news-events/news-releases/wildling-mice-could-help-translate-results-animal-models-results-humans. Accessed 9 April 2020.

- Passage 20, "Big Sagebrush Recovery After Fire Inhibited by Its Own Biology," is adapted from the article of the same name published by the United States Geological Survey. 25 July 2019, USGS. https://www.usgs.gov/news/big-sagebrush-recovery-after-fire-inhibited-its-own-biology. Accessed 9 April 2020.

- Passage 21, "Fossilized Footprints Lead Scientists Down a Prehistoric Path," is adapted from the article of the same name by Kayla Graham and published by EveryONE. 27 January 2015, PLOS ONE. https://blogs.plos.org/everyone/2015/01/27/fossilized-footprints-lead-scientists-prehistoric-path/. Accessed 9 April 2020.

- Passage 22, "Precious Time," is adapted from the article of the same name by Ivy F. Kupec and published by the National Science Foundation. 24 June 2015, NSF. https://nsf.gov/discoveries/disc_summ.jsp?cntn_id=135464. Accessed 9 April 2020.

- Passage 23, "Seaweed and sea slugs rely on toxic bacteria to defend against predators," is an excerpt from the article of the same name by Samantha Mascuch and Julia Kubanek and published by The Conversation. 13 June 2019, The Conversation. https://theconversation.com/seaweed-and-sea-slugs-rely-on-toxic-bacteria-to-defend-against-predators-118579. Accessed 9 April 2020.

- Passage 24, "Writing the First Human Genome by 2026 Is Synthetic Biology's Grand Challenge," is an excerpt from the article of the same name by Jason Dorrier and published by SingularityHub. 10 October 2016, SingularityHub. https://singularityhub.com/2016/10/10/writing-the-first-human-genome-by-2026-is-synthetic-biologys-grand-challenge/. Accessed 9 April 2020.

- Passage 25, "Scientists devise catalyst that uses light to turn carbon dioxide to fuel," is adapted from the article of the same name by Jared Sagoff and published by the Argonne National Laboratory. 3 December 2019, United States Department of Energy. https://www.anl.gov/article/scientists-devise-catalyst-that-uses-light-to-turn-carbon-dioxide-to-fuel. Accessed 9 April 2020.

- Passage 26, "Researcher studies unsolved problem of interacting objects," is adapted from the article of the same name by Marlene Cimons and published by the National Science Foundation. 10 March 2014, NSF. https://www.nsf.gov/discoveries/disc_summ.jsp?cntn_id=130738&org=MPS&from=news. Accessed 9 April 2020.

- Passage 27, "The mosquito breeder," is adapted from the article of the same name by Ed Yong and published by Mosaic Science. 25 March 2014, Mosaic. https://mosaicscience.com/story/mosquito-breeder/. Accessed 9 April 2020.

- Passage 28, "Variants in Three Genes Account for Most Dog Coat Differences," is adapted from the article of the same name published by the National Institutes of Health. 27 August 2009, NIH. https://www.nih.gov/news-events/news-releases/variants-three-genes-account-most-dog-coat-differences. Accessed 9 April 2020.

- Passage 29, "Global Storms on Mars Launch Dust Towers Into the Sky," is adapted from the article of the same name by Andrew Good and Alana Johnson and published by NASA. 26 November 2019, NASA. https://www.nasa.gov/feature/jpl/global-storms-on-mars-launch-dust-towers-into-the-sky. Accessed 9 April 2020.

- Passage 30, "Robotic Exoskeletons, Like This One, Are Getting More Practical," is an excerpt from the article of the same name by Jason Dorrier and published by SingularityHub. 18 December 2019, SingularityHub. https://singularityhub.com/2019/12/18/robotic-exoskeletons-like-this-one-are-getting-more-practical. Accessed 9 April 2020.

About the Figures: The various visual resources that accompany the passages in this section are primarily meant to facilitate critical thinking skills and may not reflect historical data.

Part 3

Science, Paired

Reading Strategy
Part 3: Science, Paired

Essential Tactics

The paired Science passages cover the same range of topics as the single Science passages, as described on Page 88. Stylistically, these readings can also be much more accessible than paired History passages, which often present test-takers with relatively obscure vocabulary and complex syntax. Still, paired Science can be more difficult for readers who are accustomed to a straightforward pro-con structure, which appears with great regularity in paired History but NOT in paired Science. These readings, instead, can give you a sound sense of the many different ways in which two SAT passages can play off one another.

Possible combinations include

- Sharp disagreement (two contradictory theories or experiments)

- Moderate disagreement (two passages that point out exceptions or convey skepticism)

- One neutral or balanced author, one extremely biased author

- One passage providing essential background, one pointing out a new approach or a new aspect of the topic

- One passage explaining a finding, one analyzing a specific point or repercussion of that finding

As this list of statements indicates, there will ALMOST ALWAYS be a core relationship between the two passages that can be summed up in a fairly concise statement. Your task is to determine what this relationship is—since the SAT features questions on exactly this topic—and then to determine a few of the smaller similarities and differences that the passages involve.

For any paired passage that you come across, ask yourself the following core questions.

1. What is the main idea and main tone (positive or negative, if relevant) of each passage?

2. How can the relationship between the passages be summed up in a single phrase or sentence?

3. In what smaller ways are the passages the same or different?

You will find that thinking analytically about this information will prepare you for the standard passage questions. Here is a list of the Paired Passage questions that have appeared prominently on the SAT.

- Relationship between the passages (opposition, agreement, one expanding upon the other, etc.)

- Purposes of the passages (sometimes BOTH passages serving the same purpose, despite other differences)

- Point of similarity (even if the passages are in overall disagreement) or point of difference (even if the passages are in overall agreement)

- Techniques used by the authors (often similarity, though noting differences may be required)

- How the author of one passage would respond to an element of the other passage (possibly a main idea or a main point, possibly a detail)

These questions will always be COMPLETELY evidence-based; in fact, the three or four questions that focus on passage comparison may include a Command of Evidence item. You must keep this rule firmly in mind even when dealing with question types that seem to require imagination or interpretation, as the final question type ("How would the author . . . ") appears to at first glance. In reality, this question type does NOT require any sort of cleverness. Simply determine one author's position, using either an effective overall read or a relevant set of lines, and use THAT information to determine a hypothetical response.

Working with paired Science passages is also made easier by similarities between these readings and the single Science entries. On the whole, paired passages adapt the standard "inquiry, experiment, outcomes" structure to account for the new, comparison-based analysis that you will need to perform.

Here are some of the passages and relationships that have appeared on recent SAT official tests; these items should give you a sense of the kind of overarching passage relationship statements that you should develop from reading comprehension.

- Passage 1 - the nature and possible economic outcomes of mining in space; Passage 2 - the conceptual and regulatory difficulties that would surround space mining practices (balanced overview to moderate negative, Test 1)

- Passage 1 - apparent effect of online activity on cognitive processes and habits; Passage 2 - skepticism about claims that online engagement changes mental activity (disagreement on some key points, Test 2)

- Passage 1 - description of soil-based cultivation of the antibiotic teixobactin; Passage 2 - some praise and clear reservations related to soil-based cultivation (process overview to assessment of value, Test 9)

Reading 31

Questions 1-10 are based on the following passages.

Passage 1 is adapted from "How do seismologists locate an earthquake?" an article that presents common research procedures. Passage 2 is adapted from "Oklahoma Study Reveals Possible, Previously Unknown Sources of Earthquakes," a 2018 news release. Both of the relevant articles were published by the United States Geological Survey.

Passage 1

When an earthquake occurs, one of the first questions is "where was it?" The location may tell us what fault it was on and where damage (if any)
Line most likely occurred.
5   Unfortunately, Earth is not transparent and we can't just see or photograph the earthquake disturbance like meteorologists can photograph clouds. When an earthquake occurs, it generates an expanding wavefront from the earthquake
10 hypocenter at a speed of several kilometers per second.

    We observe earthquakes with a network of seismometers on the earth's surface. The ground motion at each seismometer is amplified and
15 recorded electronically at a central recording site. As the wavefront expands from the earthquake, it reaches more distant seismic stations. When an earthquake occurs, we observe the times at which the wavefront passes each station. We must find
20 the unknown earthquake source knowing these wave arrival times.

    We want to find the location, depth, and origin time of an earthquake whose waves arrive at the times measured on each seismogram. We want
25 a straightforward and general procedure that we can also program in a computer. The procedure is simple to state: guess a location, depth, and origin time; compare the predicted arrival times of the wave from your guessed location with the
30 observed times at each station; then move the location a little in the direction that reduces the difference between the observed and calculated

times. Then repeat this procedure, each time getting closer to the actual earthquake location
35 and fitting the observed times a little better. Quit when your adjustments have become small enough and when the fit to the observed wave arrival times is close enough.

Passage 2

    Oklahoma has been the site of thousands of
40 earthquakes associated with wastewater injection activity, or induced seismicity, but few of the earthquake sequences have occurred on mapped faults, making seismic hazards difficult to estimate.
45   The USGS and the Oklahoma Geological Survey (OGS) used the newly acquired airborne magnetic data to image rocks where the earthquakes are occurring miles beneath the surface. The magnetic field maps reveal
50 boundaries or contacts between different rock types, some of which are linear, similar to faults. A number of these types of contacts, (referred to as "lineaments" in the magnetic field map), are aligned with sequences of earthquakes.
55 This suggests that some of them represent ancient faults that have been reactivated due to wastewater injection, which generates, or "induces" earthquakes.

    "We are hoping that the results will be used
60 to guide more detailed studies at local scales to assess potential earthquake hazards," said USGS scientist Anji Shah, lead author for the study. Additionally, the data show that there is a dominant "grain" direction to the magnetic
65 contacts (like wood grain) in the deep rocks where the earthquakes are occurring. This "grain" was formed hundreds of millions of years ago and may be composed in part by faults that are oriented favorably to move in response to
70 natural background stresses within the earth. This alignment of deep features may contribute to the high levels of seismicity occurring in response to wastewater injection.

    "There is nothing like a new data set to excite
75 geoscientists looking for answers to some of the mysteries of induced seismicity in Oklahoma,"

*See Page 228 for the citations for these texts.

CONTINUE

said Dr. Jeremy Boak, OGS Director. "We look forward to discussing these results among ourselves and with the interested technical
80 community. We also hope to bring these data to bear on addressing the persistent seismic activity and sharing our interpretations with Oklahomans and other stakeholders regarding this challenging issue."

1

Passage 1 suggests that scientists want the procedure used by earthquake mapping software to be

A) site-specific.

B) historically informed.

C) interesting to the local community.

D) widely applicable.

2

Which choice best supports the notion that earthquake modeling software finds the approximate, NOT exact, hypocenter of each earthquake?

A) Lines 5-8 ("Unfortunately, . . . clouds")

B) Lines 22-24 ("We want . . . seismogram")

C) Lines 24-26 ("We want . . . computer")

D) Lines 36-38 ("Quit when . . . enough")

3

As used in line 36, "Quit" most nearly means

A) stop.

B) give up.

C) pause.

D) exit.

4

It can be inferred from Passage 2 that which of the following would be true if wastewater had not been injected into the ground in Oklahoma?

A) Fewer lineaments in Oklahoma would remain dormant.

B) More lineaments in Oklahoma would remain dormant.

C) The magnetic contacts in Oklahoma would have a different grain direction.

D) A lower percentage of earthquakes in Oklahoma would occur on previously-mapped faults.

5

Which choice provides the best evidence for the answer to the previous question?

A) Lines 39-44 ("Oklahoma . . . estimate")

B) Lines 52-54 ("A number . . . earthquakes")

C) Lines 55-58 ("This suggests . . . earthquakes")

D) Lines 66-70 ("This 'grain' . . . the earth")

6

According to Passage 2, it is difficult to estimate seismic hazards from wastewater injection in Oklahoma because

A) most earthquakes in Oklahoma caused by wastewater injection occur on previously-known fault lines.

B) most earthquakes in Oklahoma caused by wastewater injection occur on fault lines that were previously undetected.

C) some ancient faults have been reactivated by wastewater injection.

D) the magnetic contacts in the ground are aligned to natural stresses in the rock.

CONTINUE

7

As used in line 64, "dominant" most nearly means

A) overpowering.

B) prevalent.

C) aggressive.

D) victorious.

8

One key difference between the two passages is that

A) Passage 1 discusses an indirect method of data collection while Passage 2 does not.

B) Passage 2 discusses an indirect method of data collection while Passage 1 does not.

C) Passage 1 discusses fault lines while Passage 2 does not.

D) Passage 1 discusses a procedure while Passage 2 discusses potential applications of data.

9

Passage 1 resembles Passage 2 in that both passages discuss

A) ancient fault lines.

B) seismometers.

C) mapping of the origins of earthquakes.

D) how to share results with local communities.

10

The OGS in Passage 2 would most likely respond to lines 2-4 ("The location . . . occurred") of Passage 1 by stating that

A) it would be difficult to predict the damage caused by earthquakes that did not originate on previously-known fault lines.

B) it is more important to predict than to retrospectively assess damage caused by earthquakes.

C) earthquakes are caused by wastewater injection, so geologists should focus more on wastewater injection sites.

D) airborne data is necessary to map earthquakes accurately.

CONTINUE

Part 3: Science, Paired

Reading 32

Questions 1-10 are based on the following passages.

Passage 1 is adapted from Marian Weidner, "Catching up with the author: Gareth Whiteley on snake venom and antivenom research," an article published* in 2016 by Speaking of Medicine, the official blog of the PLOS medical journals. Passage 2 is adapted from Léa Surugue, "Why is it so hard to stop people dying from snakebite?" an article published* in 2019 by Mosaic.

Passage 1

Venomous snakes are widely dispersed across the globe, occupying a range of habitats in both terrestrial and marine environments. A major part
Line of venomous snakes' predatory success is the
5 venom proteins which cause rapid cardiovascular or neurological immobilisation and death of their prey. For humans, being in the wrong place at the wrong time can have disastrous consequences—snakebites against humans are often an accidental
10 reaction to a perceived threat. Exposure to venom proteins can lead to disability, death, or other serious medical complications. Each year over 94,000 people die from snakebites globally—mostly in remote, disadvantaged areas where
15 snakebite incidence remains relatively high.

The development of effective snakebite therapies, or antivenom, relies on researchers' understanding of the unique protein composition of different snake venoms. Currently, genetic
20 sequencing of venom proteins and isolation of mRNA requires sacrifice of the snake and removal of the venom gland. This methodological challenge limits the scope of research in this area and is undesirable for ethical and environmental
25 reasons, under which a given species of snake may be endangered or assigned protected status.

In a PLOS Neglected Tropical Diseases research article published last June, Gareth Whiteley and colleagues present a new protocol
30 to improve the yield of high quality RNA isolated from venom collected from live snakes. They were able to capture significant isoform

diversity from the RNA and demonstrated that the isoforms they identified were identical to
35 isoforms extracted through traditional methods from venom glands of sacrificed snakes. These improved methods allow reliable access to venom composition data from venom acquired from live snakes, empowering researchers to expand the
40 scope of their research while obviating the need to sacrifice snakes for venom research. The hope is that this breakthrough will save lives of both snakes and people!

Passage 2

It's warm where the snakes live. The air in
45 the herpetarium is humid, and on the walls, faded posters sum up the history of antivenom production. The morning is coming to an end, and in transparent boxes, neatly piled up, 163 snakes—spanning 49 different species—are
50 waiting to be fed.

These reptiles, housed here at the Centre for Snakebite Research & Interventions at the Liverpool School of Tropical Medicine, make up the largest and most diverse collection of
55 venomous snakes in the UK. It's their job to provide venom for antivenom manufacturers and to help find new ways to treat snakebite.

Today, it's the turn of the black mamba to be "milked"—that is, to have its venom extracted.
60 Paul Rowley is the team's lead herpetologist, an expert in snake handling and husbandry. Slowly, he opens the box to let the mamba out. From behind a large glass window, I follow his careful, deliberate movements as he handles the
65 snake. It's impressive, a couple of metres long. It's hard to say if it's more brown or grey, but it is definitely not black. The snake actually gets its name from the colour of the inside of its mouth.

Despite its length, the black mamba moves
70 surprisingly quickly. Rowley and his assistant have to work together to restrain it, pinning the animal down on the table. Holding its head tightly, they then massage its venom glands to extract the venom as the snake bites on a small container
75 topped with clingfilm. The whole process takes less than five minutes.

*See Page 228 for the citations for these texts.

CONTINUE

179

Copyright 2020 PrepVantage, online at prepvantagetutoring.com

"Most snakes will instinctively bite as soon as they are presented with something," says Nick Casewell, a research fellow at the centre. "As
80 soon as you move the head of the snake towards a Petri dish, usually the snake will immediately bite, and you will get venom, too. But it is variable how much venom you get on a particular day."

Milking a snake is the first step in creating
85 antivenom. The process is over 120 years old, and has changed very little in that time. You inject small, non-toxic doses of venom into an animal—usually a horse or a sheep—to stimulate an immune response. The animal then starts
90 producing antibodies against the venom's toxins, and you draw some of its blood. Finally, you isolate and purify these antibodies, and make them into a stable solution that can be given to patients as an injection.

1

The author of Passage 1 suggests that venom research could be expanded if

A) venom did not contain specific proteins.

B) snakes were more prevalent in the most developed countries.

C) venomous snakes were not geographically dispersed in an uneven manner.

D) killing snakes were not necessary in harvesting their venom.

2

Which choice provides the best evidence for the answer to the previous question?

A) Lines 1-3 ("Venomous . . . environments")

B) Lines 12-15 ("Each year . . . relatively high")

C) Lines 16-19 ("The development . . . venoms")

D) Lines 22-26 ("This methodological . . . status")

3

As used in line 29, "present" most nearly means

A) describe.

B) perform.

C) develop.

D) invent.

4

The author of Passage 1 states that a benefit of the newer methods of harvesting venom is that

A) they enable more substantial protein harvesting.

B) they yield higher quality RNA.

C) the snakes survive the process.

D) they are cheaper than traditional methods.

5

The focus of Passage 2 shifts from

A) a profile of researchers to a discussion of the attributes of snakes.

B) an overview of a profession to a synopsis of its drawbacks.

C) a description of a facility to an explanation of the procedures employed there.

D) a research question to a potential answer.

6

Which of the following choices best supports the notion that antivenom production relies on a set of practices passed down through time?

A) Lines 45-47 ("on the walls . . . production")

B) Lines 55-57 ("It's . . . snakebite")

C) Lines 77-78 ("Most . . . something")

D) Lines 91-95 ("Finally . . . injection")

180

CONTINUE

7

As used in line 64, the phrase "careful, deliberate" primarily emphasizes

A) the high level of training needed to be a herpetarium worker.

B) the small margin of error for immobilizing a snake.

C) the detailed nature of antivenom research.

D) the predatory motions of snakes.

8

The relationship between the two passages is that

A) Passage 2 presents a counterargument to the central claim of Passage 1.

B) Passage 2 clarifies the science behind the research project discussed in Passage 1.

C) Passage 2 shows how a key development from Passage 1 being used.

D) Passage 2 criticizes the methods of a researcher mentioned in Passage 1.

9

A difference between the two passages is that

A) Passage 1 discusses benefits to people and snakes while Passage 2 considers benefits to people only.

B) Passage 1 discusses benefits to people and snakes while Passage 2 considers benefits to snakes only.

C) Passage 1 discusses benefits to people only while Passage 2 considers benefits to people and snakes.

D) Passage 1 discusses benefits to snakes only while Passage 2 considers benefits to people and snakes.

10

How would the author of Passage 1 most likely respond to lines 79-83 ("As soon . . . day") of Passage 2?

A) The procedure has evident failings because the snake will have to be sacrificed.

B) Genetic sequencing cannot be performed on the type of sample considered in Passage 2.

C) Sufficiently diverse RNA will be isolated regardless of procedure.

D) The handlers must take precautions while working with the snake.

CONTINUE

Reading 33

Questions 1-10 are based on the following passages.

Passage 1 is adapted from Janine Mendes-Franco, "Is the Caribbean apocalypse-proof?" Passage 2 is adapted from Emma Lewis, "A rash of 'travel bans' as the Caribbean gets serious about coronavirus." Both of these articles were first published* by Global Voices in 2020.

Passage 1

In one of the most curious stories to be shared on social media platforms in the Caribbean at the start of 2020, the United Kingdom-based tabloid
Line The Sun claimed that "scientists have worked out
5 the safest places for you to be if a sudden global pandemic threatens to wipe out humanity."

As it turns out, many of those supposed safe spots happen to be islands, with five out the top 20 located in the Caribbean. The highest-ranked
10 of the regional nations was The Bahamas—ironically, still reeling from a disaster of its own in the form of Hurricane Dorian—followed by Trinidad and Tobago at Number 8, Barbados at Number 9, Cuba at Number 11, and Jamaica
15 bringing up the rear at Number 18.

The article is careful to state, however, that apart from the top three (Australia, New Zealand, and Iceland), other countries "ranked less than 0.5, so were less suitable for securing
20 [humanity's] survival." Sadly, Number 1-ranked Australia has been battling debilitating wildfires since June 2019, so even if the continent were inclined to offer itself as an end-of-days refuge—questionable given its record on migration—it
25 currently has its hands full (and indeed requires both international sympathy and aid). Some of the features that contributed to the final scores included things like "a good physical location, natural resources, and political harmony."
30 Caribbean netizens were, for the most part, amused by the study, in which countries were ranked based on "the ability to avoid contagion from other areas." The "no man is an island"

philosophy clearly carries no weight when it
35 comes to the apocalypse—if doomsday looms, apparently, an island is exactly where you want to be. The infographic accompanying the article did not help to instill confidence in the findings, however, what with Cape Verde appearing
40 slightly north of where it is actually located and Madagascar showing up twice—once off the coast of Brazil. The research, first published in the international journal *Risk Analysis*, was conducted by Matt Boyd and Nick Wilson.
45 Wilson, a public health physician at the University of Otago in New Zealand, suggested that biotechnology discoveries could potentially result in a genetically-engineered pandemic threatening human survival. "Though carriers
50 of disease can easily circumvent land borders," he told The Sun, "a closed self-sufficient island could harbour an isolated, technologically-adept population that could repopulate the earth following a disaster."

Passage 2

55 Caribbean island nations are as concerned about who crosses their borders as any other nation. So, when the World Health Organization (WHO) declared the coronavirus—officially named COVID-19—as a global health emergency,
60 regional governments began taking concrete action. To date, no case of COVID-19 has been confirmed in the Latin America/Caribbean region, according to the Pan American Health Organization, which is helping the region prepare
65 for any possible cases.

Jamaica is one of several Caribbean territories—including Antigua and Barbuda, The Bahamas, Dominica, and Trinidad and Tobago—to impose travel restrictions to and from China,
70 after COVID-19 was traced back to a market in Wuhan, China, a city of 11 million people.

As of February 8, 2020, Barbados had not imposed a ban but insisted that it is conducting rigorous screening at all ports of entry. Such
75 measures will have economic implications for the region, which is heavily dependent on tourism—an industry which is reportedly thriving, as

CONTINUE ➤

thousands of visitors fly to one or more islands on a daily basis. This gradual increase in travel
80 restrictions as the virus has spread to over 20 countries will have a dampening effect on the global travel industry, at the height of tourist season in the Caribbean.

1

The author of Passage 1 would argue that the article on global "safe spots" that appeared in The Sun is

A) fundamentally authoritative despite its often outlandish style.

B) reliant on simplifications of intricate ideas in modern medicine.

C) sensationalized for the sake of engaging a diverse readership.

D) defective in how it presented even basic information about its topic.

2

Which choice provides the best evidence for the answer to the previous question?

A) Lines 3-6 ("the United . . . humanity")

B) Lines 9-15 ("The highest-ranked . . . Number 18")

C) Lines 37-42 ("The infographic . . . Brazil")

D) Lines 45-49 ("Wilson . . . survival")

3

On the basis of Passage 1, which hypothetical piece of information would effectively support the ideas set forward by Nick Wilson?

A) Most of the technologies used by island nations were not pioneered by the residents of those countries.

B) Genetically-engineered pathogens have so far been successfully confined to laboratories.

C) Island nations normally establish extensive trade networks to provide their citizens with essential goods.

D) Modern virus epidemics have spread largely as the result of overland transit between cities.

4

The main purpose of Passage 2 is to

A) propose a improvements to public health policies common to several nations.

B) chart how a single area of the world reacted to an international calamity.

C) describe the process of scientifically modeling the spread of an epidemic in the context of a single well-documented case.

D) justify the idea that economic and scientific progress are inextricable.

5

As used in lines 55-56, "concerned about" most nearly means

A) irritated by.

B) preoccupied with.

C) inseparable from.

D) petrified by.

CONTINUE

183

6

The words "confirmed" (line 62) and "traced" (line 70) help to place emphasis on

A) dangers that are increasing in extent.

B) research that is seen as innovative.

C) facts that have been firmly verified.

D) disputes that have finally been resolved.

7

The author of Passage 2 would most likely predict that one impact of the COVID-19 crisis will be

A) economic liabilities for countries that rely on tourism revenue.

B) improved methods of rapidly producing antiviral vaccines.

C) legislation to restrict the flow of immigrants.

D) new technologies that chart viral transmission.

8

Which statement best describes the relationship between the two passages?

A) Passage 1 critiques a source that is apparently flawed; Passage 2 employs new evidence to offer a defense of the same source.

B) Passage 1 considers the safety criteria for a region from different perspectives; Passage 2 shows how the same region responded to a threat to public health.

C) Passage 1 presents a series of guidelines that can be applied in managing crises; Passage 2 illustrates how a few nations successfully adhered to those guidelines.

D) Passage 1 implies that modern public health crises are mostly negligible in effect; Passage 2 underscores the severity of a recent crisis to challenge this belief.

9

One significant difference between how the two passages address the topic of public health crises is that Passage 1

A) portrays an outbreak as a hypothetical occurrence, while Passage 2 addresses a recorded crisis.

B) suggests that data collection can help to mitigate outbreaks, while Passage 2 indicates that much existing data is unreliable.

C) assesses the damage from several past outbreaks, while Passage 2 focuses on an ongoing problem.

D) sets forth information in a mostly unbiased manner, while Passage 2 voices criticisms of a specific approach.

10

Which choice best indicates that the societies on Caribbean islands are currently structured around the "no man is an island" philosophy mentioned in Passage 1?

A) Lines 57-59 ("The World . . . emergency")

B) Lines 61-63 ("To date . . . region")

C) Lines 70-71 ("COVID-19 . . . people")

D) Lines 74-79 ("Such . . . basis")

CONTINUE ▶

Part 3: Science, Paired

Reading 34

Questions 1-10 are based on the following passages.

Passage 1 is adapted from "Toward an unhackable quantum internet." Passage 2 is adapted from "Tiny optical cavities could make quantum networks possible." The original forms of these texts first appeared as news releases* from the National Science Foundation in 2020.

Passage 1

A quantum internet could be used to send un-hackable messages, improve the accuracy of GPS, and enable cloud-based quantum computing.
Line For more than twenty years, dreams of creating
5 such a quantum network have remained out of reach in large part because of the difficulty of sending quantum signals across large distances without loss. Now, Harvard and MIT researchers have found a way to correct for signal loss with
10 a prototype quantum node that can catch, store and entangle bits of quantum information. The research is the missing link toward a practical quantum internet and a major step forward in the development of long-distance quantum networks.
15 "This demonstration is a conceptual breakthrough that could extend the longest possible range of quantum networks and potentially enable many new applications in a manner that is impossible with any existing
20 technologies," said Mikhail Lukin, co-director of the Harvard Quantum Initiative. "This is the realization of a goal that has been pursued by our quantum science and engineering community for more than two decades." The National Science
25 Foundation-funded research is published in *Nature*.

Every form of communication technology—from the first telegraph to today's fiberoptic internet—has had to address the fact that
30 signals degrade and are lost when transmitted over distances. Repeaters, which receive and amplify signals to correct for this loss, were first developed to amplify fading wire telegraph signals in the mid-1800s. Two hundred years
35 later, repeaters are still an integral part of our long-distance communications infrastructure. The new device combines the three most important elements of a quantum repeater—a long memory, the ability to efficiently catch information from
40 photons, and a way to process it locally.

"If we compare the quest for a secure quantum internet to the 1960s mission to deliver Americans to the surface of the moon and return them safely to Earth," says Filbert Bartoli, director of NSF's
45 Division of Electrical, Communications and Cyber Systems, "the demonstration of quantum repeaters may be of comparable significance to the demonstration of detachable rocket boosters, which allowed astronauts to escape Earth's
50 atmosphere, or to the heat resistant shields that allowed them to return safely to Earth and not burn up on reentry to Earth's atmosphere."

Passage 2

Engineers at Caltech have shown that atoms in optical cavities—tiny boxes for light—could
55 lead to the creation of a quantum internet. Their National Science Foundation-funded work was published in the journal *Nature Physics*.

Quantum networks would connect quantum computers through a system that operates at a
60 quantum, rather than classical, level. In theory, quantum computers will one day be able to perform certain functions faster than classical computers by taking advantage of the special properties of quantum mechanics. As they can
65 with classical computers, engineers would like to be able to connect multiple quantum computers to share data and work together in a quantum computer network.

"While important in their own right, quantum
70 computer networks also represent an important step toward realizing the goal of a secure quantum internet," explained Fil Bartoli, director of NSF's Division of Electrical, Communications and Cyber Systems. Networks would open the door to several
75 applications, including solving computations that

*See Page 228 for the citations for these texts.

185

CONTINUE

Copyright 2020 PrepVantage, online at prepvantagetutoring.com

are too large to be handled by a single quantum computer and establishing unbreakably secure communications using quantum cryptography.

A quantum network needs to be able to
80 transmit information between two points without altering the quantum properties of the information being transmitted. One current model works like this: a single atom or ion acts as a quantum bit (or "qubit") storing information via one of its
85 quantum properties, such as spin.

To read that information and transmit it elsewhere, the atom is excited with a pulse of light, causing it to emit a photon whose spin is entangled with the spin of the atom. The photon
90 can then transmit the information entangled with the atom over a long distance via fiber optic cable.

Researchers led by Caltech's Andrei Faraon, an applied physicist and electrical engineer, constructed a nanophotonic cavity, a beam that is
95 about 10 microns long—a fraction of an inch— with periodic nano-patterning, sculpted from a piece of crystal. In this cavity, scientists can excite an ytterbium ion and efficiently detect the resulting photon it emits, whose spin can be used
100 to read the information stored in the ion's spin.

"Advances like this fundamental research in quantum information science are important milestones to enable the long-term development of quantum technology," added Alex Cronin, a
105 program officer in NSF's Division of Physics.

1

As used in line 10, "node" most nearly means

A) growth.

B) location.

C) repeater.

D) database.

2

The tone of lines 21-26 ("This is . . . Nature") can best be described as

A) proud.

B) arrogant.

C) resigned.

D) apprehensive.

3

According to the passage, all of the following are characteristics of quantum repeaters EXCEPT

A) the potential to process information locally.

B) the ability to duplicate very large data sets.

C) the capacity to catch information.

D) a long-lasting memory structure.

4

Which of the following choices best supports the notion that non-quantum communication must contend with signal degradation?

A) Lines 4-8 ("For more . . . without loss")

B) Lines 15-20 ("This demonstration . . . technologies")

C) Lines 31-34 ("Repeaters . . . mid-1800s")

D) Lines 36-40 ("The new . . . locally")

CONTINUE

Part 3: Science, Paired

5

The purpose of the last paragraph (lines 41-52) of Passage 1 is to

A) use an analogy to underscore the significance of a development.

B) employ a comparison to explain the technical side of an unprecedented situation.

C) point out differences between two fields of study.

D) provide instances from scientific history from the 1960s that led to quantum computing.

6

As used in line 89, "entangled with" most nearly means

A) twisted into.

B) bonded to.

C) dependent on.

D) combined with.

7

According to Passage 2, photons are useful in quantum computing because they

A) are easily ejected from atoms.

B) typically prove faster than electricity.

C) preserve information as they travel.

D) are lightweight.

8

Which choice provides the best evidence for the answer to the previous question?

A) Lines 74-78 ("Networks . . . cryptography")

B) Lines 79-82 ("A quantum . . . transmitted")

C) Lines 86-88 ("To read . . . emit a photon")

D) Lines 101-105 ("Advances . . . of Physics")

9

The primary developments addressed in the two passages are

A) quantum repeaters in Passage 1 and nanophotonic cavities in Passage 2.

B) quantum repeaters in Passage 1 and computer networks in Passage 2.

C) quantum internet in Passage 1 and quantum cryptography in Passage 2.

D) detachable rocket boosters in Passage 1 and nano-patterning in Passage 2.

10

Both passages mention

A) the discovery of new subatomic particles.

B) cloud computing as an increasingly popular technology.

C) the realization of a step in creating a quantum internet.

D) the necessity of improving GPS accuracy.

CONTINUE

Part 3: Science, Paired

Reading 35

Questions 1-10 are based on the following passages.

Passage 1 is adapted from "How the Flu Virus Can Change: 'Drift' and 'Shift'," a 2019 article from the Centers for Disease Control. Passage 2 is adapted from "Human antibody reveals hidden vulnerability in influenza virus," a 2019 news release* from the National Institutes of Health.

Passage 1

One way influenza viruses change is called "antigenic drift." These are small changes (or mutations) in the genes of influenza viruses
Line that can lead to changes in the surface proteins
5 of the virus: HA (hemagglutinin) and NA (neuraminidase). The HA and NA surface proteins of influenza viruses are "antigens," which means they are recognized by the immune system and are capable of triggering an immune response,
10 including production of antibodies that can block infection. The changes associated with antigenic drift happen continually over time as the virus replicates. Most flu shots are designed to target an influenza virus' HA surface proteins/antigens. The
15 nasal spray flu vaccine (LAIV) targets both the HA and NA of an influenza virus.
     The small changes that occur from antigenic drift usually produce viruses that are closely related to one another, which can be illustrated
20 by their location close together on a phylogenetic tree. Influenza viruses that are closely related to each other usually have similar antigenic properties. This means that antibodies which your immune system creates against one influenza virus
25 will likely recognize and respond to antigenically similar influenza viruses (a condition called "cross-protection").
     However, the small changes associated with antigenic drift can accumulate over time and result
30 in viruses that are antigenically different (farther away on the phylogenetic tree). It is also possible for a single (or small) change in a particularly important location on the HA to result in antigenic

drift. When antigenic drift occurs, the body's
35 immune system may not recognize and prevent sickness caused by the newer influenza viruses. As a result, a person becomes susceptible to flu infection again, as antigenic drift has changed the virus enough that a person's existing antibodies
40 won't recognize and neutralize the newer influenza viruses.
     Antigenic drift is the main reason why people can get the flu more than one time, and it's also a primary reason why the flu vaccine composition
45 must be reviewed and updated each year (as needed) to keep up with evolving influenza viruses.

Passage 2

The ever-changing "head" of an influenza virus protein has an unexpected Achilles heel,
50 report scientists funded by the National Institute of Allergy and Infectious Diseases (NIAID), one of the National Institutes of Health. The team discovered and characterized the structure of a naturally occurring human antibody
55 that recognizes and disrupts a portion of the hemagglutinin (HA) protein that the virus uses to enter and infect cells. The investigators determined that the antibody, FluA-20, binds tightly to an area on the globular head of the HA
60 protein that is only very briefly accessible to antibody attack. The site was not expected to be vulnerable to such a strike.
     James E. Crowe, Jr., M.D., of Vanderbilt University Medical Center, Nashville, Tennessee,
65 and Ian A. Wilson, D. Phil., of The Scripps Research Institute, San Diego, California, led the team. They isolated FluA-20 antibody from a person who had received many influenza immunizations. In a series of experiments,
70 they showed that FluA-20 can "reach into" an otherwise inaccessible part of the three-part HA trimer molecule and cause it to fall apart, thus preventing the spread of virus from cell to cell. This discovery came as a surprise because this
75 region of trimeric HA was thought to be stable and inaccessible to antibodies. Moreover, this region—unlike the rest of HA's head—varies little

---

*See Page 228 for the citations for these texts.

CONTINUE

Part 3: Science, Paired

from strain to strain. In theory, antibody-based
therapeutics directed at that precise region would
80 be effective against many strains of influenza
A virus. Similarly, vaccines designed to elicit
antibodies against this target might provide
long-lasting protection against any influenza
strain, potentially eliminating the need for annual
85 seasonal influenza vaccination.
      In mouse studies, FluA-20 prevented infection
or illness when the animals were exposed to
four different influenza A viral subtypes that
cause disease in humans. Two viruses used in
90 the experiments, H1N1 and H5N1, are Group 1
influenza subtypes, while the two others, H3N2
and H7N9, are members of Group 2. Current
influenza vaccines must contain viral components
from both subtypes to elicit matching antibodies.
95 A single vaccine able to generate potent antibodies
against members of both groups could provide
broad multi-year protection against influenza.

1

Over the course of Passage 1, the author's focus shifts
from

A) stating a theory to offering empirical support for
   that theory.

B) describing a problem to offering a potential
   solution.

C) explaining a phenomenon to exploring its
   significance.

D) defining a term to offering an alternative
   definition.

2

As used in line 13, the word "target" most nearly
conveys a sense of

A) specificity.

B) shape.

C) vulnerability.

D) harmfulness.

3

Which of the following best supports the notion that
not all regions of a virus are equally significant in
antibody-virus recognition?

A) Lines 11-13 ("The changes . . . replicates")

B) Lines 31-34 ("It is . . . drift")

C) Lines 34-36 ("When . . . viruses")

D) Lines 42-43 ("Antigenic drift . . . time")

4

As used in line 44, "composition" most nearly means

A) components.

B) layout.

C) document.

D) efficacy.

5

According to Passage 1, which of the following is
most analogous to the relationship between viral
surface proteins and phylogenetic relationships
between viruses?

A) Closely-related people have identical features.

B) Closely-related people have similar features.

C) Distantly-related people have identical features.

D) Distantly-related people have similar features.

189

Copyright 2020 PrepVantage, online at prepvantagetutoring.com

CONTINUE

Part 3: Science, Paired

6

Which choice provides the best evidence for the answer to the previous question?

A) Lines 6-9 ("The HA . . . response")

B) Lines 21-23 ("Influenza . . . properties")

C) Lines 23-27 ("This means . . . protection")

D) Lines 28-31 ("However . . . phylogenetic tree")

7

The function of the last paragraph (lines 86-97) of Passage 2 is to

A) suggest an area of further study.

B) reach a conclusion about the utility of a specific process.

C) provide a counterexample to cast doubt on a claim.

D) set forth an example to support ideas from the previous paragraph.

8

The relationship between the two passages is that

A) Passage 1 pinpoints a flaw in the line of reasoning central to Passage 2.

B) Passage 1 discusses a theory while Passage 2 focuses on that same theory's significance.

C) Passage 2 analyzes data presented in Passage 1.

D) Passage 2 provides a potential solution to a problem discussed in Passage 1.

9

A specific example of how antibodies disable viruses is presented in

A) Passage 1 only.

B) Passage 2 only.

C) both Passage 1 and Passage 2.

D) neither Passage 1 nor Passage 2.

10

The author of Passage 2 would most likely respond to the last paragraph (lines 42-47) of Passage 1 with

A) complete acceptance.

B) complete rejection.

C) agreement with the premise but disagreement with the conclusion.

D) objection to the premise but approval of the conclusion.

CONTINUE

Reading 36

Questions 1-10 are based on the following passages.

Passage 1 is an excerpt from Carl Meyer, "Western Australia's shark culls lack bite (and science)," published in 2013. Passage 2 is an excerpt from Ryan Kempster and Shaun Collin, "Finally, a proven way to keep great white sharks at arm's length," published in 2016. Both of the original articles appeared* in The Conversation.

Passage 1

After a spate of fatal shark attacks over the past two years, Western Australia has released a radical new shark plan that will see large sharks removed and destroyed in designated "safe
5 zones." The plan includes drum lines (baited hooks attached to drums) monitored daily, and solicits commercial fishers to hunt sharks larger than 3 metres. Nationally threatened and legally protected Great White Sharks are expected to be
10 one of the targeted species. But do these sort of measures actually reduce shark attacks, and how can we assess the results? How do we measure if shark programs work?

There are passionate, well-intentioned people
15 on both sides of the shark culling debate. We are unlikely to ever reach consensus on the philosophical question of whether it is ethical to kill large predators in order to make the natural environment a safer playground for humans.
20 What everyone can and should do is demand a rigorous, fact-based approach to this controversial issue. Unanswered questions remain in Western Australia's shark plan: how will the state define success of these programs and how will success be
25 measured? What are the impacts of culling likely to be on various Australian shark populations and their natural prey, and how will these be assessed?

True effectiveness cannot be assessed by simply counting the number of sharks captured
30 and killed. Demonstrable effectiveness means a measurable decrease in shark bite incidents in response to culling activities. Hawaii shark control programs of the 1960s and 1970s, for example,
were not demonstrably effective. These programs
35 were expensive, culled 4,668 sharks and yet failed to produce measurable decreases in shark bite incidents.

The challenges of reducing shark bites at specific locations were clearly illustrated by the
40 events at Barbers Point on the Hawaiian island of Oahu. The 1967-69 shark control program removed 33 tiger sharks at that one location alone, yet soon after the program finished a shark bite occurred at Barbers Point.

Passage 2

45 A wearable electric shark deterrent can effectively repel great white sharks, according to our independent tests of the device. The manufacturers of the A$749 Shark Shield Freedom 7TM say that it works by emitting an
50 electric field around the wearer. This causes uncomfortable muscle spasms in sharks that swim too close and discourages them from coming into contact.

Our research, published in the journal PLoS
55 ONE, shows that the device does indeed make sharks keep their distance. Upon first encounter with a Shark Shield, all approaching great white sharks were effectively deterred, staying an average of 1.3m away from a baited canister with
60 the device attached. After multiple approaches, individual great white sharks showed signs of habituation to the Shark Shield, coming an average of 12cm closer on each successive approach. Despite this increase in tolerance, 89%
65 of white sharks continued to be deterred from biting or interacting with the bait.

We carried out our testing in Mossel Bay, South Africa, in 2014. We used custom-built cameras equipped with bait and either an inactive
70 (control) or active Shark Shield. Using a video analysis technique traditionally used to measure the size of fish, we were able to determine exactly how closely the sharks approached the device.

We analysed a total of 322 encounters
75 involving 41 individual white sharks, ranging from 2m to 4m long. Only one great white shark came into contact with the bait in the presence of

*See Page 228 for the citations for these texts.

CONTINUE ➡

an active Shark Shield, and only after multiple approaches. The interaction in question simply
80 involved a bump of the bait canister rather than a full bite. In contrast, bites were common during control trials.

Although the effectiveness of the Shark Shield probably varies between shark species, it
85 is encouraging to note its effect on great white sharks, the species implicated in the majority of fatal incidents worldwide. This suggests it could be an important safety consideration for a range of ocean users such as surfers, divers, spear fishers,
90 and open-water swimmers.

1

As used in line 7, "soliciting" most nearly means

A) manipulating.

B) advertising.

C) hiring.

D) tempting.

2

The author of Passage 1 defines success in the shark control measures discussed as

A) a decrease in the number of sharks.

B) an increase in sharks' natural prey.

C) a consensus among experts.

D) a decrease in the number of shark bites.

3

Which choice provides the best evidence for the answer to the previous question?

A) Lines 15-19 ("We are . . . humans")

B) Lines 23-27 ("how will . . . assessed")

C) Lines 28-30 ("True effectiveness . . . are killed")

D) Lines 30-32 ("Demonstrable . . . activities")

4

Passage 2 is written from the perspective of

A) a competitor of Shark Shield Freedom.

B) independent scientists.

C) the manufacturer of Shark Shield Freedom.

D) an advocate of safety measures.

5

According to the analysis that appears in Passage 2, Shark Shield Freedom is

A) slightly less effective with repeated exposures.

B) slightly more effective with repeated exposures.

C) substantially less effective with repeated exposures.

D) substantially more effective with repeated exposures.

CONTINUE

6

Which choice provides the best evidence for the answer to the previous question?

A) Lines 56-58 ("Upon first . . . deterred")

B) Lines 60-66 ("After . . . the bait")

C) Lines 76-78 ("Only one . . . Shark Shield")

D) Lines 79-82 ("The interaction . . . control trials")

7

As used in line 88, "range" most nearly means

A) group.

B) altitude.

C) variety.

D) distance.

8

A difference between the discussions of shark bite reduction measures in the two passages is that

A) Passage 1 offers an example of an effective measure while Passage 2 focuses on an ineffective measure.

B) Passage 1 considers an example of an ineffective measure while Passage 2 mostly depicts an effective measure.

C) Passage 1 assesses experimental evidence while Passage 2 does not.

D) Passage 1 discusses a procedure while Passage 2 avoids investigations of this sort.

9

A similarity between the two passages is that both authors consider

A) experimental versus control trials.

B) Hawaii's shark control program.

C) technological solutions.

D) specific species of sharks.

10

Which statement best summarizes the relationship between the two passages?

A) Passage 2 offers a potential solution to a problem discussed in Passage 1.

B) Passage 2 questions an assumption from Passage 1.

C) Passage 2 refutes the central claim of Passage 1.

D) Passage 2 answers an ethical question posed in Passage 1.

CONTINUE

Part 3: Science, Paired

Reading 37

Questions 1-10 are based on the following passages.

Passage 1 is adapted from "Biologists Develop Large Gene Dataset for Rice Plant" (2007); Passage 2 is adapted from "Love basmati rice? Scientists have now sequenced its genome" (2020). Both passages originally appeared as news releases* from the National Science Foundation.

Passage 1

Scientists have reported development of a large dataset of gene sequences in rice. The information will lead to an increased understanding of how
Line
5 genes work in rice, an essential food for much of the world's population.

Plant biologist Blake Meyers at the University of Delaware and colleagues report their results in the March 11 online issue of the journal *Nature Biotechnology*.

10 Using advanced gene sequencing technologies and high-powered computer-based approaches, Meyers and colleagues examined both normal gene expression (via messenger ribonucleic acids, or mRNAs) as well as small ribonucleic acids

15 (small RNAs) in rice. The analysis of rice was based on gene sequences representing nearly 47 million mRNA molecules and three million small RNAs, a larger dataset than has been reported for any other plant species.

20 Small RNAs are considered one of most important discoveries in biotechnology in the last 10 years. Because they are so much smaller than mRNAs, small RNAs went unnoticed for many years, or were considered biologically

25 unimportant, said Meyers. Small RNAs are now known to play an important role in gene regulation, he said, adding that deficiencies in small RNA production can have a profound effect on development.

30 "Small RNAs also have been associated with other important biological processes, such as responses to stress," Meyers said. "Many of small RNAs in rice have related sequences in the many

important cereal crop plants, including maize and
35 wheat."

Research on small RNAs "is a leading edge in plant biotechnology," said Machi Dilworth, Director of the National Science Foundation (NSF)'s Division of Biological Infrastructure,
40 which, along with the U.S. Department of Agriculture, funded the research. "This work will contribute to an understanding of the role of small RNAs in gene expression not only in rice, but in all plants."

Passage 2

45 Using an innovative genome sequencing technology, National Science Foundation-funded researchers have assembled the complete genetic blueprint of two basmati rice varieties, including one that is drought-tolerant and resistant to
50 bacterial disease. The findings, published in Genome Biology, also show that basmati rice is a hybrid of two other rice groups.

Basmati—derived from the Hindi word for "fragrant"—is a type of aromatic long-grain rice
55 grown in southern Asia. Despite the economic and cultural importance of basmati and related aromatic rice varieties, their evolutionary history is not fully understood.

"Rice is one of the most important staple
60 crops worldwide, and the varieties in the basmati group are some of the most iconic and prized rice varieties," said Jae Young Choi of New York University and the study's lead author. "But until recently, a high-quality reference genome for
65 basmati rice did not exist."

Whole-genome sequencing—which determines an organism's complete DNA sequence—is an important tool for studying plants and improving crop varieties. Prior research assembled the
70 genome for basmati rice using short-read sequencing—in which DNA is broken into tiny fragments and then reassembled—but there were missing sequences and gaps in the data.

The researchers at NYU's Center for Genomics
75 and Systems Biology sequenced the genome of two members of the basmati rice group using nanopore sequencing technology.

---

*See Page 228 for the citations for these texts.

CONTINUE

The sequencing confirmed that basmati rice is a hybrid of two other rice groups. Most genetic
80 material in basmati comes from japonica (a rice group found in East Asia), followed by the rice group aus (found in Bangladesh).

"This discovery offers new insights into how adaptation to environments and cultural
85 preferences might have shaped the domestication of basmati rice, an aromatic rice variety that's often a preferred choice," says Gerald Schoenknecht, a program director in NSF's Division of Integrative Organismal Systems.

1

According to Passage 1, rice is an ideal plant in terms of the study of gene expression because

A) more small RNAs and mRNAs have been sequenced for rice than for other plants.

B) rice uses small RNAs to regulate its genes whereas most other plants do not.

C) other plants are descended from rice and consequently possess similar RNA.

D) rice uses small RNAs for a larger number of biological processes than other plants do.

2

Which choice provides the best evidence for the answer to the previous question?

A) Lines 18-19 ("a larger . . . species")

B) Lines 25-28 ("Small RNAs . . . regulation")

C) Lines 30-32 ("Small RNAs . . . said")

D) Lines 41-44 ("This work . . . plants")

3

As used in line 61, the words "iconic" and "prized" serve to

A) underscore how widely prioritized modern agriculture is.

B) show how highly regarded basmati rice is.

C) suggest how deeply respected Jae Young Choi is.

D) allude to the remarkable economic value of certain varieties of rice.

4

According to Passage 2, whole-genome sequencing is superior to short-read sequencing because

A) short-read sequencing does not sequence the entire genome, while whole-genome sequencing does.

B) short-read sequencing is much more expensive to perform than whole-genome sequencing is.

C) short-read sequencing is much more time-consuming to execute than whole-genome sequencing is.

D) short-read sequencing results in repeated sequences, while whole-genome sequencing does not.

5

In can be inferred from Passage 2 that the agricultural yield of basmati rice is sometimes diminished by

A) a lack of information about the evolution of rice.

B) genetic defects in the rice crop itself.

C) the nature of basmati rice as a hybrid of two other types of rice

D) droughts and bacterial infections.

CONTINUE

195

6

Which choice provides the best evidence for the answer to the previous question?

A) Lines 47-50 ("researchers have . . . disease")

B) Lines 55-58 ("Despite . . . understood")

C) Lines 74-77 ("The researchers . . . technology")

D) Lines 78-79 ("The sequencing . . . groups")

7

As used in line 85, "shaped" most nearly means

A) confined.

B) encouraged.

C) built.

D) influenced.

8

A difference between Passage 1 and Passage 2 is that

A) Passage 1 references changes in sequence databases over time while Passage 2 only alludes to data that is currently available.

B) Passage 1 discusses the importance of facts that were previously thought to be insignificant while Passage 2 considers information that has long been viewed as valuable.

C) Passage 1 only mentions rice varieties while Passage 2 mentions other crops as well.

D) Passage 1 addresses the topic of gene sequencing while Passage 2 avoids this realm of inquiry.

9

Both Passage 1 and Passage 2

A) address the cultural forces responsible for artificial selection in rice.

B) reveal both a problem and a potential solution to that problem.

C) end with a discussion of what can be learned from research that involves rice.

D) explore how different types of rice are phylogenetically related to one another.

10

Which of the following is mentioned in Passage 1 but NOT in Passage 2?

A) The linguistic derivation of a word

B) Research applications to plants other than rice

C) The culinary status of rice around the world

D) The economic importance of rice

CONTINUE

Reading 38

Questions 1-10 are based on the following passages.

Passage 1 is adapted from Bill Steigerwald, "'Goldilocks' Stars May Be 'Just Right' for Finding Habitable Worlds" (2019). Passage 2 is adapted from Lonnie Shekhtman, "How Earth Climate Models Help Scientists Picture Life on Unimaginable Worlds" (2020). The original forms of these texts first appeared as news releases* from NASA.

Passage 1

Scientists looking for signs of life beyond our solar system face major challenges, one of which is that there are hundreds of billions of stars in our galaxy alone to consider. To narrow the search,
5 investigators must figure out what kinds of stars are most likely to host habitable planets.

A new study finds that a particular class of stars called K stars, which are dimmer than the Sun but brighter than the faintest stars, may be particularly
10 promising targets for searching for signs of life.

Why? First, K stars live a very long time—17 billion to 70 billion years, compared to 10 billion years for the Sun—giving plenty of time for life to evolve. Also, K stars have less extreme activity in
15 their youth than do the universe's dimmest stars, called M stars or "red dwarfs."

M stars do offer some advantages in the search for habitable planets. They are the most common star type in our galaxy, comprising about 75
20 percent of all the stars in the universe. They are also frugal with their fuel, and could shine on for over a trillion years. One example of an M star, TRAPPIST-1, is known to host seven Earth-size rocky planets. But the turbulent youth of M
25 stars presents problems for potential life. Stellar flares—explosive releases of magnetic energy—are much more frequent and energetic from young M stars than from young Sun-like stars. M stars are also much brighter when they are young, for
30 up to a billion years after they form, with energy that could boil off oceans on any planets that might someday be in the habitable zone.

Passage 2

In a generic brick building on the northwestern edge of NASA's Goddard Space Flight Center
35 campus in Greenbelt, Maryland, thousands of computers packed in racks the size of vending machines hum in a deafening chorus of data crunching. Day and night, they spit out 7 quadrillion calculations per second. These
40 machines collectively are known as NASA's Discover supercomputer, and they are tasked with running sophisticated climate models to predict Earth's future climate. But now, they're also sussing out something much farther away:
45 whether any of the more than 4,000 curiously weird planets beyond our solar system discovered in the past two decades could support life.

Scientists are finding that the answer not only is yes, but that it's yes under a range of surprising
50 conditions compared to those on Earth. This revelation has prompted many of them to grapple with a question vital to NASA's search for life beyond Earth. Is it possible that our notions of what makes a planet suitable for life are too
55 limiting?

The next generation of powerful telescopes and space observatories will surely give us more clues. These instruments will allow scientists for the first time to analyze the atmospheres of the
60 most tantalizing planets out there: rocky ones, like Earth, that could have an essential ingredient for life—liquid water—flowing on their surfaces.

For the time being, it's difficult to probe far-off atmospheres. Sending a spacecraft to the closest
65 planet outside our solar system, or exoplanet, would take 75,000 years with today's technology. Even with powerful telescopes, nearby exoplanets are virtually impossible to study in detail. The trouble is that they're too small and too drowned
70 out by the light of their stars for scientists to make out the faint light signatures that they reflect—signatures that could reveal the chemistry of life at the surface.

In other words, detecting the ingredients of the
75 atmospheres around these phantom planets, as many scientists like to point out, is like standing in Washington, D.C., and trying to glimpse a

---

*See Page 229 for the citations for these texts.

CONTINUE ➡

Part 3: Science, Paired

firefly next to a searchlight in Los Angeles.
This reality makes climate models critical to
80 exploration, said chief exoplanetary scientist Karl
Stapelfeldt, who's based at NASA's Jet Propulsion
Laboratory in Pasadena, California.
    "The models make specific, testable predictions
of what we should see," he said. "These are very
85 important for designing our future telescopes and
observing strategies."

1

Based on the information in Passage 1, which of the
following would have the longest possible lifespan?

A) A K star

B) An M star

C) A star that resembles the Sun

D) A rocky planet that harbors life

2

Which of the following, if true, would contradict the
author's conclusions about K stars and M stars in
Passage 1?

A) In most areas of the universe, M stars appeared at
least 10 billion years before K stars did.

B) Scientists have not succeeded in locating
habitable exoplanets outside the galaxy that
contains Earth.

C) M stars give off less light than Sun-like stars do
but are nonetheless extremely volatile.

D) In the galaxy that also contains Earth, M stars
are slightly outnumbered by stars known as
"white dwarfs."

3

As used in line 15, "dimmest" most nearly means

A) most primitive.

B) least interesting.

C) most mysterious.

D) least luminous.

4

In line 37, the reference to a "deafening chorus"
serves to

A) acknowledge the spirit of diligence and creativity
that motivated a group of scientists.

B) suggest the intensity of a set of operations by
creating a parallel with human activity.

C) indicate that future developments in an area of
inquiry will be both pleasing and predictable.

D) offer a musical analogy that the author revisits in
order to clarify additional concepts.

5

It can be inferred from Passage 2 that the direct
precursors of the "instruments" in line 58 are

A) devices that will comprise "the next generation"
(line 56) of telescopes and observatories.

B) the types of "spacecraft" (line 64) that could be
sent to exoplanets.

C) the "powerful telescopes" (line 67) that are
limited in usefulness.

D) "faint light signatures" (line 71) detected by
scientists.

CONTINUE

Part 3: Science, Paired

6

The descriptions in Passage 2 characterize climate modeling as a procedure that

A) will produce planetary images that non-experts will find understandable.

B) has prompted investment in new telescopes.

C) is best applied to the largest exoplanets.

D) appears feasible even when visual observation of planets is problematic.

7

Which choice provides the best evidence for the answer to the previous question?

A) Lines 53-55 ("Is it . . . limiting?")

B) Lines 56-58 ("The next . . . clues")

C) Lines 79-82 ("This reality . . . California")

D) Lines 84-86 ("These . . . strategies")

8

Which choice best describes the relationship between the two passages?

A) Passage 1 assesses star systems that may exhibit conditions conducive to life; Passage 2 considers the technological advances that could enable more authoritative study of such systems.

B) Passage 1 provides systematic descriptions of two types of stars; Passage 2 contends that these same star types have not been observed in any reliable manner.

C) Passage 1 outlines a variety of conditions that would enable life to flourish on exoplanets; Passage 2 construes some of these criteria as questionable while promoting alternatives.

D) Passage 1 encourages a focus on fewer star systems in the search for extraterrestrial life; Passage 2 endorses this spirit of selectivity.

9

Both authors imply that one key trait of planets hospitable to life is

A) the presence of liquid water.

B) a diameter that is smaller than that of Earth.

C) an orbit centered on a star similar to the Sun in brightness.

D) an atmosphere that includes breathable oxygen.

10

Which choice from Passage 1 provides the best evidence for the answer to the previous question?

A) Lines 7-10 ("A new . . . life")

B) Lines 14-16 ("K stars . . . dwarfs")

C) Lines 24-25 ("But . . . life")

D) Lines 28-32 ("M stars . . . zone")

CONTINUE

Reading 39

Questions 1-10 are based on the following passages and supplementary material.

Passage 1 is an excerpt from Kevin Bennett, "No, turkey doesn't make you sleepy—but it may bring more trust to your Thanksgiving table" (2017). Passage 2 is an excerpt from Andrew Neff, "Turning to turkey's tryptophan to boost mood? Not so fast" (2019). Both of these articles were originally published* by The Conversation.

Passage 1

'Tis the season for giblets, wattles, and snoods—oh my. On Thanksgiving and Christmas, Americans consume about 68 million turkeys—
Line one for about every five of us. In fact, 29 percent
5 of all turkeys gobbled down in the U.S. are consumed during the holidays.

And where turkey is being eaten, there is inevitably talk of tryptophan—a naturally occurring chemical found in turkey and other
10 foods. This building block of protein often takes the blame for eaters feeling sleepy soon after the Thanksgiving meal.

Science has cleared tryptophan, though—it's not the culprit when it comes to drowsiness after
15 the feast. There are far more important factors leading to those post-turkey comas, not least of which is my Uncle Clarence's story about parking at the airport. Add that to free-flowing booze combined with a load of carbohydrates followed
20 by plenty more booze and you have a foolproof recipe for dozing off on the couch. Turkey, chicken, lamb, and beef all contain roughly the same amount of tryptophan—ranging from 0.13-0.39 grams per 100 grams of food—yet the
25 sleepiness myth has never surrounded those other foods.

So tryptophan is off the snooze-inducing hook. But researchers in the Netherlands suggest that it does have a different psychological effect: they've
30 discovered that doses of tryptophan (chemically known as L-tryptophan and abbreviated TRP) can promote interpersonal trust—that feeling you get

when you look somebody in the eye, shake her hand, and think, "I can cooperate with this person
35 and she would reciprocate."

In a study published in the journal *Psychological Science*, pairs of volunteers were each given an oral dose of 0.8g of TRP or a placebo. For comparison, a 100g standard serving
40 of turkey about the thickness of a deck of playing cards contains about 0.31g of tryptophan. Each duo then sat in separate cubicles and played a game in which one person (the truster) was given US$7 and had to decide how much to transfer to
45 the other person. The transferred money was then multiplied by three and the trustee could give back part of the tripled money. The more money you're willing to give away in the first place, the greater your return in the end—but you have to trust
50 the other person to cooperate. A very simple and profitable game if played right.

The researchers found that the TRP group gave $4.81 on average and the placebo group offered only $3.38. This is a sizable 42 percent increase in
55 transferred money between the two groups.

Passage 2

Every Thanksgiving, myths of the quasi-magical powers of tryptophan rise again.

There's the turkey/drowsiness myth: Eating lots of juicy turkey meat supposedly makes people
60 feel tired because it contains an amino acid called tryptophan. This molecule travels into the brain, where it's converted into a neurotransmitter called serotonin, which in turn is converted into a hormone called melatonin. Voila! Sleepiness.
65 But science and the internet agree: It's not the turkey's tryptophan to blame for your post-feast nap. All protein sources, and even vegetables, contain some tryptophan; turkey isn't at all special in this regard.
70 So the sleepiness myth of turkey may be fading, but other legends around tryptophan's effects in the brain are taking hold. Some people are eyeing tryptophan supplements as an unconventional treatment for depression. Others
75 are curious whether eating foods that are high or low in tryptophan could be useful for influencing mood. Recently, some scientists have even

---

*See Page 229 for the citations for these texts.

CONTINUE ➡

proposed that gut bacteria are driving changes in emotion by producing or breaking down
80 tryptophan.

This tryptophan/mood connection is an area of ongoing research. And while some are captivated by tryptophan's potential, it's not clear whether the excitement is warranted.

85 There is some scientific evidence that eating tryptophan can alter your mood. For example, back in 2000, researchers found that when people ate an isolated protein that was very high in tryptophan, they felt less stress while doing
90 math problems. However, placebo-controlled clinical trials haven't, in general, shown much of a connection. A few studies have found that supplementing with pure tryptophan provided little to no benefit for people with depression.
95 Some studies have even looked at what happens when you remove tryptophan from people's diets, but found little to no effect.

Correlations from a Study of 155 Adults in the United States

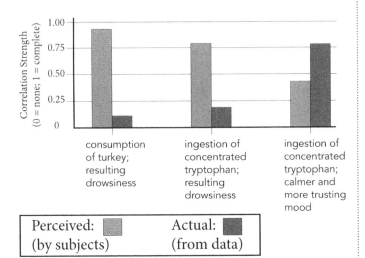

Perceived: (by subjects)   Actual: (from data)

1

The author of Passage 1 argues that the drowsiness that accompanies a Thanksgiving meal may be attributed to

A) the demands of an invigorating conversation.

B) the consumption of large quantities of alcohol.

C) similarities between turkey and other meats.

D) frequent discussion of the sleepiness myth.

2

Which choice provides the best evidence for the answer to the previous question?

A) Lines 7-10 ("And . . . foods")

B) Lines 13-15 ("Science . . . feast")

C) Lines 15-18 ("There . . . airport")

D) Lines 18-21 ("Add . . . couch")

3

As described in Passage 1, the study of the effects of TRP was designed to feature which of the following elements?

A) Well-defined protocols for settling disputes among the participants.

B) Participants with similar academic backgrounds

C) Self-reporting mechanisms that were short-lived

D) An experimental group that did not ingest TRP

4

As used in line 48, "give away" most nearly means

A) willingly hand over.

B) represent as a bargain.

C) unintentionally reveal.

D) abruptly disregard.

CONTINUE

5

The author of Passage 2 regards the "legends around tryptophan's effects in the brain" (lines 71-72) as

A) intriguing possibilities that should nonetheless be regarded with considerable skepticism.

B) new versions of the connection between turkey and drowsiness that have led unwitting scientists to promote questionable conclusions.

C) products of a flawed belief that most food sources can bring about psychological changes.

D) dramatic but fundamentally reliable testimonies derived from a consensus among researchers.

6

Which choice provides the best evidence for the answer to the previous question?

A) Lines 58-61 ("There's . . . tryptophan")

B) Lines 74-77 ("Others . . . mood")

C) Lines 82-84 ("And . . . warranted")

D) Lines 95-97 ("Some . . . effect")

7

The author of Passage 1 and the author of Passage 2 use the word "myth" (line 25 and line 58) in order to describe

A) a widespread notion that is appealing primarily due to its comical quality.

B) a problem that requires a solution which continues to elude even practiced researchers.

C) a misconception that has been complicated by factual investigation.

D) a set of beliefs that persist despite new public awareness of scientific breakthroughs.

8

The primary purpose of each passage is to

A) describe experiments designed to debunk the connection between tryptophan and drowsiness.

B) assess the influence of tryptophan on humans while soundly rejecting one common assumption.

C) conclusively correlate tryptophan ingestion with feelings of generosity.

D) argue against the idea that tryptophan can pose long-term risks in terms of individual health.

9

The relationship between the statements in lines 21-26 ("Turkey . . . foods") and lines 67-69 ("All . . . regard") is that

A) the statement in Passage 2 contradicts the statement in Passage 1.

B) the statement in Passage 1 introduces a divisive tone continued in the statement in Passage 2.

C) the statement in Passage 2 indicates that the statement in Passage 1 is not confined to meat consumption.

D) the statement in Passage 1 involves a hypothesis that was validated by the statement in Passage 2.

10

Which of the following groups has NOT presented a finding or argument that would be supported by the data from the graph?

A) The "researchers in the Netherlands" mentioned in line 28

B) The "internet" commentators mentioned in line 65

C) The "researchers" mentioned in line 87

D) Those who conducted the "studies" mentioned in line 95

CONTINUE ➔

Part 3: Science, Paired

Reading 40

Questions 1-10 are based on the following passages and supplementary material.

Passage 1 is an excerpt from Vanessa Bates Ramirez, "This Self-Driving AI Is Learning to Drive Almost Entirely in a Virtual World." Here, the author describes her ride in a self-driving car produced by the company AImotive; she was accompanied by a human "safety" driver and by the CEO of AImotive itself. Passage 2 is an excerpt from David Pring-Mill, "Everyone Is Talking About AI—But Do They Mean the Same Thing?" Both articles were published* in 2020 by SingularityHub.

Passage 1

. . . After another brief—and thankfully uneventful—hands-off cruise down the highway, the safety driver took over, exited the highway,
Line and drove us back to the office.
5   I climbed out of the car feeling amazed not simply that self-driving cars are possible, but that driving is possible at all. I squint when driving into a tunnel, swerve to avoid hitting a stray squirrel, and brake gradually at stop signs—all
10 without consciously thinking to do so. On top of learning to steer, brake, and accelerate, self-driving software has to incorporate our brains' and bodies' unconscious (but crucial) reactions, like our pupils dilating to let in more light so we can
15 see in a tunnel.
      Despite all the progress of machine learning, artificial intelligence, and computing power, I have a wholly renewed appreciation for the thing that's been in charge of driving up till now: the
20 human brain.
      CEO Laszlo Kishonti seemed to feel similarly. "I don't think autonomous vehicles in the near future will be better than the best drivers," he said. "But they'll be better than the average driver.
25 What we want to achieve is safe, good-quality driving for everyone, with scalability."
      AImotive is currently working with American tech firms and with car and truck manufacturers in Europe, China, and Japan.

Passage 2

30   When it comes to matters of scientific integrity, the issue of accurate definitions isn't a peripheral matter. In a 1974 commencement address at the California Institute of Technology, Richard Feynman famously said, "The first principle is
35 that you must not fool yourself—and you are the easiest person to fool." In that same speech, Feynman also said, "You should not fool the layman when you're talking as a scientist." He opined that scientists should bend over backwards
40 to show how they could be wrong. "If you're representing yourself as a scientist, then you should explain to the layman what you're doing—and if they don't want to support you under those circumstances, then that's their decision."
45   In the case of AI, this might mean that professional scientists have an obligation to clearly state that they are developing extremely powerful, controversial, profitable, and even dangerous tools, which do not constitute
50 intelligence in any familiar or comprehensive sense.
      The term "AI" may have become overhyped and confused, but there are already some efforts underway to provide clarity. A recent PwC
55 report drew a distinction between "assisted intelligence," "augmented intelligence," and "autonomous intelligence." Assisted intelligence is demonstrated by the GPS navigation programs prevalent in cars today. Augmented intelligence
60 "enables people and organizations to do things they couldn't otherwise do." And autonomous intelligence "establishes machines that act on their own," such as autonomous vehicles.
      Roman Yampolskiy is an AI safety researcher
65 who wrote the book *Artificial Superintelligence: A Futuristic Approach.* I asked him whether the broad and differing meanings might present difficulties for legislators attempting to regulate AI.
70   Yampolskiy explained, "Intelligence (artificial or natural) comes on a continuum and so do potential problems with such technology. We typically refer to AI which one day will have the full spectrum of human capabilities as

*See Page 229 for the citations for these texts.

CONTINUE

203

Copyright 2020 PrepVantage, online at prepvantagetutoring.com

75 artificial general intelligence (AGI) to avoid some confusion. Beyond that point it becomes superintelligence. What we have today and what is frequently used in business is narrow AI. Regulating anything is hard; technology is no 80 exception. The problem is not with terminology but with complexity of such systems even at the current level."

Occurrences on Test Drives, 2019
(40 miles of residential California streets)

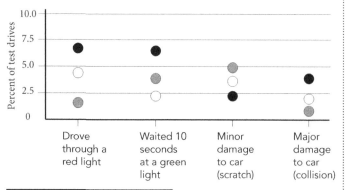

Human Only: ○
AI-Assisted: ◑
Autonomous AI: ●

1

As used in line 2, "uneventful" most nearly means

A) forgettable.

B) fast.

C) boring.

D) safe.

2

In Passage 1, the author's opinion of autonomous vehicles is that they

A) must have been difficult to develop.

B) lack any meaningful human capabilities.

C) have various human abilities but are nonetheless vastly inferior to human drivers.

D) are for the most part superior to human drivers.

3

Which choice provides the best evidence for the answer to the previous question?

A) Lines 7-9 ("I squint . . . stop signs")

B) Lines 10-13 ("On top . . . reactions")

C) Lines 16-20 ("Despite all . . . human brain")

D) Lines 22-23 ("I don't . . . best drivers")

4

As used in line 39, the phrase "bend over backwards" most nearly functions to convey

A) the importance of a priority.

B) the burden of an obligation.

C) the flexibility of science.

D) the unfairness of a standard.

5

Which of the following choices best supports the notion that the technology itself, rather than nomenclature, makes AI hard to regulate?

A) Lines 30-32 ("When it . . . matter")

B) Lines 52-54 ("The term . . . clarity")

C) Lines 79-80 ("Regulating . . . exception")

D) Lines 80-82 ("The problem . . . current level")

CONTINUE ➤

Part 3: Science, Paired

6

How does the tone of Passage 1 compare to the tone of Passage 2?

A) Passage 1 is dryly technical throughout, while Passage 2 employs a tone that repeatedly shifts from formal to easygoing.

B) Passage 1 combines lofty phrases and colloquial word choices, while Passage 2 is entirely somber and anxious.

C) Passage 1 employs an extremely personable approach, while Passage 2 mixes academic and anecdotal writing.

D) Passage 1 alternates between academic and informal tones, while Passage 2 is primarily conversational and whimsical.

7

The topic of Passage 1 contrasts with the topic of Passage 2 because Passage 1 focuses on

A) the flaws of fully autonomous vehicles, while Passage 2 focuses on the successes of artificial intelligence generally.

B) the human brain, while Passage 2 focuses on computers and their applications.

C) current technology, while Passage 2 focuses on future technology.

D) a technology and its capabilities, while Passage 2 focuses on terminology and ethics.

8

Roman Yampolskiy would most likely respond to lines 22-23 ("I don't . . . best drivers") by

A) disagreeing completely.

B) assenting, but with the caveat that future AI may outperform even the best human drivers.

C) pointing out that confusion in terminology led Kishonti to an invalid conclusion.

D) rejecting elements of Kishonti's reasoning while assenting to Kishonti's conclusion.

9

Based on the graph, which of the following drivers is typically least responsive to traffic signals?

A) Human only

B) AI-assisted

C) Human only and AI-assisted (roughly identical)

D) Autonomous AI

10

Does the graph align more closely with the content of Passage 1 or Passage 2, and does it primarily indicate that AI outperforms or underperforms human drivers?

A) Passage 1, outperform

B) Passage 1, underperform

C) Passage 2, outperform

D) Passage 2, underperform

STOP
**If you have finished this section, consult the relevant answers and explanations.
Do not turn to any other section.**

Answer Key
Part 3: Science, Paired

Reading 31		Reading 32		Reading 33		Reading 34		Reading 35	
1.	D	1.	D	1.	D	1.	C	1.	C
2.	D	2.	D	2.	C	2.	A	2.	A
3.	A	3.	A	3.	D	3.	B	3.	B
4.	B	4.	C	4.	B	4.	C	4.	A
5.	C	5.	C	5.	B	5.	A	5.	B
6.	B	6.	A	6.	C	6.	C	6.	B
7.	B	7.	B	7.	A	7.	C	7.	D
8.	D	8.	C	8.	B	8.	B	8.	D
9.	C	9.	A	9.	A	9.	A	9.	B
10.	A	10.	C	10.	D	10.	C	10.	A

Reading 36		Reading 37		Reading 38		Reading 39		Reading 40	
1.	C	1.	A	1.	B	1.	B	1.	D
2.	D	2.	A	2.	D	2.	D	2.	A
3.	D	3.	B	3.	D	3.	D	3.	B
4.	B	4.	A	4.	B	4.	A	4.	A
5.	A	5.	D	5.	C	5.	A	5.	D
6.	B	6.	A	6.	D	6.	C	6.	C
7.	C	7.	D	7.	C	7.	C	7.	D
8.	B	8.	B	8.	A	8.	B	8.	B
9.	D	9.	C	9.	A	9.	C	9.	D
10.	A	10.	B	10.	D	10.	D	10.	B

Answer Explanations

Passage 31, Pages 176-178

1. <u>D</u> is the correct answer.

Passage 1 explains that scientists "want a straightforward and general procedure that [they] can also program in a computer" (lines 24-26). This content indicates that researchers want earthquake mapping software which is broadly applicable, rather than narrowly focused. Choose D as the best answer. A can easily be eliminated since the notion of site-specific software is directly contradicted by the content of the passage (which calls for broad applicability). B and C can also be eliminated, since the software would primarily be used by specialized researchers, NOT the broader community, and since it can focus on earthquakes that are presently occurring, without relying on historical data.

2. <u>D</u> is the correct answer.

Lines 36-38 state that a useful mapping tool should "Quit when your adjustments have become small enough and when the fit to the observed wave arrival times is close enough." This content indicates that modeling software only needs to approximate the location of an earthquake's hypocenter; choose D as appropriate. A identifies why locating an earthquake hypocenter is challenging and contrasts such a process with an easier type of scientific observation, while B articulates a goal that effective earthquake modeling software could achieve. C articulates additional features which make a modeling tool useful to researchers. None of these other answers reflect a desire for a model to be approximate rather than exact (despite referencing the topic modeling overall), and therefore they should all be eliminated.

3. <u>A</u> is the correct answer.

In line 36, "quit" refers to the moment at which a researcher could stop making calculations and be content with the data that have been gathered. Choose A to reflect this meaning. B (inappropriately implying stopping before a satisfactory conclusion has been reached), C (inappropriately implying stopping for a temporary period of time), and D (inappropriately implying departing from a location or situation) all introduce improper contexts and therefore should be eliminated.

4. <u>B</u> is the correct answer.

Lines 55-58 state that "ancient faults [. . .] have been reactivated due to wastewater injection, which generates, or "induces" earthquakes." This content indicates that if wastewater were not injected, more of the lineaments would remain dormant. Choose B as appropriate. A can readily be eliminated since this choice is directly contradicted by the content of the passage. C and D can also be eliminated since the grain of magnetic contacts might make a site susceptible to becoming reactive after wastewater injection but does NOT change in response to wastewater injection. Less wastewater injection might lead to fewer earthquakes, but such a situation would NOT necessarily alter the locations of those earthquakes.

5. C is the correct answer.

See the previous answer explanation for analysis of the correct line reference. A describes a pattern of earthquake activity and the associated challenges, while B identifies a correlation between lineaments and sequences of earthquakes. D describes how the "grain" of magnetic contacts originated. None of these other answers indicate that lessening wastewater injections would lead to faults remaining dormant (thus presenting both the correct topics AND the correct logic), and therefore they should all be eliminated.

6. B is the correct answer.

Passage 2 quickly identifies a challenge relevant to estimating seismic hazards in Oklahoma: "few of the earthquake sequences have occurred on mapped faults" (lines 41-43). Choose B to reflect this content. A can be readily eliminated since this answer is explicitly contradicted by the content of the passage. Be careful not to choose C or D, since there is evidence that ancient faults are reactivated by wastewater injection, but this situation is NOT what makes seismic hazards difficult to predict. There is also evidence that magnetic contacts are aligned with natural stresses, but again, this situation is NOT a contributing factor to what makes seismic hazards unpredictable.

7. B is the correct answer.

In line 64, "dominant" refers to how a specific pattern appears in the majority of cases. Choose B to reflect this content. A (inappropriately implying something asserting power or control over someone or something else), C (inappropriately implying an attitude of being willing to inflict harm on others), and D (inappropriately implying triumphing over a competitor) all introduce improper contexts and should be eliminated.

8. D is the correct answer.

Passage 1 focuses on describing a procedure for identifying the location of the hypocenter of an earthquake, while Passage 2 describes how new imaging technology could be applied to make it easier to identify and predict seismic hazards in Oklahoma. Choose D to reflect this relationship between the two passages. A and B can both be eliminated since BOTH passages arguably address indirect methods of data collection (extrapolation for earthquake sources in Passage 1, magnetic monitoring below the surface in Passage 2). C can be eliminated since BOTH passages discuss fault lines as an important element of seismic research.

9. C is the correct answer.

Both passages are focused on research related to the mapping of the origins of earthquakes: Passage 1 describes the desire of researchers to be able to identify the location of the point where an earthquake originates, while Passage 2 describes how researchers are making progress towards identifying locations where earthquakes are likely to originate. Choose C to reflect this shared commonality between the passages. A and B can be eliminated since only Passage 2 discusses ancient fault lines, and only Passage 1 discusses seismometers. D can also be eliminated since both passages discuss research which will primarily be of interest of scientists and technical specialists, NOT the wider community even though the research may be practically useful.

10. <u>A</u> is the correct answer.

Passage 1 states in lines 2-4 that being able to identify the origin of an earthquake makes it possible to determine the fault line where the quake occurred and to predict where damage most likely occurred. The OGS data discussed in Passage 2 was collected in response to the challenge of earthquakes occurring in locations outside of known and identified fault lines. A most accurately describes the relationship between the two passages. B and C can be eliminated since, while Passage 2 does focus on prediction, it does NOT state that prediction is more important than assessing damage. Passage 2 also establishes wastewater injection as a factor which may lead to earthquake occurrences, but NOT as a sole or even primary cause. D can also be eliminated since the research described in Passage 2 relied on airborne date, but the passage does NOT necessarily indicate that gathering this data is the only method by which earthquakes can be mapped.

Passage 32, Pages 179-181

1. <u>D</u> is the correct answer.

Lines 22-26 state that "this methodological challenge [that the genetic sequencing of venom proteins requires killing the snake] limits the scope of research in this area and is undesirable for ethical and environmental reasons." This content indicates that venom research could be expanded if harvesting venom did not require killing snakes; choose D as appropriate. A can be eliminated since the passage discusses the specific proteins contained in snake venom but does NOT connect these proteins to a difficulty of conducting the research. B and C can be eliminated since the geographic areas where snakes tend to live are discussed in the passage, but geographic origin was NOT logically connected to how challenging it was to conduct research.

2. <u>D</u> is the correct answer.

See the previous answer explanation for analysis of the correct line reference. A describes how snakes live in many different regions, while B describes the annual global death toll associated with snakebites. C describes the scientific information that is required in order for researchers to effectively develop snakebite therapies. None of these other answers raise the central topic of killing snakes (though B mentions HUMAN deaths) and therefore they should all be eliminated.

3. <u>A</u> is the correct answer.

In line 29, "present" refers to how researchers used a publication to outline or articulate a new protocol. Choose A to reflect this meaning. B (inappropriately implying carrying out a task or expectation), C (inappropriately implying gradually creating an outcome or product), and D (inappropriately implying innovating to offer a product or service for the first time) all introduce improper contexts and should therefore be eliminated.

4. <u>C</u> is the correct answer.

Passage 1 describes a new research protocol which showed promising results for conducting research using venom harvested from live snakes. One key benefit of this process is that snakes are not killed during this process; choose C as appropriate. A and B can be eliminated since the new protocol demonstrated comparable levels of protein and high quality rNA, but did NOT show improvement in these areas. D can be eliminated because the costs of protocols involving living or dead snakes are NOT contrasted in this passage (which mostly considers killing a snake as a necessity).

5. <u>C</u> is the correct answer.

Passage 2 begins with a description of a physical space, and then goes on to describe the scientific procedures which are conducted there. Choose C to reflect this content. A and B can be eliminated because the passage does NOT begin with either a description of researchers or of any particular profession (topics that are at most introduced in the LATER stages of the discussion). D can be eliminated because Passage 2 describes a scientific procedure but does NOT focus on the broader topic of any particular question or answer.

6. <u>A</u> is the correct answer.

Lines 45-47 explain that "on the walls, faded posters sum up the history of antivenom production." Because the posters are depicted as old, and as representing the history of antivenom production, this content indicates that techniques for producing antivenom have a significant lineage. Choose A as the best answer. B describes the goals of the research center, while C describes how snakes have an instinct to bite whenever they encounter something unfamiliar. D describes the final steps involved in preparing an antivenom solution. None of these other answers suggest that techniques for producing antivenom have been passed down over time, and therefore they should all be eliminated.

7. <u>B</u> is the correct answer.

In line 64, the phrase "careful, deliberate" is used to describe the way in which a researcher handles a venomous snake. The phrase highlights the caution which the researcher exercises, along with the fact that handling snakes requires expertise and caution. Choose B to reflect this content. A and C can be eliminated since it is NOT clear from the passage what type of training is required in order to work with snakes, and since the focus is on the caution to avoid getting bitten, NOT on the need to be detail-oriented when conducting scientific research. D refers to the snake itself, not to the cautious action of the researcher HANDLING the snake.

8. <u>C</u> is the correct answer.

Passage 1 focuses on how a new development allowing for venom to be collected from live snakes offers a bright prospect for advancing research into treatments for snake bites, while Passage 2 describes the process of collecting venom from live snakes. C best describes this relationship, and should be identified as the correct answer. A and B can be eliminated because the claims of both passages support rather than contradict one another, and Passage 2 provides more detailed description of a protocol but NOT the scientific theory behind it. D can be eliminated because the passages consider DIFFERENT groups of researchers, rather than offering direct assessment of the same few research teams.

9. <u>A</u> is the correct answer.

Passage 1 explores attempts to find research protocols which would allow for antivenom therapies (benefiting humans) to be developed using live snakes (benefiting snakes). Passage 2 focuses only on the process behind extracting snake venom and using it to develop antivenom therapies (benefiting humans). A most accurately represents this relationship between the passages, and should be identified as the correct answer. B and C can be eliminated since Passage 2 does NOT describe any benefit to snakes, and Passage 1 DOES consider benefits to snakes. D can be eliminated because Passage 1 considers benefits to both people AND snakes.

10. C is the correct answer.

Lines 79-83 state that, typically, it is fairly easy to get a sample of venom from a snake due to the biting instinct of snakes, although the exact amount of venom varies. Passage 1 explains that the new research protocol involving venom extracted from live snakes allows for consistent isolation of diverse RNA regardless of the volume of the venom sample. Choose C to reflect this relationship. A and B can be eliminated since the procedure described in Passage 2 does NOT require the snake to be sacrificed, and since these types of sample are collected precisely so that scientists can perform genetic sequencing. D can also be eliminated because, while it is true that precautions must be taken by handlers of venomous snakes, such caution is not relevant to a statement about the amount of venom collected being variable.

Passage 33, Pages 182-184

1. D is the correct answer.

Lines 37-42 state that "The infographic accompanying the article did not help to instill confidence in the findings . . . " and then go on to provide examples of inaccuracies presented in a map-based infographic. This content indicates that the article discussed in Passage 1 was not successful at presenting accurate information; choose D as the best answer. A and B can be eliminated because the passage does NOT present the article as containing accurate information, and since it is not clear based on the passage alone whether or not the article misrepresents medical (as opposed to GEOGRAPHIC) information. C can be eliminated because the passage is critical of the article but does NOT explicitly criticize the article (which is factually flawed in its presentation) for being sensational or for other stylistic matters.

2. C is the correct answer.

See the previous answer explanation for analysis of the correct line reference. A establishes a claim made in a recent newspaper article, while B identifies the Caribbean nations ranked as safe places in the event of a pandemic. D identifies a researcher who contributed to the article's findings and a threat that he identified. None of these other answers provide evidence that the author of the passage is skeptical of the accuracy of the article (and often reference the article WITHOUT offering clear criticisms), and therefore they should all be eliminated.

3. D is the correct answer.

Wilson states that "carriers of disease can easily circumvent land borders" (lines 49-50) and then argues that individuals isolated on an island would be less likely to become infected. This content indicates that Wilson believes that viruses spread primarily due to transit between landlocked regions; choose D as appropriate. A can be eliminated since Wilson mentions that a disease-resistant island population would also need to be technologically savvy, but does NOT comment on HOW island residents typically access technology. B and C can be eliminated because Wilson argues that genetically engineered pathogens could lead to a mass pandemic (suggesting that they could escape from a lab) and since the impact of trade networks (while broadly related to the theme of international contact) does NOT logically connect to Wilson's arguments about how islands could provide safe havens during a pandemic.

4. <u>B</u> is the correct answer.

Passage 2 describes how various Caribbean nations are currently responding to the COVID-19 global health emergency. Choose B to reflect this content. A and C can be eliminated because the passage describes actions which are currently being taken but does NOT make further recommendations, and since the author focuses on responses to the epidemic in terms of major events, NOT on how the spread of the disease is being modeled for study. D can be eliminated because the passage indicates that scientific progress towards curbing the spread of disease may be in conflict with economic progress (based on tourism as a source of funds).

5. <u>B</u> is the correct answer.

In lines 55-56, "concerned about" refers to how Caribbean nations are currently paying close attention to who is crossing their borders and to what protocols might need to be put in place. Choose B to reflect this context. A (inappropriately implying personal frustration), C (inappropriately implying a refusal to move away from someone or something), and D (inappropriately implying intense fear or panic) all introduce improper contexts for a discussion of a careful policy and should therefore be eliminated.

6. <u>C</u> is the correct answer.

In lines 62 and 70, language is used to establish a focus on known facts and events which have been documented in terms of the spread of a public health problem, the COVID-19 crisis. Choose C to reflect this content. A and B can be eliminated because the passage does NOT focus on whether the dangers associated with the virus are increasing (despite worsening ECONOMIC effects); moreover, the author does NOT focus on innovative research into COVID-19 (but rather on measures that different countries are taking in response to the crisis). D can be eliminated since the passage identifies areas where different perspectives exist but does NOT resolve areas of dispute.

7. <u>A</u> is the correct answer.

Passage 2 discusses how some nations are closing their borders in an effort to prevent the spread of the virus, and how this practice will impact economies which are dependent on tourism. Since this impact is likely to be negative, choose A as the best answer. B and C can be eliminated since the passage does NOT discuss efforts to produce a vaccine or efforts to introduce legislation to prevent immigration (focusing instead on attempts to prevent tourists from entering different regions). D refers to a relevant problem (transmission of a virus) but then raises a solution (new technology) that the author of Passage 2 does not explicitly discuss.

8. <u>B</u> is the correct answer.

Passage 1 discusses, in a critical manner, an article which asserts that the Caribbean would most likely be a very safe region during a viral pandemic, while Passage 2 discusses how that same region responded once an actual pandemic broke out in 2020. Choose B to most accurately reflect this relationship. A and C can be eliminated Passage 2 does NOT discuss the source discussed in Passage 1 (despite the common geographical topic), and Passage 1 does NOT describe any guidelines for managing a public health emergency (despite the rankings of which countries would be best at dealing with such an emergency). D can be eliminated because Passage 1 presents a presumably misguided conclusion about a potential public health emergency but does NOT imply that health crises are negligible; this passage simply critiques a source relevant to crises.

9. <u>A</u> is the correct answer.

Passage 1 discusses an article which presented conclusions based on speculation about what would happen in the hypothetical advent of a viral pandemic, while Passage 2 discusses a specific event: the outbreak of COVID-19 in 2020. Choose A to reflect this relationship. B and C can be eliminated since Passage 2 avoids a strongly critical tone (in contrast to Passage 1) and does not evaluate any specific examples of previous virus outbreaks (a topic that both passages mostly avoid). D can be eliminated because an important purpose of Passage 1 is to criticize an article for exaggerated and inaccurate claims.

10. <u>D</u> is the correct answer.

In reference to the Caribbean, lines 74-79 state that "measures will have economic implications for the region, which is heavily dependent on tourism—an industry which is reportedly thriving . . . " This content indicates that Caribbean nations are not self-contained and independent; instead, they rely on interactions with other nations to sustain their economies. Choose D as appropriate. A describes a specific world health emergency while B identifies a region where no cases had yet been detected. C describes the location which has been established as the point of origin for COVID-19. None of these other answers describe how Caribbean nations are interdependent with other regions (often referencing locations WITHOUT raising the theme of connection), and therefore they should all be eliminated.

Passage 34, Pages 185-187

1. <u>C</u> is the correct answer.

In line 10, "node" refers to a prototype that can correct for the loss of quantum signals by catching, storing, and repeating those signals. Choose C to reflect this meaning. A (inappropriately implying a protuberance of organic matter), B (inappropriately implying a specific position), and D (inappropriately implying a location where forms of data are collected and stored) all introduce improper contexts and should be eliminated.

2. <u>A</u> is the correct answer.

Lines 21-26 celebrate what has been achieved with the development of the node prototype and indicate that this breakthrough is very impactful and valuable. This tone can best be described as proud; choose A as appropriate. Be careful not to choose B, since while these lines do applaud the value of the innovation, evidence is provided to indicate that this development was very challenging and will be genuinely useful. C and D can be eliminated since they both carry negative connotations, whereas the content of these lines presents the recent innovation in extremely positive terms.

Answer Explanations, Part 3

3. <u>B</u> is the correct answer.

The passage designates "the three most important elements of a quantum repeater—a long memory, the ability to efficiently catch information from photons, and a way to process it locally" (lines 38-40) The ability to duplicate information is NOT explicitly listed as characteristic of a repeater and should not be assumed from the name "repeater" itself, so that B can be identified as the correct answer. A, C, and D all describe characteristics which ARE typically associated with quantum repeaters, and therefore they should all be eliminated.

4. <u>C</u> is the correct answer.

Lines 31-34 state that "Repeaters, which receive and amplify signals to correct for [transmission] loss, were first developed to amplify fading wire telegraph signals in the mid-1800s." This content indicates that, since much older technologies also had to contend with signal loss, this challenge is not unique to quantum communication. Choose C as appropriate. A describes why it has been challenging to develop a quantum internet, while B describes the potentially valuable impacts enabled by this new technological development. D describes the important characteristics associated with the new quantum node. None of these other answers refer to the problem of signal loss impacting non-quantum technology (since most focus on quantum technology alone), and therefore they should all be eliminated.

5. <u>A</u> is the correct answer.

The last paragraph of Passage 1 compares the quest for a secure quantum internet to the mission to land a human on the moon. Indeed, the moon landing is a famous example of a scientific and technological breakthrough, so this analogy serves to underscore the importance of this advancement in quantum communication. Choose A as the best answer. B and C can be eliminated since the comparison does NOT serve to explain the technical side of the quantum development, and since the passage focuses on an analogy between two key scientific achievements, NOT two distinct fields of study. D can readily be eliminated since the comparison (though related to the history of technology) does NOT serve to provide specific history for quantum computing.

6. <u>C</u> is the correct answer.

In line 89, "entangled with" refers to how the spin of a photon is intertwined with and reliant upon the spin of the atom from which the photon was emitted. Choose C to reflect this meaning. A (inappropriately implying two objects being braided or twined together), B (inappropriately implying one object being fused onto another), and D (inappropriately implying two objects becoming indivisible and indistinguishable) all wrongly refer to physical processes of a DIFFERENT sort and should thus be deleted.

7. <u>C</u> is the correct answer.

Lines 79-82 state that "A quantum network needs to be able to transmit information between two points without altering the quantum properties of the information being transmitted." This content indicates that the ability to preserve information is an important requirement of quantum computing. Since photons are able to provide this quality, they are valuable. Choose C as the best answer. A and B can be eliminated since the passage does discuss photons being ejected from atoms but does NOT specify whether this process occurs easily, and since the passage does NOT specify whether photons are faster than electricity. D can be eliminated because, even though photons may be lightweight, the relative weight of a photon is not presented as an advantage within the passage.

8. B is the correct answer.

See the previous answer explanation for analysis of the correct line reference. A describes the benefits associated with operational quantum computer networks, while C describes how information could be extracted from the atom in which it is stored. D describes the connection between current research and long-term scientific progress. None of these other answers describe why photons are beneficial to the development of a quantum network, and therefore they should all be eliminated.

9. A is the correct answer.

Each passage focuses on one scientific innovation with implications for the development of quantum networks: Passage 1 discusses the development of quantum repeaters (lines 46-52), while Passage 2 focuses on the development of nanophotonic cavities (lines 92-100). Choose A as appropriate. B can be eliminated since the topic of Passage 2 is more specialized than the topic of computer networks overall. C and D can be eliminated since Passage 1 has a more precise focus than the quantum internet, and since detachable rocket boosters are only mentioned in Passage 1 by way of analogy and are not a key topic of discussion.

10. C is the correct answer.

In discussing quantum repeaters (Passage 1) and nanophotonic cavities (Passage 2), the authors both focus on steps towards the ULTIMATE goal of a quantum internet (mentioned in line 1 and line 55). Choose C as appropriate. A and B can be eliminated since the passages discuss new applications for subatomic particles, but NOT the discovery of these particles, and focus on a new technology which could prove superior to cloud computing (a topic that is mostly avoided). D can be eliminated since improving GPS accuracy (lines 2-3) is only mentioned very briefly as one potential benefit associated with the development of a quantum internet.

Passage 35, Pages 188-190

1. C is the correct answer.

The author of Passage 1 begins by explaining the concept of antigenic drift in viruses and then concludes the passage by noting that this concept is relevant because it explains why vaccines need to be updated and why individuals can catch the flu multiple times. Choose C to reflect this content. A and B can be eliminated since antigenic drift is a confirmed scientific phenomenon, NOT a hypothesis, and since no specific particular solution is identified in the passage (which mainly provides background for a health liability). D can be eliminated since the passage relies on a SINGLE definition of antigenic drift but explains some of the complexities of this occurrence.

2. A is the correct answer.

In line 13, "target" refers to how a specific vaccine is designed to react and respond to predetermined aspects of the influenza virus. Choose A to reflect this content. B (inappropriately implying the spatial dimensions and contours of an object), C (inappropriately implying weakness or areas susceptible to harm), and D (inappropriately implying the ability to cause hurt or damage to someone or something else) all introduce improper contexts and should therefore be eliminated.

3. <u>B</u> is the correct answer.

Lines 31-34 state that "It is also possible for a single (or small) change in a particularly important location on the HA to result in antigenic drift." This content indicates that some regions of a virus are more sensitive than others; choose B as appropriate. A describes the gradual and ongoing nature of antigenic drift, while C describes a consequence of antigenic drift. D connects a feature of some viruses to a practical impact on human health. None of these other answers suggest that some regions of a virus are more sensitive than others, and therefore all of these choices should be eliminated.

4. <u>A</u> is the correct answer.

In line 44, "composition" refers to the proportion of ingredients contained within a vaccine. Choose A to reflect this content. B (inappropriately implying spatial dynamics and organizations), C (inappropriately implying a record of information for future consultation), and D (inappropriately implying effectiveness or an ability to produce desired results) all introduce improper contexts and should therefore be eliminated.

5. <u>B</u> is the correct answer.

Lines 21-23 state that "Influenza viruses that are closely related to each other usually have similar antigenic properties." This content is comparable to a statement that closely related individuals usually have similar features; choose B as the best answer. Be careful not to choose A, since closely related viruses have similar but NOT identical antigenic properties. C and D can also be eliminated since they discuss cases in which the relevant analogy would involve viruses which are distantly related to one another, while the passage only discusses viruses which closely resemble one another.

6. <u>B</u> is the correct answer.

See the previous answer explanation for analysis of the correct line reference. A provides a definition of an antigen and explains how an antigen functions, while C describes how the human immune system responds to similar viruses. D describes one result of the antigenic drift process. None of these other answers articulate the relationship wherein related viruses have similar properties, and therefore they should all be eliminated.

7. <u>D</u> is the correct answer.

The second-to-last paragraph states that "vaccines designed to elicit antibodies against this target might provide long-lasting protection against any influenza strain" (lines 81-84), and the final paragraph builds on this idea by providing a specific example of a case in which a single vaccine provided protection against multiple influenza strains. A and B can be eliminated since no new area of study is introduced in this paragraph, and since the utility of the vaccine process has already been established at this point. C can also be eliminated since the final paragraph provides additional support for the claim of the previous paragraph and thus does NOT contradict it.

8. <u>D</u> is the correct answer.

Passage 1 discusses the phenomenon of antigenic drift and explains that this problem can lead to a need to constantly update influenza vaccines, as well as a need for vaccines to be limited in how many strains they protect against. Passage 2 discusses a possibility for ensuring that the same vaccine can protect against multiple strains of influenza, thus presenting a potential solution to this problem. Choose D as appropriate. A and B can be eliminated since the reasoning across both passages is consistent, and since Passage 1 discusses a known phenomenon and NOT a theory. C can be eliminated since no common data is discussed in the two passages, which nonetheless have the same general topics (health and antigens).

9. <u>B</u> is the correct answer.

The final paragraph of Passage 2 discusses FluA-20, an antibody that has shown the ability to disable several different viruses. Since Passage 2 provides a specific example of an antibody and of how it disables viruses, and Passage 1 (which offers an overview of trends) does not, choose B as the best answer. A and C can both be eliminated since Passage 1 describes the process and results of antigen drift without focusing on any specific virus and antibody in particular. D can be eliminated since Passage 2 DOES provide discussion of a specific antibody.

10. <u>A</u> is the correct answer.

The final paragraph of Passage 1 explains that, because of antigen drift, vaccines must be continuously updated in order to remain effective. Passage 2 accepts both this premise (viruses gradually altering over time) and the conclusion (the tendency of vaccines to become ineffective), and then describes a potential solution to this problem; choose A as appropriate. B, C, and D (which all indicate disagreement in varying degrees) can all be eliminated since there is alignment in both premise and conclusion across Passage 1 and Passage 2.

Passage 36, Pages 191-193

1. <u>C</u> is the correct answer.

In line 7, "soliciting" refers to how local fishers are employed specifically to capture sharks. Choose C to reflect this meaning. A (inappropriately implying someone being forced or coerced), B (inappropriately implying something being promoted or publicized), and D (inappropriately implying someone being seduced or lured) all introduce improper contexts and should be eliminated.

2. <u>D</u> is the correct answer.

Lines 30-32 state that "Demonstrable effectiveness means a measurable decrease in shark bite incidents in response to culling activities." Choose D to reflect this content. Be careful not to choose A, because the author identifies a decrease in the number of sharks as a false measure of success, which does NOT necessarily correlate to fewer bite incidents. B and C can also be eliminated since there is no discussion of measuring the numbers of prey, and since success is defined as a quantifiable result, not simply a matter of expert opinion.

3. <u>D</u> is the correct answer.

See the previous answer explanation for analysis of the correct line reference. A presents a complex moral question which is difficult to resolve, while B raises some critical questions about an endeavor. C identifies a perspective which the author disagrees with. None of these other answers directly clarify what the author believes to be the measure of success for shark control programs, and therefore they should all be eliminated.

4. <u>B</u> is the correct answer.

Passage 2 describes a product known as Shark Shield Freedom and provides objective analysis of its success based on independent studies. This content indicates that the passage is written from the perspective of independent scientists; choose B as appropriate. A and C can both be eliminated, since the manufacturer would likely be interested in unilaterally promoting the product, while a competitor would likely try to detract from its positive features. Be careful not to choose D, since the author does view shark safety measures as beneficial but is focused on assessing the impact of ONE particular measure rather than on advocating for shark safety in general.

5. <u>A</u> is the correct answer.

Lines 60-66 state that "After multiple approaches, individual great white sharks showed signs of habituation to the Shark Shield, coming an average of 12cm closer on each successive approach." This content indicates that as sharks became more used to the Shark Shield, it became less effective; however, they came only slightly closer. Choose A to reflect this content. B and D can readily be eliminated since these answers are explicitly contradicted by the content of the passage. C can also be eliminated, since the sharks were still generally repelled by the device and only ventured slightly closer; it would be an overstatement to say that the device became substantially less effective.

6. <u>B</u> is the correct answer.

See the previous answer explanation for analysis of the correct line reference. A describes how sharks responded to their first exposure to the Shark Shield device, while C describes one outlying test case in which a shark did actually come into contact with the device. D qualifies a discussion of one test case by explaining that, even when a shark was not fully deterred, it still behaved in a less aggressive manner. None of these other answers (despite in some ways referencing the Shark Shield) indicate that the Shark Shield became less effective with repeated exposure, and therefore they should all be eliminated.

7. <u>C</u> is the correct answer.

In line 88, "range" refers to an array of different individuals who might be at risk of shark attacks. Choose C to reflect this content. A (inappropriately implying individuals sharing a common purpose or identity), B (inappropriately implying a height above sea level), and D (inappropriately implying a measurement from one point to another) all introduce improper contexts and should be eliminated.

8. <u>B</u> is the correct answer.

Passage 1 is critical of shark protection programs which focus on culling sharks, arguing that such programs are not effective. Passage 2 focuses on a specific device which seems to effectively increase shark safety. Choose B to reflect this relationship between the passages. A can be readily eliminated since it reverses the relationship between the passages. C and D can also be eliminated since Passage 2 discusses experimental results (controlled testing of the Shark Shield device) while Passage 1 does not, and Passage 1 does not offer a detailed explanation of any type of procedure (since the focus is on the broad problems with a method).

9. <u>D</u> is the correct answer.

At the end of Passage 1, the author mentions specific efforts to cull tiger sharks (line 42), while the experiments discussed in Passage 2 specifically addressed Great White sharks (line 75). Since both passages discuss specific shark species, choose D as the best answer. A and B can be eliminated Passage 1 does NOT discuss experiments or control trials, and Passage 2 looks at shark safety specifically in South Africa, NOT Hawaii.

10. <u>A</u> is the correct answer.

Passage 1 identifies both the problem of shark attacks posing a threat to human safety and the problem of misguided efforts to safeguard humans by culling sharks. Passage 2 offers a potential technological solution that would both protect humans and allow sharks to live on without much interference. Choose A to reflect this relationship between the two passages. B and C can be eliminated since Passage 2 supports (and thus does NOT question or refute) an assumption that efforts OTHER than shark culling are worthwhile and should be explored. D can be eliminated, since Passage 2 does NOT offer an answer to the ethical questions raised in Passage 1, but does offer a potential solution which might allow humans and sharks to live in harmony.

Passage 37, Pages 194-196

1. <u>A</u> is the correct answer.

Lines 18-19 explain that, in regards to rice, scientists possess access to "a larger dataset than has been reported for any other plant species." This content indicates that more sequencing has taken place for rice than for other plants; choose A as the best answer. B and D can be eliminated since the passage does NOT state that RNAs function differently in rice than in other plants (which in fact COMPARABLE to rice despite the larger dataset for rice itself). C can also be eliminated since, while the passage does state that other plants have similar RNA, this reality is NOT explicitly linked to these plants being descended from rice.

2. <u>A</u> is the correct answer.

See the previous answer explanation for analysis of the correct line reference. B describes the significance of small RNA and the impact of deficiencies in this area, while C quotes an expert explaining additional functions of small RNA in plants. D summarizes the potential overall impact of a research project. None of these other answers imply that more data is available about RNA in rice than in other plants (since some avoid comparison altogether), and therefore they should all be eliminated.

3. <u>B</u> is the correct answer.

In line 61, the words "iconic" and "prized" describe the way in which basmati rice is regarded as a highly valued rice variety; choose B as appropriate for this positive meaning. A and C can also be eliminated because the words refer specifically to basmati rice, NOT to either modern agriculture or a particular researcher. Be careful not to choose D, since the passage indicates that basmati rice is highly-regarded but NOT necessarily that it carries significant economic value.

4. <u>A</u> is the correct answer.

In lines 66-73, Passage 2 differentiates between whole genome sequencing ("which determines an organism's complete DNA sequence") versus short-read sequencing ("in which DNA is broken into tiny fragments and then reassembled") and states that the former is preferable, since the latter can result in "missing sequences and gaps in the data." Choose A to reflect the content of the passage. B and C can both be eliminated since the passage does not compare either the cost or time requirement (NOT to be confused with accuracy) of the different types of sequencing. D can also be eliminated since the passage implies that short-read sequencing may result in missing sequences, NOT in repeated sequences.

5. <u>D</u> is the correct answer.

Lines 47-50 state that the research project described in the passage focused on "two basmati rice varieties, including one that is drought-tolerant and resistant to bacterial disease." The fact that these two specific varieties exist, and were chosen for study, indicates that some basmati rice is susceptible to drought and bacterial infestation; choose D as appropriate. A and B can be eliminated since the passage does NOT indicate that a lack of knowledge about the evolution of basmati rice (as opposed to practical problems) leads to lower yield, and since there is no discussion of genetic defects in the rice. C can be eliminated since, while basmati is a hybrid of two other rice varieties, this characteristic is NOT linked to lower agricultural yield.

6. <u>A</u> is the correct answer.

See the previous answer explanation for analysis of the correct line reference. B describes an area where scientific knowledge is still lacking, and C describes a key feature of the methodology behind the research project presented in the passage. D describes a conclusive finding that resulted from the research project. None of these other answers identify factors which might result in a lower yield from a basmati rice crop (though some do describe research involving rice), and therefore they should all be eliminated.

7. <u>D</u> is the correct answer.

In line 86, "shaped" refers to how a number of different factors led to the current characteristics associated with basmati rice. Choose D to reflect this meaning. A (inappropriately implying restrictions or limitations), B (inappropriately implying emotional support and positive feedback), and C (inappropriately implying construction of a physical object) all introduce improper contexts and should therefore be eliminated.

8. <u>B</u> is the correct answer.

Passage 1 discusses the significance of small RNAs, which were previously not considered to be an important factor in genetic functioning, while Passage 2 discusses the genetic sequencing of basmati rice, which is an important and valued crop. Choose B to reflect this relationship. A and C can be eliminated since Passage 2 focuses on newly-discovered sequences, as opposed to pre-existing data, while both passages focus solely on rice as the crop which was researched. D can be eliminated since both passages present discussions of research related to gene sequencing.

220

9. <u>C</u> is the correct answer.

Passage 1 concludes with a discussion of how research into small RNA sequencing in rice can lead to a better understanding of all plants, while Passage 2 concludes with discussion of how the genetic sequencing of basmati rice can lead to a better understanding of its origins and evolution. Since both passages conclude with a discussion of what can be learned based on rice research, choose C as appropriate. A and B can be eliminated since Passage 1 does NOT explore cultural factors involved in the domestication of rice crops, while neither of the research studies focus specifically on generating a solution to a known problem (not to be confused with gathering information). D can be dismissed since only Passage 2 discusses different varieties of rice and how they are related to one another.

10. <u>B</u> is the correct answer.

Passage 1 specifies that research into small RNAs which is currently being applied to rice can have implications for other plants as well, whereas Passage 2 discusses different varieties of rice but NO other plants. Choose B to reflect this difference between the two passages. A and C can be eliminated since ONLY Passage 2 provides an etymology of a word (the term "basmati") and discussion of the cultural significance of rice as a staple crop. D can also be eliminated since the economic significance of rice is ONLY mentioned in Passage 2 and not in Passage 1.

Passage 38, Pages 197-199

1. <u>B</u> is the correct answer.

The passage explains that M stars "could shine on for over a trillion years" (lines 21-22). Since the passage notes that K stars can shine for 17 billion to 70 billion years, and that the Sun can shine for about 10 billion years, M stars are shown to have the longest lifespan. Choose B as the best answer. A and C can be eliminated since K stars and stars similar to the Sun are described as having relatively short. D can be eliminated since the lifespan of planets that in fact harbor life (as opposed to stars) is not discussed in the passage, so that the lifespan of such a planet could be logically higher OR lower than that of an M star.

2. <u>D</u> is the correct answer.

The passage describes M stars as being the most common type of star in the galaxy where Earth is located. If it were found that M stars were outnumbered by a different type of star, the author's hypothesis that galaxies hospitable to life tend to have a high proportion of M stars would be challenged. Choose D as the best answer. A can be eliminated since the author notes that M stars live for considerably longer than K stars, and therefore it would NOT be surprising if they were found to exist long before K stars. B can be eliminated since scientists have indeed not yet been able to locate habitable planets outside of Earth's galaxy; this information thus would not contradict the assumptions of the passage. C can be eliminated because the passage already contains information about M stars being dimmer than the Sun and yet extremely volatile.

3. <u>D</u> is the correct answer.

In line 15, "dimmest" refers to M stars giving off less light than other types of star. Choose D as appropriate. A (inappropriately implying the least evolved or least sophisticated of a group), B (inappropriately implying a topic that would not generate intellectual excitement or curiosity), and C (inappropriately implying a lack of information) all introduce improper contexts and should therefore be eliminated.

4. <u>B</u> is the correct answer.

In line 37, "a deafening chorus" refers to the sound produced by working computers; by referencing a "chorus," the author creates a comparison to the sound produced by humans. Choose B as the best answer. A and C can be eliminated since the description refers to the working of computers, NOT to the research efforts of scientists (a topic noted elsewhere in the passage), and since the description refers to ongoing efforts, NOT to predictions about future research developments. D can be eliminated since the analogy is only mentioned extremely briefly and is NOT used to clarify additional concepts, which are mostly presented without imagery.

5. <u>C</u> is the correct answer.

In line 58, "instruments" is used to refer to the "next generation of powerful telescopes and space observatories." These devices have not yet been developed, but they represent a potential advancement beyond the telescopes which are available today. Today's telescopes can thus be considered the precursors to ones which will be developed in the future. Choose C as the best answer. A and B can be eliminated since next-generation devices represent a future development, NOT a precursor, and since spacecraft could be more complicated machines than the "devices" discussed here. D can be eliminated since light signatures are what these devices are intended to detect and examine, NOT what has led to their development.

6. <u>D</u> is the correct answer.

Lines 79-82 quote an expert explaining, in terms of observational difficulty, that "This reality makes climate models critical to exploration." This content indicates that the difficulty of observing exoplanets increases the importance of using climate models. Since this content indicates that climate modeling is feasible despite other obstacles, choose D as appropriate. A and B can be eliminated because the purpose of using climate models is NOT to produce planetary images, and such modeling does NOT rely on the development of specialized telescopes. C can be eliminated because climate modeling can be applied to any planet, regardless of size.

7. <u>C</u> is the correct answer.

See the previous answer explanation for analysis of the correct line reference. A uses a rhetorical question to introduce a research topic, while B describes the hope for a better technology and what it will be able to achieve. D only describes the valuable impact of climate modeling. None of these other answers connect the value climate models to the difficulty of observing exoplanets, and therefore they should all be eliminated.

8. <u>A</u> is the correct answer.

Passage 1 discusses which star systems might be most likely to harbor life, with the author concluding that K stars may have distinct benefits, while Passage 2 discusses how improvements to technology may make it more plausible to closely study these distant star systems. Choose A as appropriate. B and C can be eliminated since Passage 1 does discuss two types of stars, but ONLY through in relation to one key issue (whether or not they are likely to support life on nearby planets), while Passage 1 does NOT provide an extensive description of the conditions required for a planet to sustain life despite its general focus. D can be eliminated since Passage 1 indicates that some types of star system may be more likely to harbor life than others but does NOT conclude that only a select or small number of star systems merit research and exploration more broadly.

9. <u>A</u> is the correct answer.

Lines 28-32 state that, in relation to other stars, "M stars are also much brighter when they are young, for up to a billion years after they form, with energy that could boil off oceans on any planets that might someday be in the habitable zone." This content indicates that one reason that young M stars are unlikely to support life on nearby planets is that their energy would make it impossible for these planets to have surface-based water. This content (along with lines 60-62 of Passage 2) indicates that the presence of water is necessary for a planet to host life; choose A as the best answer. B and C can both be eliminated since no particular planetary diameter is discussed as being important for supporting life, and Passage 1 does not arrive at a conclusion as to which type of star is most likely to be at the center of the orbit of a life-supporting planet. D can be eliminated because the presence of breathable oxygen as a prerequisite for life is NOT discussed in both passages; the discussion of Earth-like conditions mainly involves a focus on water and rocky terrain.

10. <u>D</u> is the correct answer.

See the previous answer explanation for analysis of the correct line reference. A describes the type of star which may be likely to be accompanied by life-supporting planets, while B compares the volatility and activity of K and M stars. C describes why some features associated with M stars could make it hard for nearby planets to support life. None of these other answers connect the presence of liquid water to the ability to support life (despite the reference to the issue of planetary life in C), and therefore they should all be eliminated.

Passage 39, Pages 200-202

1. <u>B</u> is the correct answer.

In reference to a Thanksgiving meal, lines 18-21 state that "Add that to free-flowing booze combined with a load of carbohydrates followed by plenty more booze and you have a foolproof recipe for dozing off on the couch." This content indicates that consumption of alcohol may cause the drowsiness that accompanies a Thanksgiving meal. Choose B as appropriate. A and C can be eliminated since the passage suggests that Thanksgiving conversation tends to be dull, NOT invigorating, and since, while the passage does establish that turkey is quite similar to other meats, this fact would NOT explain the drowsiness associated with a meal in which turkey is typically consumed as the primary meat. D can be eliminated since (in an illogical statement involving actual topics) nothing about discussing the sleepiness myth would cause sleepiness itself.

2. <u>D</u> is the correct answer.

See the previous answer explanation for analysis of the correct line reference. A identifies the naturally occurring chemical which is the focus of the passage, while B discounts a widely held misconception. C adds a sarcastic note to introduce the notion that many factors might combine to lead to post-Thanksgiving sleepiness. None of these other answers connects the consumption of alcohol to post-Thanksgiving sleepiness (though C does BROADLY and less precisely mention the sleepiness that attends a Thanksgiving meal), and therefore they should all be eliminated.

3. D is the correct answer.

The study discussed in Passage 1 featured a control group who ingested a placebo rather than an oral dose of TRP (lines 36-39). Choose D to reflect this content. A and B can be eliminated since there was no mention of disputes occurring between participants (who instead often worked in harmony), and since no mention of the academic backgrounds of the participants was present (only of their decisions within the experiment). C can be eliminated since the behavior of the participants could be objectively observed and recorded, and there was no self-reporting required as explicitly described in the passage.

4. A is the correct answer.

In line 48, "give away" refers to the amount of money which participants were willing to offer to a partner in the game. Choose A to reflect this meaning. B (inappropriately implying a context in which money could be saved or a product could be purchased), C (inappropriately implying information being shared without a specific plan or design to do so), and D (inappropriately implying suddenly ignoring or rejecting) all introduce improper meanings and should therefore be eliminated.

5. A is the correct answer.

Lines 82-84 state that "And while some are captivated by tryptophan's potential, it's not clear whether the excitement is warranted." This content indicates that the author of the passage is curious about, but not wholly convinced by, the scientific possibilities associated with tryptophan. Choose A as the best answer. B and C can be eliminated since the author notes that the connection between sleepiness and turkey has been conclusively discredited, while the new possibilities concerning tryptophan do NOT rely on a connection between MOST food sources and psychological changes (since ONLY food sources containing tryptophan are considered). D can be eliminated because the author refers to hypotheses and theories which are being promoted, but which are NOT necessarily reliant on personal testimonials.

6. C is the correct answer.

See the previous answer explanation for analysis of the correct line reference. A describes one false belief associated with tryptophan, while B describes a potential area of scientific exploration. D describes past studies and the results which they revealed. None of these other answers display the author's attitude of curious skepticism towards tryptophan (since some only present clear negatives), and therefore they should all be eliminated.

7. C is the correct answer.

The authors of both passages refer to "myth" to reference unsubstantiated beliefs which were examined using scientific research; to "complicate" such a belief would (in a somewhat lesser-used meaning of the word) be to find that the belief is problematic. Choose C as the best answer. A and B can be eliminated since the idea that consuming tryptophan can have physiological effects is NOT comical (although the author of Passage 1 describes a Thanksgiving dinner in a lighthearted manner) and does NOT present any particular problem (other than misconceptions) to be solved. Be careful not to choose D, since false beliefs about tryptophan do persist, but there have NOT been any scientific breakthroughs that were DESIGNED mainly to undermine these beliefs.

8. <u>B</u> is the correct answer.

Both passages clearly reject the assumption that the consumption of tryptophan leads to drowsiness, and then go on to assess other ways in which tryptophan might impact human health and behavior. Choose B as appropriate. A and C can be rejected since the passages discount the connection between tryptophan and drowsiness and do NOT seek to explore it further, and since the connection between tryptophan and generosity is ONLY explored in Passage 1. D can be rejected because neither passage refers to an assumption that tryptophan can have negative health effects (not to be confused with unreliable but mostly harmless myths).

9. <u>C</u> is the correct answer.

Lines 21-26 state that many different kinds of meat contain similar levels of tryptophan, while Lines 67-69 state that vegetables (and not just meat) contain tryptophan. The lines from Passage 2 clarify that the statement about turkey not being the only food to contain tryptophan includes foods other than meat; choose C as appropriate. A and B can be eliminated since the two statements are complementary and NOT contradictory, and since the tone of both statements is objective and neutral. D can be eliminated since the two statements both represent firmly-established conclusions, NOT a hypothesis or supporting evidence.

10. <u>D</u> is the correct answer.

Line 95 mentions a study in which tryptophan was removed from the diet of participants. This study would not be reinforced by the data shown on the graph, since all of the data presented in the graph involves cases in which tryptophan WAS consumed by study participants. Choose D as the best answer. A can be eliminated since the research referenced in line 28 showed a correlation between consumption of tryptophan and feelings of trust, and a similar correlation is displayed on the graph. B can be eliminated since the internet commentators suggest that consuming tryptophan does not lead to sleepiness, and the graph reinforces this idea with data. C can be eliminated because the studies discussed in line 95 refer to tryptophan improving sensations of calm, and the graph reinforces this connection with correlation data.

Passage 40, Pages 203-205

1. <u>D</u> is the correct answer.

In line 2, "uneventful" refers to how the ride in the self-driving car did not involve any negative or dangerous incidents. Choose D as appropriate. A (inappropriately implying something which is unlikely to stick in someone's mind), B (inappropriately implying excessive speed), and C (inappropriately implying a lack of stimulation) all introduce improper contexts and should therefore be eliminated.

2. <u>A</u> is the correct answer.

Lines 10-13 state that "On top of learning to steer, brake, and accelerate, self-driving software has to incorporate our brains' and bodies' unconscious (but crucial) reactions." This content indicates that self-driving software is sophisticated and complex, so it follows logically that the author believes that the software was difficult to develop. Choose A as appropriate. B can be eliminated since the author mentions the software replicating many qualities of human drivers. C and D can be eliminated since the passage indicates that self-driving cars will not be consistently superior or inferior to all humans (lines 21-26), since humans display varying levels of skill as drivers.

3. <u>B</u> is the correct answer.

See the previous answer explanation for analysis of the correct line reference. A describes the unconscious responses that the author uses while driving, while C describes the author's deepened appreciation for the human brain. D describes an expert stating that self-driving vehicles will most likely never be superior to highly skilled human drivers. None of these answers indicate that self-driving software is sophisticated and difficult to develop, and therefore they should all be eliminated.

4. <u>A</u> is the correct answer.

In line 39, "bend over backwards" refers to Feynman's recommendation that scientists devote extreme effort and care to being transparent and honest in their communications with the public. This language signals that this approach is considered to be extremely important. Choose A to reflect this meaning. B and C can be eliminated since the transparency that Feynman endorses is a recommendation but NOT currently an externally enforced obligation, and since the relevant content refers to a principle which he believes should be strictly applied (NOT flexible). D can be eliminated since Feynman endorses this practice as a sound principle and does NOT consider it to be negative or unfair.

5. <u>D</u> is the correct answer.

Lines 80-82 state that "The problem is not with terminology but with complexity of such systems even at the current level." This content indicates that although different types of AI might be given different names, the problem with regulation is linked to the technology regardless of what it is called. Choose D to reflect this content. A describes the importance of accurate definitions to science overall (thus raising a much broader point), while B describes how attempts are being made to clarify terms around AI technology. C describes a more general problem with regulation. None of these other answers distinguish between confusing terms and difficulty with regulation, and therefore they should all be eliminated.

6. <u>C</u> is the correct answer.

Passage 1 is written in the first person, and describes a personal and subjective perspective. Passage 2 includes some anecdotes, but overall is more objective and descriptive in providing an overview of concepts. Choose C to accurately reflect this relationship between the passages. A and B can be eliminated since Passage 1 is personal, NOT dryly technical, and Passage 2 describes challenges around AI regulation, but does NOT discuss these challenges in a tone of anxiety. D can be eliminated since Passage 2 includes objective and academic description; thus, this passage is NOT primarily conversational and whimsical.

7. <u>D</u> is the correct answer.

Passage 1 focuses on self-driving cars (a specific AI technology) while Passage 2 discusses terminology relevant to artificial intelligence and ethical challenges associated with regulating AI. Choose D to accurately reflect the relationship between these passages. Be careful not to choose A, since Passage 1 does focus on autonomous vehicles, but Passage 2 describes many aspects of artificial intelligence, NOT just general artificial intelligence. B can be eliminated since the human brain is mentioned in Passage 1, but only in the context of a discussion about autonomous vehicles. C can be eliminated since both passages describe technology which currently exists while mentioning future possibilities, so that this answer does NOT describe a contrast.

8. <u>B</u> is the correct answer.

In line 22-23, Kishonti asserts that self-driving cars will not perform better than highly skilled human drivers. Yampolskiy asserts that there are different types of artificial intelligence with different capacities, and some of these may eventually exceed the skills and capacity of human beings. Choose B to reflect the relationship between the passages. A and C can be eliminated since Yampolskiy concedes that artificial intelligence has different levels of capacity, and since Kishonti's argument does NOT rely on specific terminology. D can be eliminated since Kishonti's rationale aligns with the rationale of Yampolskiy.

9. <u>D</u> is the correct answer.

The graph shows that autonomous AI drivers drove through red lights in almost 7.5 % of test drives, while human only and AI-assisted drivers drove through red lights with lower frequency in test drives. It is reasonable to infer from this data that autonomous AI drivers were least likely to respond to traffic signals; choose D as the best answer. A and B can be eliminated since human-only and AI-assisted drivers drove through red lights in less than 5% and less than 2.5% of test drives, respectively. C can be eliminated since human-only and AI-assisted drivers showed different rates of how frequently they drove through red lights.

10. <u>B</u> is the correct answer.

The graph indicates that autonomous AI drivers (with no human component) were more likely to drive through a red light, have a delay at a green light, or be involved in a collision. This indicates that fully autonomous AI drivers typically underperform in comparison to human drivers. This set of factors also aligns with the content of Passage 1, which emphasizes driving; choose B as appropriate. A can be eliminated because while, the data on the graph do align with the conclusions of Passage 1, the information does NOT show AI drivers outperforming human drivers. C and D can be eliminated because the data shown in the graph do NOT align with the conclusions of Passage 2, which engages in a conceptual discussion of AI generally and extends well beyond the topics of autonomous drivers and AI-assisted driving.

Answer Explanations, Part 3

NOTES

- Passage 31, Reading 1, "How do seismologists locate an earthquake?" is adapted from the article of the same name published by the United States Geological Survey. USGS. https://www.usgs.gov/faqs/how-do-seismologists-locate-earthquake?qt-news_science_products=0#qt-news_science_products. Accessed 9 April 2020.

- Passage 31, Reading 2, "Oklahoma Study Reveals Possible, Previously Unknown Sources of Earthquakes," is adapted from the article of the same name published by the United States Geological Survey. 1 June 2018, USGS. https://www.usgs.gov/news/oklahoma-study-reveals-possible-previously-unknown-sources-earthquakes. Accessed 9 April 2020.

- Passage 32, Reading 1, "Catching up with the author: Gareth Whiteley on snake venom and antivenom research," is adapted from the article of the same name by Marian Weidner and published by Speaking of Medicine. 11 November 2016, PLOS One. https://blogs.plos.org/speakingofmedicine/2016/11/11/catching-up-with-the-author-gareth-whitely-on-snake-venom-and-antivenom-research/. Accessed 9 April 2020.

- Passage 32, Reading 2, "Why is it so hard to stop people dying from snakebite?" is adapted from the article of the same name by Léa Surugue and published by Mosaic Science. 17 September 2019, Mosaic. https://mosaicscience.com/story/snakebite-antivenom-crisis-Africa-Togo/. Accessed 9 April 2020.

- Passage 33, Reading 1, "Is the Caribbean apocalypse-proof?" is adapted from the article of the same name by Janine Mendes Franco and published by Global Voices. 9 January 2020, Global Voices. https://globalvoices.org/2020/01/09/is-the-caribbean-apocalypse-proof/. Accessed 9 April 2020.

- Passage 33, Reading 2, "A rash of 'travel bans' as the Caribbean gets serious about coronavirus," is adapted from the article of the same name by Emma Lewis and published by Global Voices. 12 February 2020, Global Voices. https://globalvoices.org/2020/02/12/a-rash-of-travel-bans-as-the-caribbean-gets-serious-about-coronavirus/. Accessed 9 April 2020.

- Passage 34, Reading 1, "Toward an unhackable quantum internet," is adapted from the article of the same name published by the National Science Foundation. 26 March 2020, NSF. https://www.nsf.gov/discoveries/disc_summ.jsp?cntn_id=300266&org=NSF&from=news. Accessed 9 April 2020.

- Passage 34, Reading 2, "Tiny optical cavities could make quantum networks possible," is adapted from the article of the same name published by the National Science Foundation. 3 April 2020, NSF. https://www.nsf.gov/discoveries/disc_summ.jsp?cntn_id=300328. Accessed 9 April 2020.

- Passage 35, Reading 1, "How the Flu Virus Can Change: 'Drift' and 'Shift'," is adapted from the article of the same name published by the Centers for Disease Control and Prevention. 15 October 2019, CDC. https://www.cdc.gov/flu/about/viruses/change.htm. Accessed 9 April 2020.

- Passage 35, Reading 2, "Human antibody reveals hidden vulnerability in influenza virus," is adapted from the article of the same name published by the National Institutes of Health. 16 May 2019, NIH. https://www.nih.gov/news-events/news-releases/human-antibody-reveals-hidden-vulnerability-influenza-virus. Accessed 9 April 2020.

- Passage 36, Reading 1, "Western Australia's shark culls lack bite (and science)," is an excerpt from the article of the same name by Carl Meyer and published by The Conversation. 11 December 2013, The Conversation. https://theconversation.com/western-australias-shark-culls-lack-bite-and-science-21371. Accessed 9 April 2020.

- Passage 36, Reading 2, "Finally, a proven way to keep great white sharks at arm's length," is an excerpt from the article of the same name by Ryan Kempster and Shaun Collin and published by The Conversation in partnership with the University of Western Australia. 4 July 2016, The Conversation. https://theconversation.com/finally-a-proven-way-to-keep-great-white-sharks-at-arms-length-61986. Accessed 9 April 2020.

- Passage 37, Reading 1, "Biologists Develop Large Gene Dataset for Rice Plant," is adapted from the article of the same name published by the National Science Foundation. 13 March 2007, NSF. https://www.nsf.gov/news/news_summ.jsp?cntn_id=108455&org=NSF. Accessed 9 April 2020.

- Passage 37, Reading 2, "Love basmati rice? Scientists have now sequenced its genome," is adapted from the article of the same name published by the National Science Foundation. 12 February 2020, NSF. https://www.nsf.gov/discoveries/disc_summ.jsp?cntn_id=300012&org=NSF. Accessed 9 April 2020.

- Passage 38, Reading 1, "'Goldilocks' Stars May Be 'Just Right' for Finding Habitable Worlds," is adapted from the article of the same name by Bill Steigerwald and published by NASA. 10 March 2019, NASA. https://www.nasa.gov/feature/goddard/2019/k-star-advantage. Accessed 9 April 2020.

- Passage 38, Reading 2, "How Earth Climate Models Help Scientists Picture Life on Unimaginable Worlds," is adapted from the article of the same name by Lonnie Shekhtman and published by NASA. 24 January 2020, NASA. https://www.nasa.gov/feature/goddard/2020/how-earth-climate-models-help-scientists-picture-life-on-unimaginable-worlds. Accessed 9 April 2020.

- Passage 39, Reading 1, "No, turkey doesn't make you sleepy – but it may bring more trust to your Thanksgiving table," is an excerpt from the article of the same name by Kevin Bennett and published by The Conversation in partnership with Pennsylvania State University. 15 November 2017, The Conversation. https://theconversation.com/no-turkey-doesnt-make-you-sleepy-but-it-may-bring-more-trust-to-your-thanksgiving-table-87052. Accessed 9 April 2020.

- Passage 39, Reading 2, "Turning to turkey's tryptophan to boost mood? Not so fast," is an excerpt from the article of the same name by Andrew Neff and published by The Conversation. 21 November 2019, The Conversation. https://theconversation.com/turning-to-turkeys-tryptophan-to-boost-mood-not-so-fast-125633. Accessed 9 April 2020.

- Passage 40, Reading 1, "This Self-Driving AI Is Learning to Drive Almost Entirely in a Virtual World," is an excerpt from the article of the same name by Vanessa Bates Ramirez and published by SingularityHub. 18 December 2017, SingularityHub. https://singularityhub.com/2017/12/18/this-self-driving-ai-is-learning-to-drive-almost-entirely-in-a-virtual-world/. Accessed 9 April 2020.

- Passage 40, Reading 2, "Everyone Is Talking About AI—But Do They Mean the Same Thing?" is an excerpt from the article of the same name by David Pring-Mill and published by SingularityHub. 15 March 2018, SingularityHub. https://singularityhub.com/2018/03/15/everyone-is-talking-about-ai-but-do-they-mean-the-same-thing/. Accessed 9 April 2020.

About the Figures: The various visual resources that accompany the passages in this section are primarily meant to facilitate critical thinking skills and may not reflect historical data.

Made in the USA
Middletown, DE
06 September 2024

60500145R00130